For Kevin & Sandi,

And the greatest
word is love!

God bless you both!

Karen Moore.

# Praise for *What a Great Word!*

"The term 'short, sweet, and to the point' is often misused, but it perfectly and beautifully describes Karen Moore's new devotional. We live super-busy lifestyles and the short chapters leave us without excuse for taking a moment to consider the deep things of God. Each chapter is sweet with truth that is nourishment for the soul. And the 'to the point' target helps focus on the main thing each and every day. Recommended reading!"

—*Joel Comm,* New York Times *best-selling author*

"*What a Great Word!* Another devotional, you might think. If you are like me, I am in the Word every morning and always looking for a fresh perspective. This book will fit great into my daily readings. It does exactly what I'm looking for, and that is to come from a new place to find fresh thoughts and ideas to help me grow in and receive more from the Holy Spirit. Thank you for your gift, Karen."

—*Marty Roe, Diamond Rio*

"While reading *What a Great Word!*, I'm reminded how it is important to think and meditate on what we read in God's Word. Thank you, Karen Moore. You've made this a daily devotional that everyone can understand and walk away feeling enlightened. God bless you as you help people draw closer to the Savior."

—*George Shinn, the George Shinn Foundation*

"A few simple words can be a powerful thing. They bring hope to despair and order into chaos. They can calm both stormy seas and anxious hearts. Karen Moore's new book, *What a Great Word!*, helps to take the living words of scripture and weave them into encouraging devotionals for daily life."

—*Daniel Rice, author of* #Gospel: Life, Hope, and Truth for Generation Now

" 'God's Word is alive, active, and sharper than any two-edged sword' is a familiar verse in Hebrews. In *What a Great Word!* Karen Moore has captured what is truly alive and active about reading scripture, and has come up with a refreshingly simple, yet intensely focused way to bring new life and a new perspective to daily-devotional reading. Pick up a copy and enjoy!"

—*Joe Battaglia, author of*
The Politically Incorrect Jesus

"God chose His words carefully, wisely, and precisely. *What a Great Word!* drew my attention to the detail in God's precise promises. It strengthened my resolve to trust God to manage my life's problems, big or small. It actually helped me relax at the beginning of each day. I highly recommend this devotional for each day of the year, with an added one to grow on."

—*Brenda Golden, Entertainment Marketing/PR,*
*CEO of GoldenGab.com*

"Sometimes devotionals inspire your heart. Sometimes they edify your thinking and give you a new perspective. Other times, they simply fill your spirit with joy. Karen Moore's new book, *What a Great Word!*, does all those things for the reader and more. I look forward to spending some time with this book every morning."

—*David L. Hancock, founder and CEO of Morgan James Publishing*

"We often search the Bible for just one word from God that will give us hope and encouragement for the day. Karen Moore's new book, *What a Great Word!*, gives us those special words that help us face life's challenges and joys with encouragement, hope, and love. This is truly an inspiring book. Thank you, Karen."

—*Terry Squires, author, television host*

"Sometimes you just need a good word! What Karen Moore has done in *What a Great Word!* though is give you a fresh look at words she selected from scripture to offer a new perspective. Each word causes you to think more deeply about the passage and to focus on that word in a way you may never have done before. I look forward to getting a daily nugget of refreshment each time I open *What a Great Word!*"

—*Duane Ward, CEO, Premiere Marketing, LLC*

"My father was a newspaper man, and my mother was an English teacher, so words played an integral part in my life. My parents taught me that choosing the right word for the occasion was meaningful, but even more important was the recognition that words can either be helpful or hurtful. Karen Moore's devotional is more than just helpful. In the simplest manner, she guides the reader/contemplator to embrace a word within the Word, not just for personal edification, but also for action. I look forward every morning to discovering what word will be highlighted for the day, and I'm confident that others will feel the same."

—*Ron Doyle, Owner, TargetOne Coaching*

"I love getting up every morning and contemplating this special word of the day as I do my prayers and read God's word. I highly recommend *What a Great Word!*"

—*Pete Kersten, illustrator, Kersten Brothers Studios*

"Starting each morning with inspiring and thought-provoking words can help set the tone for your entire day in such a positive and uplifting way. Karen Moore's new book, *What a Great Word!*, gives you the tools to do just that. In our complicated world, it's so easy to get overwhelmed and discouraged. Reading a devotional like Karen's will help to feed your spirit and encourage you to see the world through the eyes of love."

—*Kathy Davis, Kathy Davis Studios,*
*Chief Visionary Officer, author, and artist*

What a *Great word*

What a

# A YEAR OF
# DAILY DEVOTIONS

# KAREN MOORE

NASHVILLE   NEW YORK

FaithWords
Hachette Book Group
1290 Avenue of the Americas, New York, NY 10104
faithwords.com
twitter.com/faithwords

First Edition: December 2018

FaithWords is a division of Hachette Book Group, Inc. The FaithWords name and logo are trademarks of Hachette Book Group, Inc.

The publisher is not responsible for websites (or their content) that are not owned by the publisher.

The Hachette Speakers Bureau provides a wide range of authors for speaking events. To find out more, go to www.hachettespeakersbureau.com or call (866) 376-6591.

Library of Congress Cataloging-in-Publication Data has been applied for.

ISBNs: 978-1-5460-3195-6 (paper over board), 978-1-5460-3194-9 (ebook)

Printed in the United States of America

LSC-C

10 9 8 7 6 5 4 3 2 1

# Introduction

Dear Friends,

Perhaps one of the greatest gifts of my marriage is my husband's practice of doing daily devotions. He gets up way before it is civilized to do so to read God's Word and pray. During that process, he listens carefully and often discovers a word that seems to perfectly fit our needs in a special way for that day.

He usually sends me a text so I can also start my day pondering that word and what God wants me to know. Often, he sends a similar text to others as well. His notes typically result in someone saying, "That's exactly what I needed today," or "That's a great word! Thank you so much for thinking of me."

I've learned so much about how powerful those simple, one-word thoughts are that I wanted to share them in a new devotional with you. You won't find as many of the typical Bible words in these devotions. I have intentionally selected the ones you are more likely to gloss over, not realizing how significant they can be. As you carry the word of the day around with you, listen for God's voice for a personal message. You can share that word with others, or you can simply know that God is near, able and willing to embrace you at any time. So get ready to ponder, pray, and consider a tiny nugget of joy each day.

I hope you let each special word whisper blessings into your life everywhere you go. *What a Great Word!* is sent to you with love...God's love and mine!

—*Karen Moore*

# WATCH

*O Lord, in the morning you hear my voice;*
*in the morning I plead my case to you, and watch.*     Psalm 5:3 NRSV

When we **watch** for something, it means we're intent on staying alert to an event or possibility. This Scripture serves as a simple guide to help us establish the order of things we do each day. We want our first words in the morning to be words of praise as we thank God for a good night's rest and for the start of a new day.

After that, we reflect on and surrender those areas of our lives that cause us anxiety or fear. David, the author of the Psalm, would likely have prepared a literal sacrifice to God each morning. In our day, we surrender our hearts and prepare to listen for God's voice.

The next and most important thing we do each day is to watch for God to show up in unexpected places and in wondrous ways. We set our hopes high and trust that our mighty God and Heavenly Creator is working on our behalf.

Wherever you are as you begin the year anew, be watching for the work of God, mindful of His goodness. Be willing to keep constant vigil over the things He would have you do. He is watching over your life every moment of the day. He has great plans for you!

*Lord, thank You for **watching** over my life as I rise to greet each new*
*day. Help me to be mindful of You, always aware that You are near.*
*Guide my heart and help me to continually watch for You each place*
*I go. I pray You will bless the work of my hands. Amen.*

# EVERY

*Every word of God is true.*
*He guards those who come to him for safety.*            Proverbs 30:5 NCV

This may be a short Proverb, but it is a mighty one! It tells us that **every** word of God is true; not "a few," not "some," or not even "most," but "every" word is true!

In our limited thinking, we often want every word of God to come true in our time frame, exactly when we need it, like right now. But what God wants is for our hearts to be ready to receive His truth and His blessing. For our own sake, God waits until we can receive what He has planned.

In the meantime, He wants us to continue to come to Him every hour of every day. He wants us to surrender the things that unnerve us and make life feel overwhelming. He wants us to draw near to Him and take refuge in His strength and in the power of His Word.

Go to God today; draw near to Him for every need you may have. Seek His protection and His healing and His steadfast love. Ask Him to help you wait and trust and believe that He is always with you. Ask Him to help you know with your whole heart that every word of God is true.

Whatever you need and wherever you are today, may God make His Presence known and guard you as you walk in His grace and mercy and truth. The One who created you knows everything about you. He guards your life.

*Lord, I ask You to be with me today as I wait for Your promise, Your Presence, and Your generous provision. Help me to know without a doubt that **every** word from You is true for me. Amen.*

# HELPER

*But you, God, see the trouble of the afflicted; you consider their grief and take it in hand. The victims commit themselves to you; you are the **helper** of the fatherless.*
Psalm 10:14 NIV

You've probably had times in your life when you needed an extra pair of hands, or even just another thoughtful person to work through an idea or a dilemma. You may have been overworked or overwhelmed and simply couldn't do everything on your to-do list. Those moments can make you feel alone. They drain your hope and your energy. Then it happens: You're pleasantly surprised because someone offers to give you some assistance, or someone sees your need and works with you to tackle those difficult circumstances.

The Psalm writer reminds us that God sees us when we are having trouble in any of its forms. He sees our struggles and our momentary feelings of hopelessness. He sees us and He steps in to lighten the load as we commit our hearts and minds to live in ways that please Him. He is our **helper**.

When you feel weak, when your strength is small, go to the One who created the Heavens and the Earth. Go to the one whose strength is perfected in weakness. He sees your need and when you surrender to Him, He can meet you right where you are and offer you His help. You won't have to ask Him twice. He's your helper, 24/7!

*Lord, I thank You for seeing my hardships and those moments when I am simply overwhelmed by the activities of life. Thank You for being a swift and steady **helper**. I commit all my ways and my work to You. Amen.*

3

# ABLE

*Now to him who is **able** to do immeasurably more than all we ask or imagine, according to his power that is at work within us, to him be glory in the church and in Christ Jesus throughout all generations, for ever and ever! Amen.*                    Ephesians 3:20–21 NIV

When you signed up to be on the team where Jesus Christ is the CEO of your life, you probably were inspired and ready to move forward quickly. You may remember the exact day or the moment when you first realized that God was real, and not only that, but He wanted to be part of your life.

But if you're like most people, that initial enthusiasm and energy may have waned a bit over time. It doesn't mean your faith is not strong—in fact, it's likely to be stronger now than when you first signed on—but life comes in and saps you of strength. It causes you to feel like you simply can't accomplish everything. And you can't.

The good news is that God has given you amazing power through the Holy Spirit and that power will indeed help you to be **able**. You will be able to reach out and touch the hearts of others. You will be able to meet your daily goals and still have time for prayer. You will be able to do all that God has called you to do because as long as you're open to being used by God, then you will be. He is able to do more through you and your work than you can even imagine. Bless His Holy Name today.

*Lord, I thank You for renewing my spirit when I'm weary from the work I do in the world. Help me to live in ways that please You and help me to be **able** to shine Your light today. Amen.*

# UNBELIEF

*And not being weak in faith, he did not consider his own body, already dead (since he was about a hundred years old), and the deadness of Sarah's womb. He did not waver at the promise of God through **unbelief**, but was strengthened in faith, giving glory to God and being fully convinced that what He had promised He was also able to perform. And therefore "it was accounted to him for righteousness."*　　　　　Romans 4:20–22 NKJV

Abraham and Sarah were in advanced years when God shared with them the good news that they would have a son. Abraham and Sarah had hoped and prayed year after year for a baby. They hoped against all odds. They hoped past anything that other human beings thought was logical. Sarah hoped even when her biological and physical clocks stopped ticking. Eventually, her hope turned to unbelief. She could no longer imagine that having a baby was possible. God had other plans, though, and her **unbelief** did not stop Him.

What hope do you have that you've moved to a back burner, imagining that it was now too late for it to come to fruition? What unbelief has kept you from continuing in the direction of your dreams or from giving opportunity a chance despite the passage of time? Unbelief is what keeps us back. Unbelief is what causes us to give up on our dreams. Unbelief is what paralyzes every hope we ever had.

Today, revisit the dreams you let go of, the ones where you imagine that nothing is possible. Open the box of your dreams with new belief, with renewed hope, and let the possibility that only God can provide shine through. God can work miracles when belief opens the door.

*Lord, I squandered my dreams, wandering around in **unbelief** because nothing happened in the time frame I imagined. Help me today to be open to Your timing and Your willingness to walk with me in renewed hope. I ask this in Jesus' name. Amen.*

# GIVE

*You must each decide in your heart how much to give. And don't give reluctantly or in response to pressure. "For God loves a person who gives cheerfully." And God will generously provide all you need. Then you will always have everything you need and plenty left over to share with others.*

2 Corinthians 9:7–8 NLT

Most of us enjoy being **givers**. We look for those moments when we can provide a surprise delight for the people we love. We anticipate the joy they might feel as they receive our generous gift, no matter what the occasion. It simply does our hearts good to know that we have been able to do something special for others.

Now imagine that you have your heart set on something special. Perhaps you've prayed for a long time to get out of debt, or to own a home, or to go back to school. Maybe you've given all you have to others, but it seems that your "giving" attitude seldom is returned to you. You should know that God sees your generosity and He wants you to enjoy His favor as well.

God loves to surprise you with little blessings. He loves to see you light up when something that you never dreamed could happen suddenly comes to fruition. He loves knowing that He helped fulfill the desires of your heart. Acknowledge His gifts with love and praise and return your heartfelt joy to Him as a small way of giving back. May God give you new ways to continue to give cheerfully and well.

*God, I love You and appreciate all that You have done for me and all that You give me each day to sustain me. Amen.*

# JUST

*The Lord is **just** in all his ways, and kind in all his doings.*
*The Lord is near to all who call on him, to all who call on him in truth.*

Psalm 145:17–18 NRSV

A good synonym for the word **just** is "right." When we think about who God is, it is helpful to realize that God is "just" or that He is "right" in all that He does. The psalmist reminds us that God is not simply just in a few things that He does, but in all things. That means there is nothing else God can be except just. We would be hard-pressed in the world we live in today to find a few people who are "just" sometimes, much less all the time.

Two things come to mind as we consider that God is always just. One is that we have greater confidence that God will deliver us from anything that is not right for us. In fact, the rest of the Psalm goes on to say that God draws near to those who call on Him in truth. A just God draws near to the people He loves and guards them. He helps them walk in His ways and strengthens them with His truth.

Number two is that you may not feel you've always been judged fairly or that the world has treated you in a way that is just and right. The good news is that God does not see you in the same way that the world sees you. He sees your heart and draws close to you. He helps you because of His own steadfast love for you and His righteousness. You may not always see His hand at work, but you can trust Him to guide you in ways that are right and just.

*Lord, let me live with honesty and integrity, and help me to do all I can to stand up for what is right and **just** wherever I am today. Amen.*

# FULL

*You visit the earth and water it, you greatly enrich it;*
*the river of God is full of water; you provide the people with grain,*
*for so you have prepared it.*                    Psalm 65:9 NRSV

The beauty of a phrase like "the river of God is **full** of water" is that it is a great reminder that God's work, His Presence, and His reality are continual; they overflow with goodness. The psalmist reminds us that God has provided all that we need to sustain life from the very beginning. He intends for each of us to live in His care and keeping. He wants us to have all that we need, physically, emotionally, and spiritually.

So today, we can each choose how we want to be made full, or filled up with to the point of overflowing. We can be full of the Holy Spirit, and overflow with His bounty of goodness and peace and patience and self-control. We can intentionally share more goodness and love and joy. When we go to the river of God's love and mercy, we discover that there is always enough to go around. He makes it clear that He has plenty to share and even more where that came from. Surrender your heart to Him today and you will be provided with His glorious fullness.

*Lord, thank You for providing for my needs beyond measure. Help me to always appreciate the overflowing love You have for me. Let my heart be humbly **full** of Your love. Amen.*

# CONTINUALLY

*The Lord will guide you **continually**,*
*and satisfy your needs in parched places, and make your bones strong;*
*and you shall be like a watered garden,*
*like a spring of water, whose waters never fail.*          Isaiah 58:11 NRSV

Isn't it amazing to imagine that God is **continually** guiding you? He doesn't guide you on Monday and then wait until Thursday to guide you again. He doesn't walk with you on Sunday right after church, and then forget about you the rest of the week. No, He is with you every moment to satisfy your needs. He is your incessant and constant source of direction.

Sometimes you may feel parched. You may feel alone and that you're doing everything you can to simply survive. You go to work, you pay your bills, you take care of your family, go to church, and start all over again on Monday. You may not feel like a watered garden. In fact, you may wonder if God even knows you exist because everything about your life feels parched and dry.

If that's the case, then read this verse from Isaiah very carefully. If you need to read it continually for several days until it sinks in that you are not alone, that you are not in a desert, parched and thirsty, then do so. You have been given, instead, a spring of living water, put inside your heart from your loving Father. You are a continual fountain, ever nourished and replenished by the One whose waters never fail. May you never thirst again.

*Lord, I turn to You **continually** for refreshment and strength. Help me to come often to You for guidance and living water. Amen.*

# ENCOURAGE

*We have different gifts, according to the grace given to each of us. If your gift is prophesying, then prophesy in accordance with your faith; if it is serving, then serve; if it is teaching, then teach; if it is to **encourage**, then give encouragement.*                                      Romans 12:6–8 NIV

The **encouragement** you give to others is a gift. You know that when the tables are turned and someone encourages you, you understand what a gift kind words spoken at the right time can truly be. A day rarely passes that you don't need encouragement for something you're trying to accomplish. Maybe you want to learn a new skill and you're not sure you have what it takes. Maybe you want to write a novel, but you're afraid publishers will reject you. Perhaps you simply want to get through your to-do list and have time to exercise as well. No matter what it is, it helps your heart and mind to receive a little encouragement.

On the reverse side, notice the difference it makes when you are the one giving the gift of reassurance, hope, or kindness to someone else. For instance: You have a friend who seems to have everything she needs to succeed in achieving a goal, but she still needs your encouragement. You see your spouse work hard to finish a project and you know that it's getting tough to have the energy to see it through. You offer a loving smile, a boost of confidence, and see that it is just what he needs to complete the work. God wants us to encourage each other to build our faith, do our work, and learn to love one another. Give the gift of encouragement. Inspire someone today and it will do your heart good.

*Lord, as I cross paths with others today, let me be the first to* ***encourage*** *them toward their hopes and dreams. Amen.*

# NEW

*The Lord says, "Forget what happened before,*
*and do not think about the past.*
*Look at the **new** thing I am going to do.*
*It is already happening. Don't you see it?"*　　　Isaiah 43:18–19 NCV

We all love to get something **new**! We like to carry a new cell phone or drive a snazzy new automobile. We love a new idea to stimulate our life direction, a new friend to increase our sense of connection, or a new book to change our thinking.

One reason we like new things is because we can get stuck in the past. We may listen to the same old tapes that have worked through our minds for years. We carry those old ideas and thoughts with us because we haven't yet discovered good replacements. We need something new. We need a change.

In Isaiah 43, we see that sometimes God does a new thing too. Isaiah tells us to stop thinking about the past. We don't need to assume that what happened before will happen again. We don't have to imagine that there is an obstacle around every corner. We only need to understand that God is doing a new thing, and it is already happening.

Can you see any new things God is doing in your life? Can you understand that He is so devoted to you that He continues to search for ways that will motivate your spirit and bring you joy? God is doing a new, innovative, original thing in your life right now. Give Him thanks and praise.

*Lord, please open my eyes to the **new** things You are doing to*
*motivate and inspire me today. Help me to see Your hand at work in*
*all that I do. Amen.*

# OPEN

*Be good to your servant,*
*that I may live and obey your word.*
***Open** my eyes to see the wonderful truths in your instructions.*
*I am only a foreigner in the land. Don't hide your commands from me!*

Psalm 119:17–19 NLT

Have you ever thought to ask God to **open** your eyes so you can clearly see His truths? Has it occurred to you that you may be walking around half asleep, only partially aware of all that God really has for you? If you honestly answer yes to either of those questions, then this could be a new day for you. This could be the day that you open your heart and mind to God as never before. What would that look like?

Perhaps you remember that Jesus said, "Let the one with eyes to see, see." It appears that He felt people were not seeing or comprehending His messages clearly. They were not truly open to all that God wanted them to know. They could not see God's hand at work in their lives.

So what will it be for you? Open or closed? Are you closed-minded and unable to recognize that God desires more for you? If so, then this is a great day for you to open the eyes of your heart and mind and surrender to His care and keeping. When you acknowledge God's gifts and open your eyes to all that He is doing, you will find a multitude of reasons to sing His praise.

*Lord, I know I've been asleep to many of the precious gifts You've given me. **Open** my eyes today to see Your hand at work every place I turn. Amen.*

# PROUD

*The end of a thing is better than its beginning;*
*The patient in spirit is better than the **proud** in spirit.*

Ecclesiastes 7:8 NKJV

This bit of Solomon's wisdom may indeed be one for us to take to heart. After all, when we start a project, especially one that we initiated, or one that is important to us, we usually do so with gusto. We are ready to take on the world and get it done. We are **proud**, in a good way, of the project before us and may even be humbled that we get to do it.

A patient spirit may benefit us even more, though. When we're patient, motivated by an opportunity, or a chance to serve, then our hearts are open to hearing other opinions or thoughts on ways to get things done. We can then choose the best advice to take on as our own.

A proud spirit that may even be arrogant or controlling seldom serves you as well. It doesn't accept advice or truly listen to the counsel of others. In fact, pride stands in the way of receiving God's advice and counsel as well.

It's great to be proud of the things you do as you raise a family, or volunteer in the neighborhood, or go to a workplace environment each day. Just remember when you're patient with yourself and others, you'll enjoy the fruit of your labors and God will bless your humble efforts.

*Father in Heaven, I do love starting new projects, and I am **proud***
*that You continue to bless me with ideas and joyful things to do.*
*Remind me to maintain a spirit of patience and humility in the work*
*I do. Amen.*

# QUICKLY

*Then he said to me, "These words are faithful and true." And the Lord God of the holy prophets sent His angel to show His servants the things which must shortly take place. "Behold, I am coming **quickly**! Blessed is he who keeps the words of the prophecy of this book."*     Revelation 22:6–7 NKJV

Often, when the word **quickly** comes up in Scripture, it is a reference to a request from an angel, as in "Go quickly!" or "Come quickly!" Sometimes it is the request of a king who commands something to be done speedily and without wasting any time.

We may interpret this word today as "Hurry up!" or "What are you waiting for?" We have to get the job done fast or make it a priority so that another step can be taken. We move with haste because we know what a difference it can make.

This quote from Revelation, which reminds us that Jesus said that He would come quickly, may be a bit different in its intention. It may address more than speed and a need to hurry up.

It reminds us that whatever we're doing with our time, we should be careful to remain faithful and true, be wise, and watch out because we never know when Jesus will return. We can be sure that for some He will come too quickly, because they have not yet anchored themselves to Him, and they are not prepared for His coming. When time is running out, moving through the hourglass at rapid speed, everything needs to be done quickly. If nothing else, the Author of time may be reminding us that the clock is always ticking with some urgency, but He has given us a Guide Book to prepare our hearts and minds. Let us be quick to heed His voice.

*Lord, I pray that You will remind me to use my time well and to get meaningful things done **quickly**. After all, they can only benefit those around me when I've completed the work You gave me to do. Amen.*

# ONLY

*The desire of the righteous ends **only** in good.*   Proverbs 11:23 NRSV

We often use a word like **only** to emphasize a point. We might say, "I only want this one thing!" What we mean is, you should listen to me because I've got one request, and so it deserves to be heard. Another way we may use this word is that we tell a beloved person, "You are my one and only." That means no one else holds the place in your heart that that one person does.

What is it that makes "only" a great word to consider in the things of God? Perhaps it is this: If we want only what God wants, or if we only, solely, wholeheartedly want to please God, then our priorities shift from mere matters of the heart, to matters of the Spirit. Our hearts are in alignment with God because we are declaring that we only want to do what will further the work of His kingdom. We want to do the good things, the right things, the only things that truly matter. When we focus on God's love for us and our love for God, according to the Proverb, then ultimately, only good will come.

When you only have eyes for God, and you have a heart to listen for His voice, then you can be sure that good will prevail according to God's plan and purpose for you.

God wants your love for Him to be a continual focus. Look for Him wherever you are and let Him know you serve Him only. He will hear the prayers of your heart and guide you toward only those things that bring life to your soul.

*Lord God, You know me better than I know myself. You know that I can often get distracted and that I may not always focus my heart's attention on You. Help me today to seek Your face and prepare my heart to serve You **only**. Amen.*

# SOURCE

*He is the source of your life in Christ Jesus, who became for us wisdom from God, and righteousness and sanctification and redemption, in order that, as it is written, "Let the one who boasts, boast in the Lord."*

1 Corinthians 1:29–31 NRSV

Life is complicated. It wraps around us with tentacles that leave us feeling parched and spent. It overwhelms our souls and distracts our hearts and minds. We get confused and we forget who we are.

We are the sanctified and the redeemed. We are the ones that God called to do His work, to become His hands and feet in our homes and our neighborhoods and the places where we make a living. We are His ambassadors.

So what do we do when news broadcasts sweep away our confidence, or when bill collectors call relentlessly seeking payment, or when we are discouraged at the tension in our family? Where do we go when we feel lost in the darkness?

We go back to the Spring. We go to the very **Source** of our lives, the Living Water of God's grace and hope and deliverance. We go and we stand before Him and let Him fill us up once again with love and honor and possibility. If your well is running dry, then stop everything and run back to the Source, your Creator, your Redeemer, your Savior, Jesus Christ for all that is good. He is waiting at the well for you.

*Lord, I am often parched, weary from the obstacles that try to keep me from moving toward the good You have for me. Help me to come to You, the Source of my life, anytime I am overwhelmed. Amen.*

# WORTHY

*They told the church about your love. Please help them to continue their trip in a way **worthy** of God.*                    3 John 5:6 NCV

**Worthy** is an interesting word with diverse definitions. Jesus is worthy of our trust and love because He is honorable and commendable and keeps His promises. He holds up a standard for us to follow, a desire for us to live in ways that will please Him, that are worthy of Him.

To be worthy of God suggests that there is something we must do, an action perhaps that may cause us to feel worthy in His sight. Christians are made worthy by our faith in Jesus Christ. It is through our belief that we become acceptable and lovable so we can stand in the Presence of a Holy God.

People we know may be worthy of our respect and admiration. They live with integrity and honor and bring joy to the hearts of others. They are trustworthy and kind, generous and prayerful. We might want to seem worthy to others, but the thing each of us desires most is to be found worthy of God. We want to be counted among those He will reveal in the last days. We want to be called up front when He goes through the listing of His beloved children. We want to be worthy of being in His will as an inheritor of all that He has planned.

Whatever you do today, remind yourself that your real goal is to share your gratitude for all God does on your behalf because He always finds you worthy of His grace and mercy every day.

*Lord, You are my hope and my prayer each day. Help me to live in a way that pleases You and is **worthy** and honorable in Your sight. Amen.*

# PEACE

*All the people of Judah were happy about the promise, because they had promised with all their heart. They looked for God and found him. So the Lord gave them **peace** in all the country.*     2 Chronicles 15:15 NCV

What comes to mind when you think of the word **peace**? Do you think of world peace and wish somehow that violence would cease? Do you wish for peace in your own home, where everyone gets along and contributes with joy to the household? Perhaps you simply think of having peace in your soul, being in a space where your heart feels relieved of stress and the worries of the day.

This Old Testament Scripture offers us a glimpse of one way to achieve all those things—peace in the world, peace in our homes, and peace in our hearts. It reminds us that the only part we have in the matter is this. We must make a commitment and a promise that comes from the heart. When we make that promise to God, He works immediately to establish peace.

When we look for God, earnestly seeking His voice, His direction, His counsel on the steps we must take, we find Him. When we find Him, then the Lord is able to do what we ask of Him. He is able then to bless our country, our homes, and our lives with His incredible peace.

Pray for peace. Pray with every fiber of love that you hold in your heart. Let God know that you seek His face today, perhaps more earnestly than you ever have before. When you do, He promises to hear you and to bring you His peace that passes all understanding.

*Lord, I do seek Your **peace** today for the country I live in, for the people in my neighborhood, and in my household, and for my heart and soul. Grant us all Your peace. Amen.*

# WISDOM

*So God said to him, "You did not ask for a long life, or riches for yourself, or the death of your enemies. Since you asked for **wisdom** to make the right decisions, I will do what you asked. I will give you wisdom and understanding that is greater than anyone has had in the past or will have in the future."*
1 Kings 3:10–12 NCV

Imagine that you hold the secrets of the universe. You understand the complexities of life like no one before you. You are the go-to person at work and at home and in your neighborhood. People don't really know how you got such **wisdom**, but they accept and appreciate you for it. For Solomon, it was the desire of his heart to be wise and God granted it to be so.

Solomon was concerned about leading God's chosen people. He wanted to be sure that he pleased God and he wanted to treat people with mercy and understanding. He wanted to see into their hearts and know what motivated them. Those were the gifts God gave him.

Think about your own life. If God asked you what He could do for you today, would you ask for better health or more money, or maybe ask to make better choices? Would you ask Him to help you lead your team at work with more kindness and skill?

Every day, God allows you to wake up to new possibility. He calls you back from the night into the day and He asks you what He can do for you. He does this because He loves you and He is at your side. He wants only good things for you, and when you pray, He hears your heart and answers.

This is your day to tell God what you want Him to do for you. Let Him know that you want to lead others with grace and understand the motives and hearts of those around you. You want to be given wisdom in all you do.

*Lord, grant me **wisdom** today, so that all I do brings glory to Your name. Amen.*

# SUCCESS

*Trust the Lord with all your heart,*
*and don't depend on your own understanding.*
*Remember the Lord in all you do, and he will give you* ***success***.

Proverbs 3:5–6 NCV

You've been defining what **success** is most of your life. When you were in grade school or high school, you felt successful when your team won, even if you were simply cheering them on, or you felt successful when you aced a test. You had lots of ways to determine what seemed like achievement or accomplishment back then.

Today, you may wonder whether true success has eluded you, or you may be surprised to have gotten as far as you have. Either way, the only real measure of success comes from your relationship with God. It is the things you do only for God or the things you do where you seek God with your whole heart that can truly be measured.

Success comes when we include God in our plans. Success, achievement, victory comes at that moment when we recognize we didn't accomplish anything of note on our own. We achieved a new level because we asked God to join us in the game. We recognize that we can't depend on ourselves alone, because no matter how smart we might be, or how skilled or gifted we are, we need God's help to succeed in ways that matter. We need our hearts to be aligned with the will of God and with the purpose He has for us if we want a real measure of success.

Today, seek God's heart for the actions you want to take. You may discover a whole new meaning of what success is for you.

*Lord, help me to seek Your direction today so that I may meet with* ***success*** *according to Your plans for me and those I love. Amen.*

# CHANGE

*The Lord has made a promise
and will not **change** his mind.*

Psalm 110:4 NCV

It's not easy for most of us to embrace **change**. We go along with it when it happens, but we don't look eagerly for the changes that might come. Change, of course, can be a good thing. It can be the one thing you've needed to continue pursuing your dreams. It can be the thing that gets you out of a rut or offers a new opportunity. God may even inspire a change in you.

However, the psalmist is describing in this Scripture what it means that God does not change. When He makes a vow or a promise, He keeps that promise, and nothing deters Him, nothing deflects His decision. He is the same today, tomorrow, and forever!

Unfortunately, as human beings, we change all the time. We change our minds, modify our direction, or take a new course. On a whim, we may decide to take a new path or do something we don't normally do. We change because that's what we need at that moment, and sometimes that means our promises go flying out the window.

Imagine, then, that God makes you a promise. God makes you a promise and since He does not change, since He doesn't become influenced by anything you can do, He doesn't change His mind. You can count on Him because He does not alter or modify or change . . . ever! Whatever God has promised you, He will do, because He does not change His mind. You can count on Him!

*Lord, help me be a person who keeps my promises. When **change** happens in my life, help me to take it in stride, knowing that You are with me and that You will always be near to help me do the right thing. Amen.*

21

# HAS

*Jesus **has** the power of God, by which he has given us everything we need to live and to serve God. We have these things because we know him.*

2 Peter 1:3 NCV

When someone has something like a house, or a car, or a condo on the beach, we might say they have ownership of it. If they have ownership, then they are free to do with it whatever pleases them. They can invite others in, they can share what they've got, or they can keep everything to themselves.

Think now about what it means that Jesus **has** the power of God. That isn't the same as if the text said that He could have it, or He might have it, or He will someday have it. It says He has the power of God. It is His to do with as He wills. It is His to give or withhold. It is His to share however He chooses because He alone owns that power.

Fortunately for us, Jesus chooses to share His power. He gives us everything we need to live in this life. He opens the way for us to understand joy and live in righteousness. He wants us to have everything that He has so we can use it to the glory of God. He does not withhold what He has from you or from any of His children.

How could His power help you live more fully and serve God better? Perhaps the best way to discover that answer is simply to go to Jesus and seek His help. Ask Him for a portion of what He has. Ask Him to restore to you a clean heart, a right heart, and a pure heart so that you can benefit by all that He has to give you. The more you come to know Him, the more He can do for you. He alone has everything you need.

*Lord, I thank You for all that You have given me. This life only **has** meaning when it is wrapped in Your care. Amen.*

# LISTEN

*Happy are those who **listen** to me, watching at my door every day, waiting at my open doorway.*
*Those who find me find life, and the Lord will be pleased with them.*

Proverbs 8:34–35 NCV

Do you ever wonder what your life would look like if you simply turned off all the noise around you, sat quietly, and waited for God to speak? All the distractions that normally keep you from hearing His voice have been put aside and you are open to what He has for you. You can even stand at the doorway as the Proverb suggests and wait patiently. It's a wonderful idea because even if we are good at *talking* to God, we are not always good at *listening* to Him.

Perhaps we don't **listen** because we are afraid of what we will hear. After all, when we're in a situation that causes us to feel defensive, we generally spend a lot of time talking, trying to plead our case. The idea here, though, is that you are not on the hot seat. You are not in a space where you are being judged or criticized. You are simply sitting quietly and allowing God to speak openly to you. You're allowing His Presence to fill your soul and your spirit so that you feel the intense love He has for you.

As you go through the day, listen for God's sweet voice. Listen with your heart so that you don't miss a thing in the message He has for you. He'll meet you at the doorway. When you listen, you will find Him—you will find life.

*Father, help me to stop the noises that fill my mind today and simply **listen** to You with love and hope and praise. Amen.*

# ADVERSITY

*A friend loves at all times, and kinsfolk are born to share **adversity**.*

Proverbs 17:17 NRSV

This Proverb is a beautiful reminder about the importance of relationships. It's hard to imagine how any of us would thrive without the love of our friends and the compassion and strength and help we receive from the people we call "family." The kind of family that steps in when the rest of the world walks out, the kind that stays with you no matter what is going on in your life, is the focus of this Scripture. This is the kin, the family, the friends who are your anchors when **adversity** comes washing over you like a tidal wave. These are the people who were born for such a moment as this, the ones who rise with compassion to walk with you through the worst moments of your life. These are the ones God orchestrated long ago to stand with you no matter what happens.

You know who those people are, the ones who are your pillars of support. You are that person in their lives as well. It is part of the way that God shows His love and how He helps us to be the hands and feet for each other. Stand today and see the grace of God at work in your life through every friend and every family member who shines a light just for you under any circumstance or moment of adversity.

*Lord, You know how I value the people who support me and encourage me through **adversity**. Please bless them mightily for all they do. Amen.*

# PURPOSE

*But I have raised you up for this very **purpose**, that I might show you my power and that my name might be proclaimed in all the earth.*

Exodus 9:16 NIV

In our heart of hearts, most of us have a great desire to feel needed, or even called. We want to have a genuine **purpose** for living and for the work we do. Sometimes we struggle in our efforts to figure out just what our purpose might be. We envy the people who have a particular talent or skill and who can then take that talent and do amazing things in the world. We look in awe at the pastors who speak from pulpits week after week with great authority. We look at others of influence and then we wonder, "So what is it that I am supposed to do? What is my purpose?"

Perhaps this Scripture is a key to unlock the box that contains your life purpose. It reminds you that whatever your purpose may be, it is God's purpose that is really behind every success that you see out in the world. God raises people up, not so that they can be measured in their own greatness, but so His name can be glorified. God is the power behind the purpose. God is the purpose! He wants you and me to be people that He can get behind, fuel with incredible energy, and guide the world to see His face. We are God's reflection, the light that He wants others to see. We bring His purpose to light.

You don't have to be an Oscar-winning actor or an amazing country music star. You don't have to be the teacher of the year or the best pastor who ever preached a sermon. You must be the one who stands before God and allows Him to use you, to fuel you, to process His power through you so that others will come to know His name. Can you imagine a purpose more glorious than that? It's a calling and a huge job, but you can do it!

*Lord, thank You for creating me to work and play and be a person who fulfills Your **purpose**. Let me shine Your light for all to see in everything I do. Amen.*

# WILL

*The Lord had said to Abram, "Go from your country, your people and your father's household to the land I will show you. "I will make you into a great nation, and I will bless you; I will make your name great, and you will be a blessing."*
Genesis 12:1–2 NIV

No matter how many times you've read this Scripture, it's possible that you may have glossed over one of the key words in it: **will**. If we really focus on that small word, we see that God has a plan for His servant, Abram. He gives Abram, whom we know as Abraham, a very clear picture of what He will do. He doesn't equivocate! He doesn't say, "If you do XYZ, then I'll do this." He doesn't say, "I might do it, or I'm thinking about doing it, or if you say your prayers just right, I'll look into it." No! He says what He will do, and nothing will change that.

God chose Abraham to do a specific job and He outlined the terms of the deal. He promised to make Abraham and his descendants into a great nation. He promised to bless Abraham personally. When God blesses someone personally it means He gives them favor. He honors them and He helps them to achieve their goals. God promises that He will make Abraham's name great.

And finally, God promised that He would make Abraham a blessing. If any of us are a blessing to others, it is because we can offer them something. We might lead them into a new possibility as Abraham did for the children of Israel. We might offer encouragement, or inspiration, or a hand to hold when life is overwhelming. As Abraham was a blessing, so you are too.

God will do wonders for the people who respond to His call. His love overshadows their weaknesses. His power sustains them and His desire to accomplish the work He calls them to do will bring them blessing. You are called to be a blessing, and God will work out the desires of your heart.

*Lord, may Your **will** be done in my life today. Amen.*

# AFRAID

*So don't worry, because I am with you. Don't be **afraid**, because I am your God. I will make you strong and will help you; I will support you with my right hand that saves you.*                               Isaiah 41:10 NIV

If love is the emotion that gives us wings, fear or being **afraid** is the one that ties us back up again. How can we fly or rise to the top or do what we've been called to do in the world if we are filled with fear?

The answer is that it is hard to fly when your wings are still tied together. You have to release the things that bind you, before you can soar. For most of us, the fears we harbor are attached to old "tapes" or stories that we play in our heads. We remember when we were criticized for something we tried to do as a kid, so that now as an adult, we still remember the criticism and can't move forward with something we are meant to do. We might be extremely accomplished in our work, but a shadowy figure from the past still manages to trip us up, causing a momentary fear.

When you're afraid to step out or try again, it's a good time to remember the One who sees you and walks with you and strengthens you. God is at your right hand and knows your heart. He knows what you want to achieve, and if you've put your plans before Him, He can help you find your way, raising you up to new levels of possibility.

Fear is actually the opposite of love. Love opens doors and fear blocks the way. Today, put your fears in God's hand. You don't have to be afraid if you trust in Him. Let His love be bigger than any fear that may emerge in your mind. After all, He is the One who lives in your heart.

*Lord, thank You today for walking with me. Let me not be **afraid** of whatever this day brings. Sustain me with Your love and Your amazing presence. Amen.*

# STUDY

*I have rejoiced in your laws as much as in riches.*
*I will **study** your commandments and reflect on your ways.*
*I will delight in your decrees and not forget your word.*

Psalm 119:14–16 NLT

We make promises every day.

We promise we will cut down on carbs, so we can lose some weight. We promise we will establish better habits and walk more. We promise that we will remember to say our prayers early in the morning. We may even promise to **study**, learn more Scripture, or train ourselves in God's word.

The psalmist says that he rejoices in the laws, that is, the commands that God has given. In fact, not only does he rejoice, but those commands give him as much joy as any form of riches he may have. He makes a promise then. He says he will study God's rules and reflect on His ways. He regards the opportunity to learn more about God as a gift to his life.

If you study something and then reflect on it, it means that you are trying to honestly take it to heart. You want to remember it, perhaps memorize it, and apply it to your life. Once the psalmist meditates on God's ways, he states again what joy he will experience and then he makes another promise, and says, "I will not forget your word."

Promise yourself that you, too, will study, reflect, consider, and then remember God's words wherever you are today. Talk about what you've learned with those around you and encourage them to get out a notebook and the Word of God. It could be a great day to study!

*Lord, help me to **study** Your commands and hold them close to my heart. I pray to always take delight in Your ways. Amen.*

# ALERT

*For you are all children of the light and of the day; we don't belong to darkness and night. So be on your guard, not asleep like the others. Stay **alert** and be clearheaded.*                    1 Thessalonians 5:5–6 NLT

We might think of an **alert** as something that happens to give us fair warning about what's ahead. We get an alert that bad weather is in the area, or we get a warning that a senior citizen is lost somewhere driving a car. Bulletins of this sort keep us aware of issues of immediate concern.

When God tells us to be alert, be awake, get prepared, it has some of those implications as well. He wants us to be aware that the Devil is always on the prowl. God wants us to keep close to Him so that He can protect us wherever we may be.

It appears that many people are walking around half asleep. They are not conscious of God's Presence. They do not know His love and protection or the light He can bring to their lives. They don't know, and they are confused about what God can really do for them.

As a Christian, though, you have already been ushered toward the light. You are not meant to loiter in the darkness. It's important to wake up to all that God has planned for you so that you can be clearheaded and capable of doing the work He's asked of you. Sometimes God wants you to be alert to the way a person acts or the way a group responds to Him. Other times, He wants you to realize that something wonderful is coming and it is meant for you. He's giving you a heads-up that He's about to act on one of your dreams. Stay alert today and seek His direction.

*Lord, I know that I'm often less than **alert**, somewhat sleepy as I go through life. Help me to be ready for all that You've planned for me. Amen.*

# BELIEVE

*I write this letter to you who **believe** in the Son of God so you will know you have eternal life.*                    1 John 5:13 NCV

What you **believe** about the world changes over time. What you believe *in* may change as well. Perhaps you believed that you would always live in the country because that's where you lived as a child. You now live in the city and you can't imagine that country life anymore. You may have believed that you would grow up to become a teacher back when you were in junior high. Now you're an architect and love the work you do. What you once believed has changed.

How does that relate to your understanding of what it means to believe in God? When you truly believe in something or in someone, as in the case of your belief in Jesus and God, then you absolutely know it to be true. You know it so well that nothing could change your mind about it. You won't outgrow it or leave it behind. It is simply a part of you. It is in your belief system, and like your DNA, it simply exists to make you the person you are. It shapes and molds everything you do.

In anyone's lifetime, there may be many beliefs, things that were believed at one time or another. Beliefs of that type prove flimsy and often simply fade away. But when you know something to be true, when you have it deeply engrained inside your heart and mind, then that is more than a simple belief; that is a way for you to believe eternally. Today, look at the things you currently believe. How many of those things are ones you know without a doubt? Your faith in God will stand out, then, as one of the few things you absolutely are certain you can count on. Believe in Jesus and you will have eternal life. That's something you know for sure!

*Lord, thank You for all You've done to shape the things I **believe** in. You know my heart and how much I count on You. Amen.*

# AIM

*However, I consider my life worth nothing to me; my only **aim** is to finish the race and complete the task the Lord Jesus has given me—the task of testifying to the good news of God's grace.* Acts 20:24 NIV

Ready! **Aim!** Fire! No, you didn't just sign up for a sharpshooting class. You signed up to be more intentional about achieving your goals. You signed up to remind yourself that your job is to finish the race and to complete the task that you have been assigned, not by your boss at work, but by your Lord and Savior, Jesus Christ. You have a purpose in Him that is like no other. It is the task of every believer. God has prepared you and made you ready to do His work. Your aim is to share the good news of God's grace.

How will you do it? You might begin by determining ways to focus your message. Will you be in a meeting with others you work with, or will you be sitting at the dinner table with friends and family, or will you simply be walking down the street and see someone who has caught your attention? Where will you aim your message?

Once you've aimed in the right direction, you can prepare to deliver the message itself. You might recall a Scripture that helps you be bold in the way you witness to others, or perhaps you will begin to pray for the person you are going to address because you want to shoot straight. You don't want them to miss the point you plan to make.

Finally, you will fire off your message with enthusiasm and gusto and love so that they can embrace what you have to say. Aim to speak with just one person today about the grace of God's love.

*Lord, help me to make it my **aim**, my intention, to draw at least one other person closer to You today. Amen.*

# DO

*Here is a simple rule of thumb for behavior: Ask yourself what you want people to do for you; then grab the initiative and do it for them! If you only love the lovable, do you expect a pat on the back? Run-of-the-mill sinners do that.*

Luke 6:31–32 MSG

Many of us are doers. We know what we **do** well, and we do it as a matter of course. When we do our work for the kingdom of God, it matters. What we do for the good of others makes an extraordinary difference.

In this passage, though, Luke is taking the idea of "doing" to a new level. He is asking us to see if what we do goes far enough. Do we thrive at doing good things for those we respect and appreciate? Do we only volunteer to do those things that don't require us to get out of our comfort zones or get our hands dirty? Do we do things for others, so we can get a few more points in Heaven?

If what we do matters, then it always matters. You can start with little things. Pick up the phone and call your mother or that friend who wonders what has happened to you. Go to the local library and sign up to read to the kids. Buy some groceries and take them to the food bank. You can make a difference. You could be the catalyst, the energy that lifts their wings.

Take a little inventory of the things you do, and see if you have been willing to stretch and bend and move toward new opportunities that also need a doer. The more you do for the lost and the lame, the more you are like Jesus. When you do what God designed you to do, you shine a light on the love of God. May God bless all that you do today.

*Lord, I know what I do well and I realize that I don't often step outside my comfort zone to draw others in. Make it clear to me when there is more that You want me to **do**. Amen.*

# FAITHFUL

*If we are not **faithful**, he will still be faithful, because he must be true to who he is.*
                                                        2 Timothy 2:13 NCV

In our generation, it may have gone out of style to be faithful. We might look at this word as being a measure of our loyalty to others or to the people we work with. It might be the standard that defines our relationship with God or with our spouse. We could hope so.

Chances are good that few of us are **faithful**. We may not intentionally step outside the boundaries of marriage or we might not share a company secret with a friend, but we might find ourselves giving in to a momentary challenge that is designed to test the strength of our faithfulness. One thing about not being faithful is quite clear: It is a choice we make.

God is faithful to us despite our actions. He continues to favor us and bring us back to the light of His love no matter how long we've walked in the darkness. He does it because He promised to be faithful, and He does not break His own promises. He must be faithful to His true nature.

There's the difficulty. We also have a true nature, and without Jesus, it's a nature that is prone to simply walk past the boundaries of honorable behavior and step into the mire of life. We are easily tempted, and we become faithless. What should we do?

Today, let's put faithlessness away. Let's move right to the light of God's love and ask Him to help us be the faithful followers we truly want to be. By His grace and mercy, He will hold us up, so we can be true people of faith. It's a choice you can make every day.

*Lord, You know those things that tempt my spirit and cause me to go astray. Help me to stand firm and be **faithful**, wrapped in Your love today. Amen.*

# VIGILANT

*Be sober, be **vigilant**; because your adversary the devil walks about like a roaring lion, seeking whom he may devour.* 1 Peter 5:8 NKJV

No matter where you live these days, it is probably necessary for you to be more **vigilant** than ever as you go about your everyday tasks. You may have once felt it was safe to leave your front door unlocked because you lived in a neighborhood where everything was peaceful. You may have felt just fine about letting your kids walk to school because it was only twenty minutes from your door. You may have done those things before, but now you're wary, more watchful, more concerned.

The Scripture from 1 Peter reminds us that we have always needed to be vigilant. Whether we lived in the country or the suburbs, we've had an adversary stalking us, looking for any opportunity to nibble away at our call to faith. You may think that you don't have to worry about that "roaring lion," but the truth is, you have to stick close to your Savior. He will guard you in truth and protect you with the armor of God. It's not always easy, because the Deceiver is clever. He works on your insecurities and your fears. He discovers where you feel the most vulnerable and attacks you from behind.

The word for you then is to stay alert, be vigilant. Remember to put on the full armor of God wherever you go and bathe your family and friends in prayer. God is always watching over you, and He will give you the strength to take on the roaring lions.

*Lord, please stay close to me and to all the people I love today. Let no one be deceived by the adversary. Help us to be **vigilant** and strengthen and renew our spirits in You. Amen.*

# WALK

*This is the account of Noah and his family. Noah was a righteous man, blameless among the people of his time, and he **walked** faithfully with God.*

Genesis 6:9 NIV

If you're thinking of getting out for a **walk** today, you might decide to invite someone along whom you can confide in, share your heart with, and bring up to speed on the general direction of your life. You may think that your best friend doesn't live close enough to walk with you, but that may not be true. Your best friend on Earth and in Heaven is always ready to walk with you. He loves it when you request His Presence and when you share all the events of your day. He loves it when you walk faithfully beside Him.

If you're not going for a walk, it won't matter, because He'll still be close to you if you simply ask Him to be there. Ask God to come with you to school, or walk with you through the grocery store, or maybe stay close beside you as you watch the kids at play. You can go on without Him, but why would you?

The Scriptures say that Noah was a righteous man and that he walked faithfully with God. In truth, one of the reasons we even remember the story of Noah is that he brought God into every plan and dream he ever had. He looked for ways that the two of them could connect and get to know each other better. Noah wanted to walk with God as his father and grandfather had done before him.

Do you want to know God like Noah did? If you do, then step up to the One who desires to share all things with you and seek His face. He will be with you anytime you invite Him along. Walk faithfully with God.

*Lord, please help me to seek Your face wherever I am today. **Walk** beside me and live within me so that I, too, can be blameless before You. Amen.*

# INTENTLY

*And in Lystra a certain man without strength in his feet was sitting, a cripple from his mother's womb, who had never walked. This man heard Paul speaking. Paul, observing him **intently** and seeing that he had faith to be healed, said with a loud voice, "Stand up straight on your feet!" And he leaped and walked.*                    Acts 14:8–10 NKJV

You can take a walk on a summer's day and notice the subtle changes in the colors of the landscape, the new wreath the neighbors hung on their front door, or the marigolds gracing a walkway, and on other days, you notice absolutely nothing. Sometimes you're **intently** taking everything in. Sometimes you're not.

Paul might not have noticed the crippled man who sat near him as he spoke to the crowd. After all, there were many people there. He could have just kept delivering his message, but something drew him to take note of the crippled man. Paul looked at him, and it appears that he kept looking at him to try to determine just what the man needed or wanted. Paul looked at the man so intently that he realized the man had the kind of faith that would make it possible for Paul to facilitate a healing. Paul knew that if he spoke to the man in a certain way, perhaps as intently as he had already studied him, the man would find the faith to stand up and walk.

The Scripture says that Paul saw the man's faith by looking at him intently, that is, closely, seriously, and with deep concentration. Do others see your faith if they look carefully, eagerly, intently at you? Would they be able to recognize that you believe in the One True God? When God's light shines, we can see it in each other if we look intently, gently affirming the Savior in each one we meet.

*Lord, help me to take in the world around me today. Let me notice the little things that matter, and especially let me look **intently** at those who are near me, eager to see Your grace within them. Amen.*

# LEARNING

*Give instruction to a wise man, and he will be still wiser;*
*Teach a just man, and he will increase in **learning**.*
*The fear of the Lord is the beginning of wisdom,*
*And the knowledge of the Holy One is understanding.*

Proverbs 9:9–10 NKJV

Your tutoring and your education never end. You always have opportunities for learning new things. You may have loved learning as you went through your high school and college years. You may have breezed through it all and never really connected to your schoolwork. The important thing is that no matter where you are in life now, you are ripe for **learning**.

Proverbs reminds us, though, that learning may not be all there is. Instruction is only as good as the material that we take in and use and come to understand. When we reach up to God, holding Him in awe as the Creator of the universe, recognizing that we are His creation, then learning has begun and wisdom will soon follow.

Wisdom suggests that we get ready to learn more, to take in all we can about the glory of our Father in Heaven. When we do that, we are ready for His instruction, ready to learn, and to grow under His loving care. With God's help, you will increase in wisdom, learning more each day from the gifts He shares with you of His Spirit. Keep on learning.

*Lord, I know that I have a lot to **learn**, a lot more to understand*
*about You. I thank You for granting me the wisdom to walk with You*
*one step at a time and learning as I go. Amen.*

# HUMBLE

*Now Moses was very **humble**. He was the least proud person on earth.*

Numbers 12:3 NCV

Take a moment, and think about the most **humble** person you know. How does the person you're picturing share their heart, or give of themselves to others? Think about the way they speak and act no matter who else is in the room. Humble people are refreshing simply because they make no effort to shine their own light.

It's interesting here to note that Moses was considered to be very humble. In fact, God looked at him and saw him as the most humble, the least proud person on Earth. What an amazing idea! It's amazing because Moses raised the bar for the rest of us in what it means to walk in humility before the Lord. He left everything behind to follow God's plan for his life.

If you're having trouble picturing people who have a humble demeanor, then think about those on the opposite side of the scale. Those are the ones we might call arrogant, bombastic, and "full of themselves." When someone is full of themselves, they can't be full of the Spirit of God. Perhaps Moses was the most humble man on Earth because He was truly full of God's Spirit. He was led by God, and He literally surrendered his life to God from the moment of his calling.

Imagine now that each one of us can walk before God with a humble heart, ready to receive His Spirit in fullness and joy. Humility always puts others first. Perhaps humility is another word for love. May you have a humble heart before God and share your love with others today.

*Lord, thank You for the example of the patriarchs like Moses. Help me to be a **humble** person who seeks to be full of Your gracious Spirit, every day. Amen.*

# COURAGE

*Be alert. Continue strong in the faith. Have **courage**, and be strong.*
1 Corinthians 16:13 NCV

It takes a lot of nerve to stand up to life some days. You have to get out of bed and summon every ounce of **courage** you can muster and head out into the world. When you feel like you have to suit up to get out there and fight the battles of the day, it takes courage. Your armor may not feel like it fits just right.

Remember when David was just a young boy and went out to meet the giant, Goliath? King Saul tried to put his armor around David to protect him, but David couldn't even stand up under its weight. He told the king he'd simply have to face the giant without armor. He had courage. He believed that God would fight for him, so he didn't need to do anything but show up and obey what God would have him do.

You may have your own giants to slay today. You may have to overcome the weight of the armor that someone else put on you. You may have to find a way around what they have done so that you can be effective. Whatever it is, it will take courage. It will take strength. The good news is that you don't have to go into any battle alone because your Heavenly Father goes before you. You and He together are a force of courage. Be alert to all that God will do in your life today.

*Lord, the battlegrounds change quickly. When it feels like I might win on one front, there's another one that needs my attention. Grant me the **courage** to go where You want me to go and to fight only the battles where You go before me. Amen.*

# DOUBT

*Jesus replied, "Truly I tell you, if you have faith and do not **doubt**, not only can you do what was done to the fig tree, but also you can say to this mountain, 'Go, throw yourself into the sea,' and it will be done. If you believe, you will receive whatever you ask for in prayer."*

Matthew 21:21–22 NIV

"If you have faith and do not **doubt**,... you can..." These words seem so clear and so simple. They even feel possible when you read them. After all, you have faith. So what's the problem?

The fig trees around the world have not been stopped in their tracks, withered up, and gone to seed. The mountain ranges are not simply picking up their grass roots organizations and moving to new territory. Is something missing? What did Jesus have that we don't?

Of course, we could provide a litany of answers to that, but the key one here has to do with this word "doubt." Jesus knew exactly where He came from. He knew His Father. He knew what He was called to do and He did it, never doubting that God was faithful to carry out through Jesus the things they had agreed to accomplish.

Now, hundreds of generations have passed, and the mountains are still rooted to their spots. Perhaps Jesus did not mean that to be a literal thing, or maybe he did, given the dried-up fig tree, but what about you and me? What are we going to do about doubt? Ah, the answer is in the same Scripture: Believe and you will receive.

Today, may you receive tenfold everything you believe with your whole heart. May you receive without a doubt the blessing that God alone has for you.

*Lord, I do believe in You with my whole heart. Help me to receive the kind of believing heart, mind, and soul that erases all **doubt** today. Amen.*

# PATIENCE

*Let your **patience** show itself perfectly in what you do. Then you will be perfect and complete and will have everything you need.*     James 1:4 NCV

The writer of James 1:4 might cause us to be more than a little concerned as we strive to figure out what it means to "let our **patience** show" in all we do. Does it mean that when the kid next to us at the restaurant is screaming to high heaven, we just nod and smile? Does it mean that the third time we call the Internet provider about our slow service and they put us on hold, we are perfectly in control? Or maybe it means when your spouse forgets an important occasion one more time, you simply stay calm. Of course, in all these situations your response may be like these examples. After all, you are very patient.

Let's look at patience, though, from another view. No matter how patient you've had to be with others in your life, imagine what it would be like if you somehow pushed God to the limit of His patience. How many times have you caused Him to be disappointed because you forgot an important occasion in your relationship with Him, or you didn't keep a promise you made, or you let the noises of life obscure the sound of His voice? How many times has God had to be patient with you?

Certainly, Jesus gave us numerous examples of what it means to have patience in all you do. Wherever you are today, consider the benefits of being patient with others and with yourself. Guided by patience, your day promises to be perfect and complete and provide everything you need. Now that's worth the effort to achieve.

*Lord, I have to admit that I can be a bit short on **patience**. Help me to be as patient with others as You so often are with me. Amen.*

# ACCEPT

*But I know you—I know that you don't have God's love in you. I have come from my Father and speak for him, but you don't **accept** me. But when another person comes, speaking only for himself, you will accept him. You try to get praise from each other, but you do not try to get the praise that comes from the only God. So how can you believe?*     John 5:42–44 NCV

When you **accept** something, an idea, a gift, or even a new friendship, you do so by embracing it with delight and joy. You receive it into your heart and you take pleasure in the experience. When God accepted you through baptism and your heart of faith, it brought you closer together. God adopted you into His family. He accepted you "as is," with all your faults and foibles.

As human beings, we're often willing to accept things that are totally untrue, making room for them in our lives and in our actions. Even when Jesus came, speaking of the truth of God, people were blinded by deceivers, more willing to accept lies than truth.

Perhaps the question that was posed in John 5 is still a good one for us to consider: If we're so willing to accept the lies of this world, then "how can [we] believe?" How will we even recognize the truth when it comes close to us? We each make many choices every day. What you accept into your life as truth becomes the way you perceive all things. When you accept God's love and grace and forgiveness as He intends, then your life will reflect His truth. May you accept the grace of God with your whole heart and mind today.

*Lord, I **accept** You into my life and seek to believe with my whole heart. Help me now to live in Your truth in all that I do. Amen.*

# DELIGHT

*Take **delight** in the Lord, and he will give you the desires of your heart.*
*Commit your way to the Lord; trust in him and he will do this.*

Psalm 37:4–5 NIV

When is the last time you focused on the things in your life that simply delight you? **Delight** is a great word because it gives us a glimpse of something that is more than joy, and perhaps less than out-and-out laughter, but something that truly lights us up from the inside. If it delights you, it makes you feel the way you may have felt when you first fell in love. You gush with joy. You feel silly with anticipation of all that is ahead. You overflow with excitement. Everything about the object of your delight makes you feel good.

Now transfer that understanding to the way you take delight in the Lord. Do you remember that feeling when you first encountered His amazing love in a real and personal way? It may have been your first realization of how big and how gracious God really is. It may have caused you to wonder what it is about this great big God that spurs Him to want to embrace everyday, ordinary, wonderful you.

The psalmist tells us that when we delight in the Lord, there's an instant return on our investment. There's a gift in it; we could even go as far as to call it a "gift with purchase." God purchased you through Jesus, then you lit up with the joy of your salvation, and as if that wasn't enough, God goes on to give you the desires of your heart. Wow! Your commitment to delight in the God of your heart goes a long way toward helping you live the life He fully designed for you. Now that should give you lots of reasons to smile with delight today!

*Lord, I do **delight** in You. I know that sometimes I don't tell You*
*enough what it means to me to love and serve You, so please know*
*that You are the delight of my heart. Amen.*

# GUARD

*"See, I am sending an angel ahead of you to **guard** you along the way and to bring you to the place I have prepared."*　　　Exodus 23:20 NIV

As you step out of bed and prepare for the day today, think a moment about the things you will do and the places you will go. Perhaps you have to take the kids to school, or maybe you have a big meeting with clients in a thriving city. Your life takes you to many places, and what could be more wonderful than to realize you are not alone? God has sent a **guard**, an angel, ahead of you. He will see to it that you get to the place He has already prepared.

The work of a guard is primarily to be a protector, to watch out for the things that might trip you up or cause you to lose sight of your goal. A guard will go ahead of you to scout out the landscape of the world you have to navigate, even if you never physically walk out your door. Sometimes a spiritual guard simply watches out for your heart, making sure that you are safely connected to all that God wants for you.

Imagine then that God has sent His angel ahead of you today. He knows every step you will take, every wrong turn, every good option that will be before you, and He does all He can do to help you get to the place you're meant to go. Yes, today it's a good thing to give God thanks and praise. He has sent a guard to watch over you in all your ways.

*Lord, thank You for guarding my steps and my direction. Bless the work of my hands and heart today, and **guard** and protect me in all I do. Amen.*

# LOVE

*But the fruit of the Spirit is love, joy, peace, forbearance, kindness,
goodness, faithfulness, gentleness and self-control. Against such things there
is no law.*
Galatians 5:22–23 NIV

Love plays out in every arena of our lives…**love** of and for God, love
of children and family and friends, and love of the work we do and the
opportunities we are given. Love abounds! With all these opportunities
for love, the world should be humming along with great joy as each person
celebrates the endless stream of love that comes their way.

Perhaps our Creator hoped or imagined or even planned for love to
make the world go 'round, but clearly some of us did not get the message. Love has taken a backseat to arrogance and greed, pride and avarice,
jealousy and hate. Those are the things that fill our headlines and run
through our minds like a ticker tape. What happened to love? How can we
bring it back into our daily lives?

Galatians 5 gives us a hint. It reminds us of the Spirit that works within
each of us to bring out our better personality traits. It refreshes our memory about the ways we can show love to each other. We can start by simply
being aware of our actions, words, and intentions toward others. We can
speak with kindness and forbearance, gentleness and peace. We can offer
a gentle word, a loving smile, and joyful conversation. Those things make
a difference in the way any message we want to deliver is received.

Whatever we do, we always have a choice. We can walk into any situation with actions and a heart that is shaped by love, or we can add to the
noise of an already difficult world. Keep love at the center of all you do
today.

*Lord, thank You for loving me so much and for faithfully shining
your light on my life. Let me walk in love and share Your love with
others today. Amen.*

# NAME

*He counts the stars*
*and names each one.*
*Our Lord is great and very powerful.*
*There is no limit to what he knows.*                    Psalm 147:4–5 NCV

Your parents probably thought hard about the different **names** they considered giving you when you were born. After all, it would be your name for the rest of your life. In our culture, we give everything names. We live on brands that commercials tell us are good for us, and each time something new comes out, a new name comes with it.

It's interesting to note that in the Old Testament, we often see that God changed people's names as He began something new in them. For example, He changed Abram to Abraham and Sarai to Sarah when He called them to lead the people. In essence, God put a new stamp on them.

In the Psalm noted here, we even see that God counted the stars and gave names to each one. When each star was born, the Creator provided a name. He wanted each one to have importance and definition.

We might draw the conclusion, then, that names are important. God has many names, and we call Him Father, Lord, and King of Kings. He calls himself "I Am." When you think about it, God helped us know Him simply by telling us His name. In those two words, we understand that everything we believe in, confide in, and trust in exists in this one name. God is in an eternal state of being, an everlasting I AM. He is always and forever. He has the only living name that will ever be. There is no limit to what He knows. Rejoice that He called you by name today.

*Lord, thank You for allowing us to call You by Your **name**, and*
*giving us Jesus as the only name by which we may be saved. Thank*
*You for calling me by name and drawing me closer to You. Amen.*

# PROTECT

*The sun cannot hurt you during the day, and the moon cannot hurt you at night.*
*The Lord will **protect** you from all dangers; he will guard your life.*
*The Lord will guard you as you come and go, both now and forever.*

Psalm 121:6–8 NCV

It would be nice if we were born with a protective coating. That coating would keep us from getting too cold or too warm. It could shield us from mosquito bites or nicks and bruises. Perhaps it would even **protect** our hearts as we got old enough to be foolish about our actions.

Since we don't actually have a protective coating, we buy insurance to protect us in case a calamity happens. We're ready if the car gets a fender bender or if our appendix bursts. We're even ready for earthquakes and fires. We know what it means to have as much protection as possible.

All of that is true, but one thing remains. Who will protect our lives as we come and go, both now and forever? Only God. Only God can keep us safe from any harm that might damage our eternal existence. Only God can watch out for us so that we're never blindsided by the enemy or find ourselves in a pit of despair from which we can never get out.

The Lord protects our lives as we come and go, as we put our lives in His hands, both now and forever. Give praise to the One who defends you, guards you, and keeps you safe for eternity.

*Father in Heaven, You know what I need to **protect** my heart and mind and soul each day. Keep me always in Your care. Amen.*

# SATISFY

*The eyes of all look expectantly to You,*
*And You give them their food in due season.*
*You open Your hand*
*And **satisfy** the desire of every living thing.*
*The Lord is righteous in all His ways,*
*Gracious in all His works.*

Psalm 145:15–17 NKJV

We spend a large portion of our time trying to **satisfy** our desires. We want to achieve a measure of significance. We want to be fulfilled in our relationships with those dearest to us. We want to know that we have lived a life of purpose and discover an oasis of contentment. These are at least some of the things that may satisfy us in the journey of life.

But what will satisfy, not just our wants, but our soul's desires? What will bring us that peace that passes all understanding so that we can bear witness within ourselves of God's truth and love? What else offers contentment beyond measure?

If you're not sure what will satisfy your spirit, take a look at what the psalmist says here. We can look to the One who is righteous in all His ways—not some of His ways, or a few of His ways, but in all of His ways. Because He is righteous, and gracious and loving, He truly wants to satisfy the desires of your heart in the timing that is best for you. Look expectantly to Him today as you go out. Look with great anticipation, for He will open His hand and provide for you and bring you contentment and peace and satisfy your spirit's desires.

*Lord, thank You that You are my provider, my gracious helping*
*hand, and the one who satisfies me. Watch over those I love as well*
*and **satisfy** the desires of their spirits. Amen.*

# SIGN

*Always remember these commands I give you today. Teach them to your children, and talk about them when you sit at home and walk along the road, when you lie down and when you get up. Write them down and tie them to your hands as a sign. Tie them on your forehead to remind you, and write them on your doors and gates.* Deuteronomy 6:6–9 NCV

We like **signs**. We post them everywhere. We put a sign in our yard that says we just got a new roof or the house is for sale. We put signs in retail shops to stimulate sales. We wear jewelry and T-shirts that declare our faith or indicate our politics. We have been conditioned to pay attention to signs.

The children of Israel were too. As you may recall from Deuteronomy 6:8–9, they were instructed to do things to remind others that God was in their midst. They wore the signs of God's commands on their clothing and on their foreheads, tied them to their hands, and they posted them over their doors and gates. Why? Because God did not want them to forget who they were. He did not want them to stop telling His stories. He wanted every generation to know Him.

Nothing has changed. God still wants us to tell His stories. He still wants us to write down the things that are important so that we remember what He has done in our lives. He still wants us to wear the signs of His favor and of His commands. God has put His sign in our hearts so that we will continue to share our hope and our faith with those around us. Share the signs of God's favor in your life every chance you get.

*Lord, You have blessed us with many ways to recognize Your Presence in our lives. Help me to share the **sign** of Your love and favor with others. Amen.*

# FRIENDS

*You are my **friends** if you do what I command you. I no longer call you servants, because a servant does not know what his master is doing. But I call you friends, because I have made known to you everything I heard from my Father.*                                                    John 15:14–15 NCV

Probably the dearest word in any language is the word **friend**. A friend is someone who chooses to be in your life. A few friends become your confidants as you navigate the waves of adversity or uncertainty. You bounce ideas off each other, share your hopes and your secrets, and if you're connected by faith, you may even pray together. You enjoy the times you spend together. You find reasons to laugh and celebrate life, and reasons to hold each other up and bring comfort when things go awry. Friends are people who enrich your life.

It is an interesting idea, then, that Jesus told the disciples that He wanted them to know He considered them to be His friends. Though they were all in the business of serving God, and Jesus knew they wanted to serve Him, He shifted their understanding of the kind of relationship they shared. He called them friends.

Imagine, then, that the Creator of all things chose you to be His friend. How will you show Him today what that friendship means to you? Will you spend time with Him in Scripture or talk with Him about the concerns of your heart?

God is there for you as a friend today and every day. You're one of His favorite people!

*Lord, I ask that we might walk together today as **friends**. Embrace me in all that I do so that I honor our friendship always. Amen.*

# STAND

*This is what the Lord says: "**Stand** where the roads cross and look. Ask where the old way is, where the good way is, and walk on it."*

Jeremiah 6:16 NCV

When you take a **stand**, perhaps to support a cause or to pick a side in a dispute, you are committing yourself to a direction. There is an old adage that says, "If you stand for something, you won't fall for just anything." When God asks us to take a stand, He, too, is saying that we need to make a commitment. He wants us to decide which way we will go. He wants us to stand for something.

In this passage from Jeremiah, God put the people at a crossroads. He asked them to look down both roads. Now when God asks us to look, it seems reasonable that He isn't suggesting that we take a quick peek and move on. Standing at a crossroads generally means that you have a very specific choice to make. One of those choices will probably serve you well. The other one may not.

For any of us, taking a stand is not easy. Usually, we can see a reasonable possibility either way we might go. We understand both sides. The problem is that sometimes we must step up and choose. We have to get beyond a casual look and really put a stake in the ground. Where do we stand?

In Joshua's day, when he called on the people of Israel to take a stand, he told them they had to choose what they would do. His question was about whether they would choose to serve God. Joshua answered it this way. "As for me and my house, we will serve the Lord." If you're at a crossroads, take a stand and choose the good way—and walk in it.

*Lord, help me to take a **stand** and choose to serve You in the way I live and work today. Amen.*

51

# AWARE

*When Jacob awoke from his sleep, he thought, "Surely the Lord is in this place, and I was not **aware** of it." He was afraid and said, "How awesome is this place! This is none other than the house of God; this is the gate of heaven."*

Genesis 28:16–17 NIV

When Jacob fell asleep and rested his head on a rock near Bethel, he had a dream. In his dream, he saw the angels of God ascending and descending on a ladder. He heard the voice of God speak directly to him. This was not a fleeting dream. This was a dream that was so real, Jacob could not do anything but respond to it. He woke up and realized God was literally in the place where he was resting his head. Jacob was suddenly very **aware** of God's presence.

In our own lives, God is always in our presence. He walks with us and works to make Himself known so that we can act in a new way or understand a message He has been trying to reveal to us. God wants us to be aware of His presence, and to be conscious of what He has already done in our lives. When we stop to think about what God has done, we're mindful of His handiwork. We're more aware that we are not wandering through the world alone. Awareness means that you're awake, conscious of what God is doing in your life right now.

Jacob took the stone he had used as a pillow and turned it into an altar. He was aware that he was resting in a sacred place. He wanted to give God thanks for sharing that space with him.

Perhaps in your life today, God is seeking a way for you to become aware of His presence. As you become more connected to Him, give Him thanks and praise for drawing so close to you.

*Lord, I confess that I am sometimes not **aware** of Your Divine presence in my daily routine. Help me to stop and seek You in all I do today. Amen.*

# HEART

*Acknowledge the God of your father, and serve him with wholehearted devotion and with a willing mind, for the Lord searches every **heart** and understands every desire and every thought. If you seek him, he will be found by you.*
                                                            1 Chronicles 28:9 NIV

It may be a bit sobering to realize that God searches every **heart** and understands every desire and every thought. If our hearts are in the right place, then we might find that comforting. If our hearts have gone astray in some way, we may not.

When you get to the heart of any situation, it often means that you're getting to the core of it, you're getting to the truth in some way. The heart of any person then is a big deal. Perhaps it's the only deal. God wants us to love Him with our whole heart, soul, and mind.

Sometimes we need to stop and do a little inventory. We need to check to see if there are thoughts and desires that we need to sweep out of our hearts. Maybe there are cobwebs of old memories that continue to deceive our hearts with unkind thoughts or destructive ideas. Maybe we should be as invested in searching our hearts as God is, so that our thoughts can be pure and our hearts can be light.

If you have an interest in discovering more of what is going on in your own heart, then it would be good to do what David did in Psalm 51:10: Ask God to create a clean heart in you. And watch Him work in you in ways you could never have seen before.

*Lord, I know that I often need Your help to clean up my old thoughts and get rid of those ideas that simply distract my **heart** from You. Give me a clean heart and right spirit today. Amen.*

# INTEGRITY

*Teach believers with your life: by word, by demeanor, by love, by faith, by*
*integrity.*                                                    1 Timothy 4:11–12 MSG

**Integrity** is one of those words we think we understand until we start to look at it the way God might look at it. After all, as honest and upright as we are about certain things, few of us could say that with every word, or with every thought, we've acted with integrity.

True integrity might require us to change a few things. Sure, we have operating principles that keep us from doing any of those outrageous sins. Even if we have some of those things lurking in our past, we've grown and become more mature in our faith, and God has forgiven the mistakes of youth. We've become better people.

However, we may still be wrestling with this idea of integrity. How do we determine the fine line that keeps us honest all the time? How do we serve as a good example to others?

Perhaps it helps to recognize that we aren't perfect human beings. We aren't going to get through life without blemishes or warts or whatever else might describe the poor choices we've made. However, the good news is that because of Jesus, God is willing to forgive us and to wipe the slate clean. He's willing to help us start fresh to be people of pure hearts with real integrity and a desire to live in ways that please Him. Integrity means that you are willing to be honest with yourself or, even better, honest with God. When you are, you'll walk with integrity, truth, and honesty each day.

*Lord, I know that I have fallen down a lot of times and You have*
*graciously picked me up again. Help me to walk in true **integrity** of*
*spirit and mind and heart today. Amen.*

# NET

*Once again, the kingdom of heaven is like a net that was let down into the lake and caught all kinds of fish. When it was full, the fishermen pulled it up on the shore. Then they sat down and collected the good fish in baskets, but threw the bad away.*                    Matthew 13:47 NIV

A **net** is a handy tool if you're catching fish or butterflies. In the days when Jesus walked along the shorelines calling his disciples, He told them that even though they were good at catching fish, He would teach them how to catch people. What He meant was that He would help them understand how a person can be brought into the kingdom of Heaven.

If we want to follow the example of Jesus and be one of His disciples today, then we are still interested in "catching" people for the kingdom of Heaven.

One of the ways to put our proverbial net to use is by the way we live in faith. The more we do good deeds, showing compassion, lending a hand, and sharing our faith, the more opportunity we have to engage the hearts of those around us. We can spread a pretty wide net, and before long, we'll find we've captivated a lot of people and helped bring them into the house of the Lord.

Are you ready to cast your net on the waters of your office, your home, and wherever else you go? There are a few people just waiting to be caught by the Spirit of God's love and mercy.

*Lord, let's catch a few more people for the kingdom today. I know that You have a very wide **net**! Amen.*

# INSPIRED

*We remember before our God and Father your work produced by faith, your labor prompted by love, and your endurance **inspired** by hope in our Lord Jesus Christ.*                    1 Thessalonians 1:2–3 NIV

It's helpful to notice on any given day the things that vie for our attention and time. We work hard and we do what we believe is right and fair and in keeping with the way God wants us to live our lives. We do all that, and it feels just fine.

Feeling **inspired**, though, is rare, and that's why it is so fulfilling and motivating when it happens. When you feel inspired to talk with someone and it goes well, you are glad that you listened to that gentle nudge from the Holy Spirit to have that conversation. When you come up with a plan that is utterly brilliant and changes the way your company does business, it feels good too. After all, your knowledge and timing and awareness of all the issues inspired you to act, and it paid off.

With that in mind, let's look at what it means for your endurance to be inspired by hope in Christ. Your endurance implies that this inspiration thing does not happen all the time. If you're enduring something, you may be in mental or physical discomfort, waiting for it to pass. You're enduring because hope inspires you to believe that things will change. You look to Jesus to guide your thoughts and your actions. Before you know it, your inspired hope pays off. Your life changes and you are prompted by love once again, able to do more work through the faith God has given you.

Look to be motivated, inspired, and entrusted with new vigor toward the things of God so that you can continue the path of walking in faith and love.

*Lord, let my heart be **inspired** by Your love today so that I can further the work of Your kingdom. Amen.*

# FEELINGS

*God's word is alive and working and is sharper than a double-edged sword. It cuts all the way into us, where the soul and the spirit are joined, to the center of our joints and bones. And it judges the thoughts and feelings in our hearts.*
                                                                      Hebrews 4:12 NCV

Many of us process the world through our **feelings**. We determine good and bad, right and wrong, and the actions we take by the way we feel. It can be the perfect way to look at things, or it can be a bit of a snare. So we still must seek God's help. God is good, and when we come to Him, stirred up by feelings, driven by the stories in our heads, He is our loving parent. He recognizes our feelings and then begins to guide us toward actions that will keep us on the path of His plan and purpose.

We may not always like God's direction, because our own feelings can be so strong, but if we are willing to wait and give God a chance to lead us, the outcome we experience will be far more rewarding.

The issue is that our feelings, our moods, our state of mind can change rather quickly. They are fickle. One moment we dislike the villain in a story, and then we discover why they are behaving as they do, and we feel sorry for them. We go from total dislike to sympathy. The fact is that feelings can't be the only guide to how you live your life. They simply aren't a reliable barometer for the decisions you make. God knows you have feelings about the things you do. He designed you that way and even today He will guide you to the place where your soul and spirit are joined and help you work through your feelings.

*Lord, my feelings are often taking control of my actions and choices. Help me to listen to those feelings only after I've put them all before You. Guide my choices. Amen.*

# TIME

*"This is the agreement I will make with them at that **time**, says the Lord.*
*I will put my teachings in their hearts and write them on their minds."*

Hebrews 10:15–16 NCV

"What **time** is it?" That seems like an innocent question. After all, you're trying to get a lot of different things accomplished in one day or in a week or perhaps in a specific frame of hours and minutes. Time is a mystery and a thief; it's a friend and a challenger. You take note of it as you pass by the mirror, remembering a different version of the person you now see. It beckons you to get in the race and then presses the button to see how far you can get in the brief interval it allows.

In the Scripture from Hebrews, we notice that God ordained a time when He would put His teachings in our hearts and write them on our minds. The Creator of the universe, the one who wrote every minute of history, declares that He has given you a time to know Him. He has caused His Spirit to intervene in your life and teach you heart-first. He has written messages in the recesses of your mind so that you will not run out of time to discover He is there. He has made Himself very clear and your timeline is His.

You have a lot of ways to spend your time today, but it could be worthwhile to check to see what time it is in your relationship with God. Have you given Him the time of day? Have you asked Him to spend very personal time with you as you pray? Have you got time to waste? He has put His Word in your heart so that it is there for all the times of your life. You'll have a great time together, and He'll add great joy to everything you are yet to do.

*Lord, I thank You for the **time** you have given me and ask that You would help me to use all my time wisely. I pray that You will be with me and those I love until the end of time itself. Amen.*

# ANXIOUS

*Be **anxious** for nothing, but in everything by prayer and supplication, with thanksgiving, let your requests be made known to God; and the peace of God, which surpasses all understanding, will guard your hearts and minds through Christ Jesus.*                                   Philippians 4:6–7 NKJV

None of us can get through this life without apprehension or anxiety. After all, we live with a lot of uncertainty and we have no control over most of the things that happen. Even if we get around those **anxious** moments about our own issues, we worry about those close to us, feeling at a loss as to how we can help them when a crisis comes.

Therefore, being "anxious for nothing" is a pretty big command. It would be nearly impossible, except for one thing. We were given the formula for how to do it. We were told exactly what to do when worry looms overhead. We go directly to God. We don't spend hours agonizing and then start praying when we're so tired we can barely stand up. No, we go right away to God, in everything. That's not in *some* things. That's not in a *few* things we're comfortable sharing. That's *everything*!

We go to God with everything and then, with prayer and sometimes with pleading or supplication, we talk. Supplication implies urgency; it is about giving God the thing that makes you worry or feel anxious. It's putting your request at the throne to the only One who can actually make a difference about your concern. So the steps are these: Go to God. Pray. Request. Thank Him! By prayer and thanksgiving, you can unburden your anxious heart. You can put down the weight of your worries and you can find God's amazing gift for you...peace! He will give you peace. Now which is it going to be? An anxious heart or a heart of steadfast peace?

*Lord, forgive me when I hold on to all the things that cause me to feel worried and **anxious**. Help me to know Your peace today. Amen.*

# GLAD

*Let the heavens rejoice, and let the earth be **glad**; And let them say among the nations, "The Lord reigns."*　　　　1 Chronicles 16:31 NKJV

Chances are that you're **glad** for your friend who receives a well-deserved promotion. Or when someone you care about needs help, you're probably glad to lend a hand however you can. Being willing to help or being genuinely happy for someone is certainly a demonstration of who you are as a Christian and as a kind person, but let's look at the word "glad" as it is intended in this Scripture.

When the writer of Chronicles suggests to us that the Heavens should rejoice and the Earth should be glad, he isn't saying "be mildly happy, somewhat okay." He's saying something much greater than that. We know this is true because he's building up to a great announcement, the banner headline for the day, the news of a lifetime: "The Lord reigns!" He's excited beyond measure.

With that in mind, the writer tells us to be glad in the sense of being eager, being excited, being all in, because this is worthy of celebration. This has all of Heaven pulling out the stops to sing songs and pound tambourines. This is a message of highest importance and we're not only glad about it, we're ecstatic. There's little in life that compares to this. Our happy dance can go on all day.

Sure, you can be glad for someone else when life is good, but you can also discover what it means to be truly glad that the Lord reigns. This one statement is the summary of all that is important in this life and the next. Let your heart be glad in a big way today.

*Lord, thank You for making me **glad** about the realization that You reign and that You are in control of all that happens to me today. Bless all those who are also glad to know You and fill their hearts with overflowing joy. Amen.*

# FEAR

*Love has been perfected among us in this: that we may have boldness in the day of judgment; because as He is, so are we in this world. There is no fear in love; but perfect love casts out fear.*　　　　1 John 4:17–18 NKJV

Oswald Chambers once wrote, "The remarkable thing about fearing God is that when you **fear** God, you fear nothing else. Whereas, if you do not fear God, you fear everything else."

Love and fear do not seem like the opposite sides of the same coin, but maybe they are. How are we to understand that "God is love" on one hand, and that "the fear of God is the beginning of wisdom" on the other? Our fear of God changes to our love of God when we get to know Him. Perhaps the fear we feel when we first begin to acknowledge His existence is simply that we don't yet understand who God is and what His love is all about. It may be that we aren't sure what "fear" means in this context. Awe? Reverence? Respect?

Any new experience can strike a bit of fear into our hearts. The first time you drove the car by yourself may have made you a little anxious. Perhaps the first time you stood up in front of a group to speak brought some trembling as well. We just aren't confident when we do new things. If God is a "new" experience for you and you're just getting to know Him, it may feel a bit scary. As you grow more connected through Scripture reading and prayer, though, you'll see that fear gives way to love. You'll know in your heart that God loves you right back, and the more you walk together, the better your relationship will be. Let perfect love for God cast out any fear you may have of Him today.

*Lord, help cast out any **fear** I have and help me to love You and live in ways that please You always. Amen.*

# OWN

*It was for my **own** good that I had such troubles. Because you love me very much, you did not let me die but threw my sins far away.*

Isaiah 38:17 NCV

Probably most of us have some experience with the phrase "I'm doing this for your **own** good." As a child, those words made us tremble a bit because it meant being disciplined in some way that didn't feel good at the time. Later, as parents, we may have found ourselves using that same phrase, only to see our kids wonder what could be good about what we were doing.

Our Heavenly parent has a much bigger agenda for us than our Earthly parents do. He is interested not only in how we live our daily lives on Earth, but even more—He's interested in our eternal well-being. He wants us to have a place of our own in Heaven.

When Isaiah declares that his trials and difficulties have been for his own good, he is grateful. He sees how much he is loved and that it was love that motivated God's actions on his behalf. In other words, Isaiah owns the idea that the discipline of God helped him. He realizes that it truly was for his benefit, for his own good. He sees that God's discipline brought life to his heart and soul.

Most of us wish we could learn our life lessons without needing discipline that is uncomfortable or that creates delays in our moving forward. We, too, must remember that God loves us so much, He won't simply let us drift away and get into deeper troubles. He helps us correct the path we are on so that we can draw closer to Him again. In fact, it is helpful to remember that God is always working to help us; He is always ready to act on our behalf for our own good.

*Lord, I admit that when things are done for "my **own** good," it feels like there can only be rough roads ahead. I trust and believe that You seek my good at all times and so I embrace what You do that is for "my own good" today. Amen.*

# STRENGTH

*Does your life in Christ give you strength? Does his love comfort you? Do we share together in the spirit? Do you have mercy and kindness?*

Philippians 2:1 NCV

We often make judgments about people based on what we perceive to be their **strengths** and their weaknesses. We recognize the gift they have for leadership or for working with words or numbers, and we offer them greater opportunities to use the strengths and skills they possess.

One thing we may not think about quite as often is the source of strength for any of us. If you pump iron every day, then you know you've earned your muscles because you worked hard to get them. If you crunch numbers every day, though, chances are you were given a gift to be able to do that easily and well. What gifts have you received from Christ to give you strength? What are the strengths that He has given you so that you can answer His call in the world?

If we look at Galatians 5:22, we might say that the gifts of the Spirit are notable strengths. After all, to have the gifts to be patient, kind, grateful, generous, loving, and to have self-control, along with the other attributes noted there, then God has given you considerable advantage to navigate the world. He has blessed you with strengths to manage life in every arena, no matter where it takes you.

Look at your own strengths today and consider how you might better use your gifts from God to help you with the work of His kingdom. You may be weak in many areas, but with God's help, you have enormous abilities to do great things, even finding more strength in mercy and kindness.

*Lord, please help me to put whatever **strength** You've given me to great use for the good of others. Amen.*

# BELONG

*So now there is no condemnation for those who **belong** to Christ Jesus. And because you belong to him, the power of the life-giving Spirit has freed you from the power of sin that leads to death.*          Romans 8:1–2 NLT

Most of us like to have a sense that we **belong** somewhere, that we fit in and are accepted. We become members of special-interest clubs. We move into communities and we join churches so we know where we belong. Sometimes even our career choices give us a sense that we are meant to be in the classroom if we're teachers, or we clearly belong in the medical profession. It's a good feeling to belong to someone in an emotional sense as well. What does it mean then to belong to Christ Jesus?

According to Romans 8, there's an instant benefit that comes with your choice to belong to Christ. You are no longer condemned. You are no longer criticized for your past behaviors or considered unworthy because of your sins. Even more than that, the Scripture goes on to point out that once you belong to Jesus, you are given a gift. You are blessed with a life-giving Spirit.

What does that life-giving Spirit do for you? It frees you from the confines of sin. If you're free from the wages of sin, then you are also freed from eternal death. Instead you are given eternal life. That's a pretty powerful life-giving Spirit. That benefit alone will make you glad that you opted for membership, that you chose to belong to Him.

Today, give praise to God and to His Son for seeking you out and asking you to join your life to theirs. You have a place to belong forever.

*Lord, it helps me to know I **belong** to You and that You are part of all that I say and do today. Keep me aware of all that it means for me to be in Your family so I can share my hope with others. Amen.*

# KNOWING

*For ever since the world was created, people have seen the earth and sky.*
*Through everything God made, they can clearly see his invisible qualities—*
*his eternal power and divine nature. So they have no excuse for not*
**knowing** *God.* Romans 1:20 NLT

It appears that God has tried every way imaginable to help us recognize
His Presence in our lives. He put a measure of His Spirit within our hearts
and He created the Earth in such a way that we simply can't miss His
handiwork. So how is it that some of us still are blind to His Divine nature?
How come we give ourselves reasons to doubt? The writer of Romans
comes right out and tells us that we have no excuse for not **knowing** God.

And for those of us who have embraced God's Presence, what difference does knowing God make in the way we live our lives? Can other people see that we have a relationship with God? Are we busy telling God's
stories to anyone who will listen?

If we know God, but we don't introduce Him to anyone else, that might
seem as though we aren't very excited about our relationship. If we knew
a celebrity or a sports hero, we'd probably talk about that without hesitation. We know the God of the universe, the One who created the planet
we live on. In fact, no one exists today that wasn't part of His planning
and His awareness. He knows you!

Today, spend some time considering what it really means to you to
know your Creator. What does knowing Him do for you? Once you know
deep in your heart what He means to you, then share your love and your
insights with others. Knowing Him makes all the difference.

*Lord, knowing You has changed my life. No matter what I do or*
*where I am, I know I can turn to You for guidance and help. Thank*
*You for* **knowing** *me. Amen.*

# ABUNDANCE

*Grace and peace be yours in **abundance** through the knowledge of God and of Jesus our Lord. His divine power has given us everything we need for a godly life through our knowledge of him who called us by his own glory and goodness.*
2 Peter 1: 2–3 NIV

When we think of those things we might like to have in copious amounts, it's likely that we think of material things like money or cars or shoes. Once we get past those thoughts of what it means to live in **abundance**, we might even go to more ideological things like having an abundance of love, or opportunities for dreams to flourish, or encouragement from those around us. Having abundance in most any form seems like a really good thing.

It may take us a little longer, though, to seek an abundance of peace or grace. If we had an abundance of peace, then we'd be content. We'd be content whether or not we had money or cars or shoes. We'd be filled with joy in any circumstance because of the knowledge of God and Jesus that helps us to see that through them we have everything we need. We would be overflowing with the best gifts life has to offer.

Are you looking for abundance? Are you seeking to discover ways to have more of what life offers? If not, I encourage you to put your energy into the never-ending flow of God's grace and His peace. It is only through His grace that you exist at all. It is only through His love and mercy that you do the work you do or live in the house you have. You receive all abundance from God's hand. May the One who called you by His own glory and goodness overwhelm you with His perfect abundance of joys unending today.

*Lord, thank You for blessing my life with **abundance**. I may not be where I want to be in all things, but I am blessed to be right where I am. Amen.*

# EXAMPLE

*Follow God's **example**, therefore, as dearly loved children and walk in the way of love, just as Christ loved us and gave himself up for us as a fragrant offering and sacrifice to God.*                    Ephesians 5:1–2 NIV

Most of us learn the important things in life through **example**. We observe how other people do things, and if we can relate to those things and interpret them in meaningful ways, it's how we choose to act as well. If we have good leaders to follow, good examples to show us the way, then we know how to live.

As it says here in Ephesians, "Christ loved us and gave himself up for us." He sacrificed Himself so that we could live. He did this out of absolute and profound love, a kind of love that few of us may ever know. Perhaps our closest understanding comes from being a parent. We bring an innocent child into the world, and it is our job to help them learn how to walk in the ways of God and in ways that will make them good-hearted human beings. We do that by offering them examples every step of the way. If they fall down, we show them how to get up again. If they forget what we told them, we find another way to illustrate our point, and ultimately, we sacrifice for them as well. Perhaps we do that by the choice of our job or the place where we live, even if it means depriving ourselves. We understand love for a child, our child, and so we do all we can to help them live full and productive lives.

That is exactly what Jesus did for all of us. He provided the way for us to live eternally. He gave us numerous examples of how to live in the world, and He showed us the deepest kind of love and mercy that could ever be. Today, let's thank and praise Him for His amazing and loving example.

*Lord, please help me to be a worthy **example** to others as I live my life. Thank You for the amazing ways You've taught me how to follow You. Amen.*

# HIDDEN

*Nothing in all the world can be **hidden** from God. Everything is clear and lies open before him, and to him we must explain the way we have lived.*

Hebrews 4:13 NCV

One of the things that causes most of us to feel some angst is knowing that there is nothing we do that is **hidden** from God. Nothing! That means God already knows everything about us. He knows the things we've done that we wish we could sweep under the rug. He knows all of our secrets. He knows the thoughts that come unbidden out of nowhere. The fact is, He knows the good, the bad, and the ugly of each one of us. That's a bit daunting.

On the other hand, might it not also be freeing? Does it not encourage you even more to talk to God about everything, no matter what it is, because He knows about it anyway? Doesn't it open the door for you to be authentic with the Creator of the universe and the lover of your soul?

Like Adam and Eve, the first thing we want to do when we make a mistake is hide. We hope God will pass by and simply not see us. We hope we can figure out how to fix our problems before He discovers what we've done. We can hope all we want, but it doesn't work that way.

God has given us choices in life so that we can decide how we want to act in any situation. We can get help if we aren't sure what to do next. We can admit when we're wrong. We can seek more guidance in all things. Nothing is hidden from Him, and that idea brings joy to our hearts when we are choosing to live in ways that please Him.

Thank Him today that you can clear the air with Him at any time you choose and open your heart to His steadfast love and grace. You've got nothing to hide!

*Lord, today I choose to live openly and lovingly as You would have me do, so nothing is hidden. Thank You for knowing me so well. Amen.*

# ASSURANCE

*Now faith is confidence in what we hope for and **assurance** about what we do not see. This is what the ancients were commended for.*

Hebrews 11:1 NIV

We live in a "doubting Thomas" world. We want to "see" everything before we believe it. We want the evidence in our hands, the proof in a document five pages long, because we simply can't take anything at face value. We have no **assurance**, no sense that we can trust the word of anyone we know.

Can you think of something that you would say with total certainty that you have "confidence in what [you] hope for and assurance about what [you] do not yet see"? The prophets and the patriarchs of old were commended for simply believing. They heard God's voice and they answered. He told them the mission He had for them and they accomplished it. In a simple word, they had faith. They had faith that came with assurance that what they believed and what they were told from God would come to pass.

Most of us simply don't have that kind of faith. Oh, we can talk about it and sing about it and even now and then act it out, but for the most part, we don't walk in faith. Culturally, we've lost faith in what we hear and see around us and we no longer have confidence that what we hope for will happen.

Now here's the thing to remember. God is the same yesterday, today, and forever. If you have been called, if you have a mission or a Divine purpose, then you can have the kind of confident faith that comes with assurance that your work will indeed be honored. What you have hoped for and believed with all your heart will come to pass. Cast away the doubts and move ahead with blessed assurance. Your assurance comes wholly from the Spirit of God.

*Lord, I confess that I have not always been able to hold on to the faith that trusts You with total **assurance**. Help me to move past my unbelief and rise to Your calling today. Amen.*

# FATHER

*For those who are led by the Spirit of God are the children of God. The Spirit you received does not make you slaves, so that you live in fear again; rather, the Spirit you received brought about your adoption to sonship. And by him we cry, "Abba, Father." The Spirit himself testifies with our spirit that we are God's children.*                    Romans 8:14–16 NIV

Some of the sweetest words in any language are those that speak of the people in our lives who nurture us and encourage our growth in positive ways. These are the people who see us as we are and love us anyway. They understand our quirks and our idiosyncrasies, and they see what we can be, even when we can't see for ourselves. It is in that spirit that we can learn how to perceive the God of the universe.

"**Father**, Papa, Daddy" are all affectionate terms for a parent. If we have a wonderful biological dad, then we can easily see the comparison. If we do not have an honored Earthly parent, then we have to imagine what a father should do, what it means to have a daddy who is good and tender and wise.

Whether we had a good Earthly example or not, God wants us to know that He is our Father. He is always available to us and He will never leave us. He wants us to realize that we are His family, chosen and beloved. And no matter how many crazy things we might do, He will not let go of us. He will protect us and instruct us and guide us wherever we need to go.

The Spirit you received from God means that you are His heir, His child, and He will embrace you with love forever. Give praise to your adoring Father today.

*Lord, thank You for being the most amazing **Father** that could ever be. Bless all those I love today with Your kindness and mercy. Amen.*

# LIVE

*"I am the living bread that came down from heaven. Whoever eats of this
bread will **live** forever; and the bread that I will give for the life of the world
is my flesh."*                                                    John 6:51 NRSV

Remember the story of the good Samaritan? He saw a poor, beaten man
lying in a ditch and offered him help. A priest had already passed by the
injured man. A Levite, one of his own, had also passed him by. The only
one who offered help was not his usual friend at all. He was a Samaritan,
a foe, a cultural enemy.

We **live** in a world today that is much like the injured, beaten man
lying in a ditch. The world is hurting, maybe even dying, because there is
so much hatred and violence. The world is suffering, and those who claim
to be its allies often pass it by. They walk on the other side of the street
because the sufferings of the world are too much to handle.

You can make a difference. You may not be able to do more than offer
a prayer in its direction, as you go on about your business. That's a start,
though. You may choose to volunteer your time, your resources, your
ideas to those in need.

It's your turn now to share the bread of life with those around you. You
can live in ways that serve others by example or by the things you do. You
might ask yourself these questions: "Am I passing anyone by today that I
could help by doing a kind deed or offering a word of encouragement? Is
there someone who needs to feel my love or God's love in a way that will
help them live more fully and more joyfully?"

Jesus saw the hurting and ailing world and He determined He would
do something about it. He would not make excuses. He would not pass by
on the other side of the street and ignore all the problems. Live in any way
you can today that will bless those who cross your path.

*Lord, please help me to show compassion and love to those I meet
and let me know when I need to lend a hand. Help me to **live** for You
today. Amen.*

# VISION

*Where there is no **vision**, the people perish.*     Proverbs 29:18 KJV

People with vision make incredible breakthroughs in science or "connect the dots" about life in ways that no one has before them. They bring a unique perspective and often create a band of followers. Other people can also be influenced by a **vision** or a dream.

Jesus was a man of vision. He offered insights about faith that few had been able to articulate before him. He gave guidance to those who were lost and healing to those who could neither see nor hear.

So what does it mean to us to consider the proverb that "without vision, the people perish"? What does it mean to realize we may never embrace the kind of vision that brings real meaning and purpose to our lives?

Some of us are afraid to be people of vision. We're uncertain about whether we want anyone to follow in our footsteps, and yet the very thought of living meaningful and purposeful lives drives us forward each day.

God has a vision *for* you and *of* you. He knows you and understands your strengths and limitations and what you can accomplish.

Listen for His voice so that you clearly understand what He would have you do. You are a part of His vision and you are His voice, His heart, His example to the world around you. You may be the direction, the vision, the guide who changes the way someone else lives from this day forward.

*Lord, help me understand the **vision** You have for my life so*
*that I always share the joy I experience each day in my personal*
*relationship with You. Bless those who walk with You and who*
*strengthen the faith of the rest of us by being true to Your call.*
*Amen.*

# THINK

*Brothers and sisters, think about the things that are good and worthy of praise. Think about the things that are true and honorable and right and pure and beautiful and respected.*                    Philippians 4:8 NCV

You may not always be aware of the things you're thinking about. After all, your mind keeps playing information in the background no matter what else you might be doing. Being able to **think** for yourself is sometimes a struggle, even inside your own head.

Perhaps one way to focus more clearly on the stories that float around in your mind is to be intentional about what it is you think about. You can choose to think good things. You can choose to think positive thoughts. You can even choose to spend time thinking about things that are more worthy of your attention and praise.

It's not easy to think about things that are true and honorable and right when every bit of news that flies across your television or digital device reminds you of the explosion of negativity all around you. It's not easy to even imagine things that are pure and beautiful because your heart is no longer innocent.

You have an option, though. You can openly and honestly share your childlike heart with God. You can curl up on His lap and let Him know what it is that you are concerned about and all the things that cause you fear. To God, you are beloved and innocent. He sees your heart and knows your thoughts. Let Him bless all the things you think about and ponder today. He'll give you a clear mind and a joyful heart.

*Lord, I know that I really want to **think** about good things, but I am easily distracted by the chaos of the world. Please help me to live and think and walk with You in childlike faith today. Amen.*

# RESTORE

*See what this sorrow—the sorrow God wanted you to have—has done to you: It has made you very serious. It made you want to restore yourselves. It made you angry and afraid. It made you want to see me. It made you care. It made you want to do the right thing. In every way you have regained your innocence.*
2 Corinthians 7:11 NCV

If you've ever tried to **restore** an old piece of wood furniture, you know that the process isn't easy. First you must remove old nails and things that get in the way of cleaning off the old stains and finishes. Then you have to sand it over and over again until it is smooth. After that, you have to treat it so that it is able to take on the new finish, and finally you have to create and execute your final design.

You saw how it would look in your mind's eye, even when it was simply a rough piece of old furniture. You knew that you could restore it and make it beautiful again. The gift of God's love for you is that He can always see your original beauty. He knows that as you go through life, you get scraped and bruised along the way. He knows that you make choices that damage your heart and mind and cause you to wonder if you're still valuable.

Your value in God's sight has never diminished, and He will work with you right now to restore you and help you become all He meant you to be. He holds up the best possible vision of you and waits lovingly for you to request His special attention. He wants to restore you to your incredible beauty so that you can shine for Him every place you go.

*Lord, I know that I need You to restore my heart and mind so that I can be a more gracious and loving light to those around me. Thank You for always seeing the best in me. Amen.*

# ALWAYS

*"And surely I am with you **always**, to the very end of the age."*

Matthew 28:20 NIV

Few things in this life are **always** true. We're prone to saying somewhat glibly, things like "You always do that," or "I always try to…" The problem is that, as human beings, we do not always do anything. We might do something often. We may even be fairly regular at completing a task or keeping things straight, but like it or not, we do not always manage to meet the high bar we imagine.

The word "always" means, literally, "all the time." All the time, means continuously, without stopping, without anything getting in the way. It means that we constantly deal with it.

Even if we use a word like "always" in the context of "I will always love you," the chances are good that there are a few days when I am simply putting up with you or barely liking you. Sure, I love you deep down, but I'm not really feeling it just now.

Let's think about what "always" means when God says it. Jesus made it clear in this Scripture in Matthew that He would always be with us. He emphasized how long that was by adding "to the very end of the age." Now, that sounds like all the time. That sounds like we can count on His Presence in our lives as a pure fact. He is permanently, continually, and always available.

Let Jesus be your always. You know you can't go wrong there.

*Lord, I don't **always** do the right things, but I know You always know what is right for me. Help me to continually seek Your Presence and grace in my life. Amen.*

# BE

*I pray that the eyes of your heart may be enlightened in order that you may know the hope to which he has called you, the riches of his glorious inheritance in his holy people.*                    Ephesians 1:18 NIV

One of the most familiar quotations in literature comes from Shakespeare's *Hamlet,* who ponders, "To be or not to be, that is the question." The character of Hamlet is indeed wondering whether it is worthwhile to continue living his life. Is it worthwhile "to be"?

In Scripture, we read phrases like "Be still" or "Be holy" or as we have here, "Be enlightened." These phrases key in on the idea that "to be" or to stand or to remain is what causes us to drown out the noises of the world and bring focus to the more important things. When we stand still, we learn what it means to observe everything around us with all our other senses. We feel and touch the world in new ways.

Our job then is to learn to "be." When we do, we grow more mature, more willing to be ourselves in whatever circumstances exist. We pray to be closer to God so that we can understand all that He wants for us and all that He wants to do with our lives. The greatest opportunity we have to be content then is to look to God to shape us and give us enlightened hearts so that we may know the hope to which He has called us and so that we can be worthy of His precious inheritance.

So be all you can be today. Be still. Listen, pray, and simply exist in God's Presence. He will indeed direct your paths and help you to open the eyes of your heart.

*Lord, I pray that You will enlighten my heart and mind and help me to be everything I need to be for You and for those I love. Amen.*

# COMPASSION

*The Lord is gracious and merciful,*
*slow to anger and abounding in steadfast love.*
*The Lord is good to all,*
*and his **compassion** is over all that he has made.*      Psalm 145:8–9 NRSV

When a crisis occurs and it is brought to your awareness through the local news or on social media or in some other way, you may find yourself sympathizing with those in difficulty. You might say that your "heart goes out to them." As people who care about others, we suffer with those who suffer and we hurt with those in pain and want to help however we can. We are people of **compassion**.

Compassion brings kindness and consideration to a whole new level. It is not simply about being a nice, well-mannered person. It is about a deep sense of caring that causes your heart to grieve for the plight of others. It makes you want to stand up for certain causes or champion the rights of those who have no one to speak for them. Compassion is beyond sympathy in that it brings us to a place of action. Compassionate hearts are prayerful.

Imagine then what it means for God to have compassion on all that He has made. It doesn't simply suggest that He's aware of His creation or that He has sympathy for us. It means that His heart is connected to us in a very real and meaningful way. It means that He sees us as we are and loves us anyway and wants only good things for us. It means He grieves when we grieve, that He suffers when our hearts are broken.

Everything God created enjoys His compassion. All of His children and His creatures, and all of creation itself, yearn for His kindness to wrap firmly around them at every opportunity.

*Lord, open my heart to be more aware of the needs of others. Let me always show **compassion** and kindness in ways that bring glory to You. Amen.*

# FAMILY

*So I bow in prayer before the Father from whom every **family** in heaven and on earth gets its true name. I ask the Father in his great glory to give you the power to be strong inwardly through his Spirit.*

Ephesians 3:14–16 NCV

The composition of those we regard as **family** has undergone sweeping changes over the past decade or two. Though family members are generally agreed to be the people who inhabit your household, or who bear your same name and lineage, those family members look very different from a generation ago. Today's families are blended and mended and mixed and reshaped in more ways than we ever once could have imagined. We make family members out of our friends and our work associates and people who share our belief systems. We love the idea of community and bonding and our sense of family gives us that, as well as providing a place where we belong.

Of course, the writer of the letter to the Ephesians is suggesting that every family past or present has one real source, one true name. Our name was given to us by our Father, the One who tied all of us together with love and forgiveness and rebirth. We have a larger, extended family in Heaven and a genuine family of believers who share our life experience right now.

Sometimes, family members are not easy to understand, or they act in ways that seem foreign to us. We wonder how we could have gotten in the same family, or even perhaps the same gene pool. We may question our heritage, but God does not. God knows His children and He will always cause our hearts to be joined in love, no matter how broadly we define the word "family."

*Lord, please bless those people who are part of my household and part of my extended **family** as well. Remind us all that we are children of the same Heavenly Father. Amen.*

# RECOUNT

*Then we your people, the flock of your pasture, will give thanks to you forever;*
*from generation to generation we will **recount** your praise.*

Psalm 79:13 NRSV

Do you have a favorite story that you love to tell? Maybe it's a great memory from your childhood that washes over you with delight every time you think of it, and even more so when you retell it. Maybe you love to share happy moments with your siblings, or with old college friends. Whatever it is, we know that each time we tell an old story, we relive the experience. It comes to life for us in a new way. It gives us energy and joy.

What if you decided today to **recount** the amazing stories of all that God has done for you in your life? Perhaps you could pick your top five God-shaped moments and then tell them to your friends and family and those you encounter. Your stories of God's grace and miraculous hand in the events you have experienced will no doubt bring you comfort or smiles of joy all over again.

Recounting, telling, sharing stories is part of what makes us recognize our connections to each other. Stories help us work out details in our own lives as we embrace each other's experiences. God has done mighty things, and every time we shine a light on those things for others to hear, we make them new in our hearts all over again. It is in this way that we can give thanks and praise to God from generation to generation. Keep telling your stories. Someone you know needs the blessing they will receive when you recount tales of the gifts you've been given.

*Lord, I offer You thanks and praise for the amazing stories You have given me to share. Each one renews my joy in being Your child. I love to **recount** each one. Amen.*

# GRATITUDE

*Let the word of Christ dwell in you richly; teach and admonish one another in all wisdom; and with **gratitude** in your hearts sing psalms, hymns, and spiritual songs to God.*                    Colossians 3:16 NRSV

You've probably had moments in your life that caused you to simply want to sing, or if you're not a singer, maybe dance, or at the very least, clap your hands in joy. Those moments are clearly ones where you are feeling grateful for your circumstances or for your life situation or maybe even for something wonderful that has happened to someone you love. When your heart is full of **gratitude**, it simply spills over into everything else you're doing.

Imagine then that you could spend one day, perhaps today, simply reminding yourself of all the things for which you are grateful. Your list is bound to go on and on once you get started, because the very fact that you rose from your bed, acknowledged the new day, and realized you've been given the chance to start again can bring you to your knees in gratitude. Be thankful that God has blessed you with the chance to do better than you did yesterday, or to spend more time with Him and to walk more closely with Him.

Celebrate today in every word you speak, every step you take, and every conscious action of your heart, and you will know a day of continuous gratitude. Let the rest of the world go by and mumble and complain and move on without you, because your heart is grateful for all God has done. As a matter of fact, you have good news to share with those around you. Go on, kick up your feet and sing out loud!

*Lord, my heart rejoices in You today and I am filled with **gratitude** for all that You are and all that You have done to sustain me and those I love. Help me to remember to give You thanks and praise all through the day. Amen.*

# GRACE

*Everyone has sinned and fallen short of God's glorious standard, and all need to be made right with God by his **grace**, which is a free gift. They need to be made free from sin through Jesus Christ.* Romans 3:23–24 NCV

Did you ever buy something that had a "free gift" with purchase? You buy the thing you wanted and then you get a bonus, a thing of added value. Of course, getting the free gift may have motivated you to buy the product to begin with.

Our faith in God also came with a "free gift." He purchased us through His Son and then He gave us a bonus, a free gift. He gave us **grace**. He gave us a carte blanche opportunity to receive Him. We receive His Son and we receive His grace. It can hardly get better than that!

Or perhaps it can get a little better. Perhaps each time we receive God's gift of grace and thank Him for it, that's better. Perhaps when we realize that He has forgiven us again for our poor choices or our fits of craziness in life, that's better. In fact, we love that we live under grace because it appears we would not be able to get along on planet Earth without it. Grace is our oxygen and it allows us to breathe despite the smog we create ourselves.

God gave you His free gift of grace so that you would discover His Presence in your life. He knew that if you could recognize how often He is available to you, protecting, guiding, forgiving, loving, that you would come to receive His Son. You would embrace His love for you in every way. Enjoy your free gift. Live in grace and peace and harmony today.

*Lord, how can I begin to thank You for allowing me to live under Your **grace** and care? Bless all those who seek Your face today. Amen.*

# TASTE

*O taste and see that the Lord is good;*
*happy are those who take refuge in him.*          Psalm 34:8 NRSV

If you go out for ice cream and the menu offers fifty different ways to serve your frozen delight, you might ask for a **taste** of a flavor you find intriguing. It's fun to get a little taste of something special. After all, you want to be sure to choose the right thing.

Getting a taste of something informs you about it. It gives you a perspective that helps you decide if you'd like more or if you'd rather move on. It's interesting in this Psalm that the reader is invited to take a taste of the Lord. He says, "taste and see that the Lord is good."

For some, a little taste is enough to start a lifetime of love. When it comes to God, we want to get beyond that first taste, that first sample of our awareness of Him and all that He has for us. We want to make connecting with Him a daily habit, a feast that continues for the rest of our lives.

The good news is that God knows if we simply have a taste of His precious love, His power and generosity and loving Spirit, that it will be so good for us. He knows we'll keep coming back for more. In fact, we'll crave Him. He is our taste of truth and reality. He is our strength and we are happy that we can take refuge in Him.

The best part of getting a taste of God's love and Spirit is that once you've gotten that taste, nothing else will satisfy your heart and mind ever again in the same way. You'll be hooked for life—eternal life, that is!

*Lord, thank You for giving me a precious **taste** of Your love and Your*
*Spirit. Thank You for nurturing my heart and my soul every day.*
*Amen.*

# WITNESSES

*Then Joshua said, "You are **witnesses** against yourselves that you have chosen to serve the Lord." "Yes, we are witnesses," they replied.*

Joshua 24:22 NIV

"Can I get a **witness**?" the speaker asks from the stage. The room lights up with those who identify with what the speaker has to say. They confirm and acknowledge and give witness to the words being said.

When Joshua asked the people of his day if they were going to serve the Lord, they all said, "Yes." Joshua then replied that they were witnesses against themselves. The people readily agreed.

Being a witness meant that they affirmed in front of God, in front of Joshua, and in front of each other that they would live the rest of their lives serving the Lord. They knew that they could never deny their actions. They knew that God would know if they did not serve Him from that point on.

Are we willing to stand up and be witnesses against ourselves? Are we willing to say aloud to God that we will indeed serve Him all the days of our lives? If we are, then God will call us His own. He will stand with us and He will hold us accountable. He keeps His word. He wants us to do the same.

You were designed by God, blessed with skills and talents, and given all you need so that you can serve Him in this life. Are you ready? Can I get a witness?

*Father, help me to always serve You in every way that pleases You. Grant that I might be like the **witnesses** of old, glorifying Your Presence each day of my life. Amen.*

# RESPECT

*"Stand up in the presence of the aged, show respect for the elderly and revere your God. I am the Lord."*      Leviticus 19:38 NIV

**Respect**, reverence, and veneration are appropriate behaviors toward the One who designed the very ground we walk on. They signify to Him that we recognize His importance, His position in our lives, and His contribution to all that we are and all we hope to be.

God equated the respect we show the elderly to the respect we show to Him as our Creator and our Lord. Now that puts things on a very different level. That means that God is taking it personally if you don't honor your elders. He wants to know that you are willing to recognize their achievements and their efforts to make life better for you. He wants to know that you honor and respect Him for choosing your elders to come before you. He wants your respect for paving the way for the life you now enjoy.

When we respect each other, we do our best to listen to ideas that may not be our own. We try harder to understand another point of view. When we give our respect, then we honor those around us for the contributions they have made. Think of those you admire the most in the world and let them know how much they mean to you. Your respect will encourage them and bless their day.

*Lord, thank You for all the people who have gone before me to make my life easier. Bless them with joy and health and let me always respect the work they do in Your name. Amen.*

# STRUGGLE

*For our **struggle** is not against flesh and blood, but against the rulers,
against the authorities, against the powers of this dark world and against
the spiritual forces of evil in the heavenly realms.*     Ephesians 6:12 NIV

**Struggle** is an equal opportunity player. It doesn't care what you do for
a living or where you build a home. It doesn't care how educated you are
or how many children you have. It doesn't even care if you go to church
Sunday after Sunday or simply visit on key holidays. It's there for you, or
perhaps it's there because of you.

Struggle comes to each of us as a contender, as a boxer in the ring. It's
ready to brag about its winning abilities, to taunt you into fighting, to get
you into the arena where it competes. We know this because struggle is
not coming first and foremost from the job you have, the family dynamic
you live in, or the people in your neighborhood. It's coming straight from
the wily One who prowls the Earth. It comes to test you and taunt you and
make you question the authority of the absolute power of God. It's spiritual warfare that attempts to whittle away at your heart and mind and soul
until you simply feel lost.

You may struggle to pay your bills, or to lose weight, or to find a great
job, or about any number of other life situations, but remember that no
matter what it looks like on the surface, it's really a challenge to distract
you from God's love and grace. It is an attempt to get you out of God's
hand. This is not your day to struggle, though. It's your day to win. Give
God thanks and praise that you are tightly held in His powerful hands.

*Lord, thank You for holding on to me and not letting me get
distracted by the things that bring **struggle** to my life. I trust in You
to help me overcome any obstacles I may face. Amen.*

# ARISE

*Arise, shine, for your light has come, and the glory of the Lord rises upon you.*

Isaiah 60:1–2 NIV

Each morning when you **arise**, do you celebrate the fact that the darkness has gone away and the light has come? Do you ever even imagine that the glory of the Lord rises upon you?

Perhaps today is a good day to get on your feet with great joy. It may not be joy because you have to hurry to get the kids off to school before you can fight the traffic to get to your job. It won't be joy because you have a long to-do list and have no idea how everything will get accomplished. It will simply be joy because you know that the glory of the Lord rises upon you. You know that wherever you go today, God is with you. He sees you and He knows how hard you work and how much you must do. Together, you will get it done.

If the glory of the Lord is with you every time you rise, then you are never alone. You don't have to handle the weight of the world on your own. You don't have to stuff your feelings down to your toes and wonder if anyone has a clue what is going on inside your heart and mind. It means that God knows you and He will do everything in His power to walk with you and create opportunities for you to shine and keep you strong.

Look for Him today wherever you go. See if you can feel His Presence in the little things you do and share His story with those you meet. Help others to realize that God is as close to them as the morning sunshine.

*Lord, it's hard to realize how much You love me. Thank You for choosing to be with me each day when I* ***arise****. Amen.*

# SPACIOUS

*When hard pressed, I cried to the Lord; he brought me into a **spacious** place.*
*The Lord is with me; I will not be afraid. What can mere mortals do to me?*
Psalm 118:5–6 NIV

It's interesting in this Psalm that when the writer is hard-pressed, struggling, feeling pressure from every side, God answers by bringing him to a **spacious** place. He gets him out of the box, that sense of being hemmed in, and He puts the writer in a place where He can breathe and think and begin to manage life again.

As human beings, we often feel the pressures of the ever-busy world around us. We have endless deadlines and the feeling that there just isn't enough time to accomplish our goals. We've no doubt done a lot of it to ourselves, setting schedules that simply are too tight, but look again at what God does. He invites us into a spacious place.

Only when you can look around and see the landscape, or get a bird's-eye view, can you see the bigger picture. You need a chance to see things from a distance, so you can get a new perspective. God gives you a more spacious place to view the world. He wants you to know that there is always another way to go and, more important, another place to turn. You can turn to Him whenever you are feeling hard-pressed and He will guide you to take a new view.

With God walking beside you, there is never a need to feel restricted by the world. Get some space today.

*Lord, thank You for helping me to breathe. I know that I often box myself in and then I can't manage my life well. I love the **spacious** places You offer me to think and pray. Amen.*

# BEND

*Therefore God also highly exalted him and gave him the name that is above every name, so that at the name of Jesus every knee should **bend**, in heaven and on earth and under the earth.*          Philippians 2:9–10 NRSV

If you're still working on what it means to be holy, or what it means to worship God in ways that go beyond simply showing up at a church service, the word **bend** as used here in Philippians may be helpful. It's interesting because this is a word with several definitions. One of its meanings is a curve in the road, something that makes you have to ease around it so that you can see clearly what might be coming toward you. Another definition is the bend in your elbow, the one that allows your hand to freely move up and down, so you can eat dinner without a struggle.

Other times, we hear this word in association with bending down or stooping, almost in a negative way, something foreboding, even. But now we rise to another meaning of the word. Now we see that something extraordinary is going to happen somewhere in the future. It's an event that will not be like any other. It will be the event that surrounds the return of Jesus, the one name that will cause every knee, not just some knees, not just Christian knees, but every knee, to bend. This moment of supreme exaltation will happen in Heaven. Every angel will bend down to honor the King. It will happen on Earth, where every living creature will wake up to the Son of glory and bend down to worship Him. And finally, it will happen even under the Earth, where living creatures in every universe will recognize and exalt and bend their knees to honor Him.

What an awesome picture this is! Imagine for a moment how that day will feel, how every being who waited patiently for the return of Christ will celebrate. We will gather together on bended knees, knowing that our hearts and minds will never be broken again.

*Lord, I **bend** down on my knees in love and worship and awe of You today. Amen.*

# SELF-CONTROL

*You are all people who belong to the light and to the day. We do not belong to the night or to darkness. So we should not be like other people who are sleeping, but we should be alert and have self-control.*

1 Thessalonians 5:5–6 NCV

What does it mean to have **self-control**? Perhaps the best way to answer that is to look at things in your life that feel somewhat "out of control." For example, if you have been working hard to save money, putting a few dollars a week into your savings account, but at the same time, you're still shopping almost daily with your high-interest credit card, you may not have enough self-control when it comes to spending your money.

We notice that we don't have self-control in those areas where we allow impulse to win out over reason, or where we "follow the crowd" rather than do what we know would be better for us to do. So what's the answer? Maybe you can be more alert to those things that get you off track. Maybe you realize you have more self-control when you know that God is with you every place you go. The truth is that you are capable of self-control in every area of your life because you are connected to Him. His grace, His love, and His kindness sustain you, but you have to wake up and embrace His Presence.

Perhaps the best way to do that is to start each day with a "thank you" to God. Let Him know that you are glad to wake up and know that you are in His care and keeping. It's a new day to shine your light. The good news is that you have control over your actions and God will bless you with greater joy. Be alert and have self-control so that you are awake to His blessings.

*Lord, I know that I have my sleepy days, just like everyone else does. Help me to be more alert to Your Presence today and to exhibit self-control in all I do. Amen.*

# FIX

*Why are you down in the dumps, dear soul? Why are you crying the blues?*

*Fix my eyes on God—soon I'll be praising again. He puts a smile on my face. He's my God.*                                    Psalm 43:5 MSG

Fix is one of those words in our language that has the possibility of being opposite sides of a coin. You can be in a fix, which usually means there's some trouble brewing, or you can fix something, which means you have a way of making something that was a problem better. You can fix the fix you're in!

The meaning of the word "fix" in the Scripture here, though, is about focus. It's about positioning yourself to know where to look when trouble comes. It's about looking at the one Source of possibility that you have for eternity and knowing that it's okay to put a smile on your face. You have every reason to stop being in the dumps, to stop crying your heart out, because you have a place to go with your sorrows. You can take them straight to God and all you have to do is fix your eyes on Him. Fix them, focus them, keep them aligned with Him, and you will begin to feel His comfort.

As your eyes adjust to His Holy light, you will discover that you have many reasons to praise Him, to thank Him for your life and even for your current situation, because you are fixed on Him and He is fixed on you. He is your God and there is no one else you can turn to for comfort when your spirit is weary.

Fix your heart and mind on the Lord, and He will lift you up to a place of joy and praise. You have every reason to smile.

*Lord, when I'm in a fix, I don't always understand how to make things better. From now on, I will fix my eyes on You, though, because I know You are all I need today. Amen.*

# IDEAS

*May we know what this new teaching is that you are presenting? You are bringing some strange **ideas** to our ears, and we would like to know what they mean.*

Acts 17:19–20 NIV

Part of the reason we find it difficult to embrace new **ideas** is because they always seem a bit strange to us. We aren't sure what they mean or whether we should consider them or not. The teachings of those who walked with Jesus were probably very strange ideas to the people of those times. They had grown up in cultures that were very different from our own. They wanted to know if they could accept these ideas as truth.

We are surrounded with ideas. We follow the thinkers of the day that we embrace on social media and we share our own thoughts with others. Ideas are a good thing. The difficulty is in knowing the good ideas from the ones that are just cleverly advertised as truth, disguised in a package that requires us to be discerning.

The people in Acts were being confronted with a brand-new way to think. They had been waiting for the promised Messiah for a long time. Now they were being told that the Messiah was Jesus and that He had been resurrected from the dead. These were big ideas back then and they are big ideas still being pondered today.

Your ideas, thoughts, and notions about God make a difference in how you perceive His importance in your daily life. You understand more about what those ideas of God mean to you when you study them further in a daily prayer time or doing devotions. Those devotional times will seem like one of your best ideas because they will bring truth and peace and joy to your life.

God's ideas are simple, pivotal truths. He shares His ideas through prayer and Scripture and other ways that draw you close to Him. Listen with your heart and you will be blessed with hope and the brightest possible ideas about how to live a life that pleases Him.

*Lord, thank You for being one of the most amazing **ideas** that could ever be. Thank You for helping me to see the truth of Your Spirit today. Amen.*

# OBSTACLE

*But Jesus was matter-of-fact: "Yes—and if you embrace this kingdom life
and don't doubt God, you'll not only do minor feats like I did to the fig tree,
but also triumph over huge **obstacles**. This mountain, for instance, you'll
tell, 'Go jump in the lake,' and it will jump."*      Matthew 21:21 MSG

**Obstacles**, difficulties, complications are simply part of the journey. They
can be emotional or physical or spiritual, and they can feel impossible to
overcome. They may be the stories in your head that keep you from believing you are worthy of the goal you have in mind. They can be an unkind
remark that stays with you from childhood, and no matter how old you
get, that remark still grieves your spirit. The critics are out there, but God
is in here, in your heart, and He can help you move on. You can define
obstacles in many ways, but you can only truly overcome them when you
choose to do so.

When you have a goal in mind, the best way to remove the hindrance
to your path is to start with God. Seek His guidance about how you should
proceed. Ask Him to help you manage the "land mines" of doubt and
fear that keep you from going forward. Ask for the support of those who
believe in your dreams and goals and want to do all they can to help you
achieve them.

This is a new day. It's a good day to let go of the negative influences, the
critical armies that strive to keep you stuck. Walk with God and together
you can overcome whatever gets in the way. The two of you are a force to
be reckoned with!

*Lord, help me to wait for Your guidance so that I don't create
**obstacles** myself to the work I hope to get done today. Amen.*

# ACT

*Who can proclaim the mighty acts of the Lord or fully declare his praise?*
*Blessed are those who **act** justly, who always do what is right.*

Psalm 106:2–3 NIV

When you were young, your mom may have said from time to time, "Act your age." In that context, she was probably trying to get you to act more appropriately for the situation you were in. She wanted you to act in a good way.

The way we act, behave, communicate with others, and communicate with God makes a critical difference in how our lives play out. Generally speaking, when our actions are good, good things are apt to follow as a response. When our actions are unjust or disrespectful or otherwise not good, then we might expect a negative impact on our lives.

God acted on our behalf when He sent Jesus to be our Redeemer. Jesus gave us a multitude of examples of what it means to be kind, to offer encouragement, and to do what we can to help others. He reminded His followers that their actions made a difference. His acts of healing, redefining Scripture, and teaching about God were intended for the good of the people in His day and in our day as well. So what about us? How will we act justly for the good of those around us?

Today, you might be more intentional about giving gifts of time, encouragement, attention, or simple kindness. You might be more prayerful about the ways you will choose to act toward each person you meet. You can do what is right. When you do, God will be pleased with your actions. He will act quickly to bless your life and the lives of those around you even more.

*Lord, I know that I don't always **act** in ways that please You. Help me to be aware of all my actions today. Amen.*

# BEGINNING

*In the **beginning** was the Word, and the Word was with God, and the Word was God. He was with God in the beginning. Through him all things were made; without him nothing was made that has been made.*

John 1:1–3 NIV

Some of our favorite childhood stories begin with the phrase "Once upon a time." As soon as we heard or read those words, we knew a special story was about to unfold.

God's story for us has a similar feel. It says, "In the **beginning**." If we're at the beginning of a new chapter in our own lives, we are excited because we're ready for a new adventure, ready to take on more of what life has to offer. God wants our story to start with Him. He wants to be sure we recognize all He has done. He wants us to hold on to the truth of what happened at the very beginning, so we remember it as we grow.

As a child, you learned to read stories by first learning letters and words. Once you understood how words come together, you were better able to enjoy the story. It's the same with your life story. Once you know what you need to begin your connection to God, then you can enjoy your story more. You have His Word!

The Word is Jesus and He was with God from the very beginning, and the Word is the Bible. The more you learn about the Word, the more you recognize His Presence in your daily life. God has been working with you to create a good story, because He's been with you from the beginning.

*Lord, thank You for helping me right from the **beginning** to recognize Your Word and the power of Jesus in my life. You've given me a great start. Amen.*

# BOLDNESS

*And this is the **boldness** we have in God's presence: that if we ask God for anything that agrees with what he wants, he hears us. If we know he hears us every time we ask him, we know we have what we ask from him.*

1 John 5:14–15 NCV

Can you remember the last time you acted with **boldness**? Maybe you stood up for an unpopular cause. Maybe you finally told your boss all the things that concerned you about your job. Whatever it was, you had to muster all the confidence you could to make it happen.

Imagine now that you are standing in the Presence of God. You have something very specific and important that you want to put before Him. You're not exactly sure how to say it or even if it aligns with His will and so you decide you simply must act with boldness. You boldly ask about the thing that concerns your heart and mind.

When we read this passage, one thing we might understand about asking boldly is that God will hear anything that agrees with what He wants. Ah, that seems tricky. How do we know what it is that God wants?

Perhaps we can't know specifically what God wants for us under every circumstance or in every situation, but we can know this much. We can know that when we have Jesus in our hearts, God will see us as His own. He will see us as a Father sees His child, and in that context, He will hear what we say.

Your Heavenly Father has already given you permission to approach Him boldly because your heart is entwined as one with H.m, through Jesus. With faith, you understand that He hears you and with boldness you know He hears your every request from Him.

*Lord, help me to walk with You in **boldness**, knowing that because of Jesus, I can talk to You about anything. Amen.*

# CHOICE

*If I preach because it is my own **choice**, I have a reward. But if I preach and it is not my choice to do so, I am only doing the duty that was given to me.*

1 Corinthians 9:17 NCV

One of the ways you continually write and edit the story of your life is through the **choices** you make. Sometimes you go for the high-quality, much-sought-after, best parts of life, and other times, you simply choose to move on and not think too much about the consequences. Unfortunately, even when you're weary, even when you decide not to choose, a choice has been made and it often comes with results you did not intend.

The writer of Corinthians gives us another perspective about making choices. He refers to his calling as needing to go out and tell God's story. Essentially, he seems to be saying that if he goes out to preach because it is his choice, something that he put his heart and mind into, then he gets rewarded for his choice. He is pleased because he is doing what he really wants to do. Preaching is his choice. However, he goes on to clarify. If he does not choose to preach, but he does it anyway, perhaps because he has a sense of obligation, then he is only doing it out of guilt or duty and that does not come with a reward because his heart is not in it.

Whether we're making vocational choices or emotional or spiritual choices, we have to understand that we are connected to the results. When the outcome is one that satisfies our hearts because we were pleased and excited with the choice we made, then it's a great day. When we make any kind of choice without including our heart as a guide, we can't help suffering disappointment. The choice is yours each day, but the best choices are attached to your heart.

*Lord, thank You that I can create my **choices**. Help me to recognize the various ways that I choose to act so that I am more deliberate about doing the things that please You. Amen.*

# DAILY

*Give us day by day our **daily bread**.*     Luke 11:3 NKJV

You've said the Lord's Prayer numerous times in your life, but today you're invited to simply consider this one word, **daily**. Give us day by day, this day, each day, our daily bread. We're not worrying about the past or frustrated about the future, we're simply seeking God's Presence for today. We're requesting that God never stop feeding us, that He continue to nourish us at all times and in every way. We don't want to miss one day of what He has to offer us.

Consider what it means for God to provide your daily, 365-days-a-year provision. What is it you're really asking for? Perhaps, in part, you're asking that He literally will put food on your table and provide physical nourishment for you and your family. That's something you hope He will do for you every day, daily.

You also need spiritual food daily. You need to be connected to Jesus, the bread of life, the one who nourishes your heart and mind. You need to know that you are safely in His care and keeping. You know how it feels when your spirits are low, so you need continual fortification from the Holy Spirit for both emotional and spiritual uplifting.

You need daily sustenance from God. You can't manage the world on your own steam. Your daily nourishment is given to you because your Father in Heaven knows what you need and He knows how to care for you. Give Him thanks and praise today for all He has done and for His daily bread.

*Lord, thank You for taking care of my needs **daily**. Help me to stay close to You and seek Your nourishing Spirit wherever I go today. Amen.*

# GARDEN

*And they heard the sound of the Lord God walking in the **garden** in the cool of the day, and Adam and his wife hid themselves from the presence of the Lord God among the trees of the garden.*  Genesis 3:8 NKJV

You can imagine that God must have a special place in His heart for **gardens** since that's where He put the first human beings. He wanted them to be surrounded by beauty and nourished from the land. Perhaps it was a little replica of Heaven, perfect in every way.

As we know, the first couple couldn't hold on to their garden paradise. They hid from God, not wanting to cultivate the relationship they shared. They choked on the weeds of their own choices.

The gardens of our lives need continual care. We can't keep up with the weeds and the storms that often wash out our hopes and dreams. We may not feel as protected and cared for as Adam and Eve, and yet we are. We must keep the garden of our hearts and spirits growing each day, planting our roots in the Savior, and seeking direction from God's light of love. With His help, we can tend to the weeds before they choke our spirits.

Listen for the sound of God walking near you today. Don't hide from Him. Talk to Him about the things you need. Embrace the *Sonshine*!

*Lord, thank You for taking care of me as though I, too, were a beautiful **garden**. Help me to get out of the weeds so that I can blossom for You. Amen.*

# WORRYING

*Look at the birds of the air; they do not sow or reap or store away in barns,
and yet your heavenly Father feeds them. Are you not much more valuable
than they? Can any one of you by **worrying** add a single hour to your life?*
Matthew 6:26–27 NIV

Consider the amount of time you spend **worrying**. Did the endless hours
fretting over something that never happened change anything? Did you
add more joy to your moments, more opportunities to do something in a
positive way, each time you were worrying?

Chances are you didn't add anything, especially not an extra hour to
your life. In fact, you may have spent countless hours with the swirling
stories going around in your head, never noticing that you were actually
volunteering for additional stress. Your worries didn't offer one shred of
possibility or opportunity. You might say that worrying simply doesn't
have productive qualities.

If you were to write down the last five things you worried about and
then also write down the actual outcomes of those things, the point would
be clear. Most of what you worried about never happened.

Of course, it's easy to say to someone else, "Don't worry!" In fact, you
probably mean it because deep down you know nothing good comes
from it. So today, replace your worries with something like this. Confession. That's right. Confess to God that you are worrying. After that, read
a Psalm or two and quiet your mind. Psalm 131:2 is a good one. Put your
life in God's hand and leave the worrying to Him. He stays awake all night
anyway.

*Lord, You know that I spend too much time **worrying**. Let me rest
in Your peace anytime worry tries to take over the hours of my day.
Amen.*

# GOING

*The Lord will keep you from all evil; he will keep your life.*
*The Lord will keep your **going** out and your coming in from this time on*
*and forevermore.* Psalm 121:7–8 NRSV

Sometimes, when you meet up with an old friend, you ask, "How's it **going**?" Usually, the response is something like, "It's going fine. It's good." The interesting part is that we have no idea what's going fine or what's good, but we're glad anyway.

The Lord is keeping track of your life, and He is watching over you every day. He keeps you from evil, and He is well aware of your comings and goings, your ups and downs, and your victories and losses. He is your safety net, your Divine protector, and He's with you wherever you go.

If you think you're all alone when you struggle with temptations or with other forms of evil, then you need to remember that when you go out, you're not going alone. When you come in, He is still there. You always have an option as you come and go, though. You can choose to walk around the little messes of life and keep going on your own, or you can remind yourself that where you go, God goes too.

Wherever you are going today, remember that you and God are a dynamic duo; you're going there together.

*Lord, only You know how it's really **going** today. Help me to hold*
*You close to me all through the day, no matter where I might be*
*going. Amen.*

# GENEROUS

*Keep open house; be **generous** with your lives. By opening up to others,*
*you'll prompt people to open up with God, this generous Father in heaven.*

Matthew 5:16 MSG

This Scripture from Matthew reads like an open invitation. We're all being invited to a party, an open house, and God is going to be there when we show up. We just must be **generous** with each other, willing to help others see what God has done through us. When we do that, we hear God's voice and see the opportunity to come to His table. Everyone is invited and each of us is a courier created to make sure everyone gets an invitation.

People who generously give, lend a hand, and open up to each other, often bring out the best in everyone around them. They are hosts who continually have an open house, a meet and greet, a backyard party, and they ask their friends and neighbors to stop by. They share what they have of God's grace and mercy and of this world's goods for the benefit of others. Everyone feels welcomed by the gift of their kindness and so they inspire others to want to be more generous as well.

It takes courage to be open, to be vulnerable in the presence of people you may not know well. It means you're willing to offer comfort or share the matters closest to your heart. Beyond that, being generous with what God has graciously given you radiates in your smile, letting others know how glad you are to be part of their lives. Your generous display of God's love is what brings others to the fold. Wherever you are today, may your heart be open to share God's most generous gifts. You're such a delightful and generous example of His love.

*Lord, I know that You have been very **generous** with me. Help me to hear Your voice so that I radiate Your love and generous spirit to others. Amen.*

# QUESTIONS

*Don't ask, "Why was life better in the 'good old days'?" It is not wise to ask such* **questions**.                                                        Ecclesiastes 7:10 NCV

Chances are good that you've been asking **questions** your whole life. When you were a child, your questions were probably focused around the word "why." Now that you're an adult, your questions are more reflective, perhaps still seeking the "why" of life, but in different ways than you did in your youth. The wisdom that the writer of Ecclesiastes would have us consider is about looking back. When we look back at our lives and continue to ask questions about what was or what might have been, we may find ourselves feeling disappointed or, worse yet, stuck. We may not know how to move on past the why questions so we can keep growing as God intends.

You, too, may have a time that you recall as the "good old days." Those were the moments when you may have felt more relaxed, more content with life, and perhaps even more fulfilled in the things you were doing. Looking back, you imagine that you were happy there. The problem is that God wants you to keep moving forward, learning from your past mistakes and discovering new vistas, finding the secrets of life that He wants to share with you. God wants you to imagine that the best days are still ahead and perhaps ask the questions that will help you get there a bit faster.

It's okay to have questions, especially if you are seeking guidance from God's Holy Spirit. It's good to have a sense of where you want to go. In fact, all of that is better than simply longing for the days that are in your past. God always has good things waiting up ahead and ready for you as soon as you arrive. May He bless your questions and help you discover the answers according to His grace.

*Lord, I do long a bit for those days when I seemed to understand life more clearly and when the* **questions** *seemed to have answers. I pray that You will hear my questions even now and help me seek Your voice today. Amen.*

# REDEEM

*But when the set time had fully come, God sent his Son, born of a woman, born under the law, to **redeem** those under the law, that we might receive adoption to sonship.*
                                                    Galatians 4:4–5 NIV

If you clip and save coupons to get cash back or discounts on your purchases, you get the feeling that you're a smart shopper. You understand the value of having something you **redeem** for your benefit. After all, you only clip the coupons on things you actually want, the things that are important to your lifestyle. Once you redeem a coupon, though, you don't get to use it again. It's a one-time-only deal.

When God created you, He knew that you had tremendous value. He wanted to find a way to make sure that He could get you back to Heaven. He wanted to give you a once-and-for-all coupon. You only have to accept the coupon and redeem it and you are set to go . . . eternally. God redeemed you through the gift of His Son. He made sure that you would not miss out on the deal so He made it simple. It's good to know that no matter how you have spent or even squandered your life up to this moment, God still offers you a chance to be redeemed. He wants you to be able to come back home and He already provided the safe passage to get there.

Perhaps you'll remember each time you redeem a small coupon for something that you purchase, that you, too, have been redeemed. God has sent His Holy Spirit to be with you forevermore.

*Lord, I thank You for offering me a way to come back to You, not only when this life is done, but each day that I awaken to Your **redeeming** spirit in my life. Amen.*

# ROCK

*For who is God besides the Lord? And who is the **Rock** except our God?*
*It is God who arms me with strength and keeps my way secure.*

Psalm 18:31–32 NIV

What is your **rock**? What would you identify as the thing that keeps you steady and fortifies you? Maybe you think your investments in stocks and bonds and annuities are rock solid. Maybe you've built your business or reputation in such a way that it seems like nothing could undermine you. Perhaps a spouse or family member is your daily support and strength.

While these things are good, they are not rock solid. Stock markets crash, businesses fail, relationships end, and loved ones pass away.

The psalmist reminds us here that there is only one Rock, only one foundation where you can build your sense of security, the only place where sustainable strength beyond measure can be derived. God is your rock. No other person, no place in the country, no amount of celebrity can keep you on solid ground. Nothing else can hold you up or make your path straight in the same way that God can do.

Investments, skills, and talents may well fortify you, even bring you great joy, but those gifts are fleeting. Those gifts have no promise of tomorrow. The place where you stand is made Holy only when you are standing on the Rock of Ages, the One who supports your every move.

*Lord, help me to put all my confidence in Your strength. Sustain me as only You can do, as the **Rock** of my life forevermore. Amen.*

# SPEECH

*It only takes a spark, remember, to set off a forest fire. A careless or wrongly placed word out of your mouth can do that. By our **speech** we can ruin the world, turn harmony to chaos, throw mud on a reputation, send the whole world up in smoke.*                    James 3:6 MSG

No matter how old you are, you probably have memories of a time when someone chastised you, perhaps even unfairly, and the words they spoke stung you and left you shaking. The tongue is a dangerous weapon sometimes, one that can cause untold damage, turning your world upside down.

The writer of James reminds us to think about the fury of our **speech**, our casting of opinions, and our tongue lashing so that we remember the damage it can bring. Without much effort at all, we can turn someone's life into chaos, simply by the words we speak. The wonder of it all, though, is that the same tongue that can cause trouble can also bring healing.

As a believer, you are intended to use your words for the good of others. When you speak into someone's life with words of encouragement and love, you add harmony and joy to their existence. You show them how valuable they are and raise their self-esteem. You do the work that God intended because you share His love in ways that bring out the best in others.

Today, as you consider the words that will come out of your mouth, check in with your heart to see if you can rephrase any words that might be damaging to someone else. Find a way to offer perspective that brings possibility and blessing to those around you. Let your speech to them be helpful and uplifting.

When people think of you, may they remember only the kindness that came from your lips.

*Lord, help me to hold my tongue when anything unkind tries to slip out and let my **speech** only bring peace and encouragement to those around me. Amen.*

# SIMPLE

*The answer's **simple**: Live right, speak the truth, despise exploitation, refuse bribes, reject violence, avoid evil amusements. This is how you raise your standard of living! A safe and stable way to live. A nourishing, satisfying way to live.*                    Isaiah 33:15–16 MSG

In recent years, many people have made an effort to simplify their lives. A simple life, one that is not continually swirling in chaos, can make a difference to the peace we feel on any given day. "Keep it **simple**" seems to be a good adage to live by.

Isaiah offers suggestions that can help us do that very thing. He reminds us that making choices to live right can go a long way toward keeping us from chaos and the things that cause continual turmoil. When we speak the truth, we speak with love in our tone and in the intention of what we say. We pull the plug on drama and give people room to breathe and to think.

We all want to raise our standard of living. We want to become better people, equipped to help those in our midst anytime they need us. We want to offer solutions to ease their cares and spread kindness wherever we go. When we do those things, we make a difference. We help make things simple. We help to change the atmosphere around us.

Today, see if you can discover more ways to live simply. When you dedicate yourself to living with kindness, you nourish your soul, you help others, and you are blessed with peace.

*Lord, please help me to choose to live a **simple** life. Help me to bring peace to any situation I might find myself in today. Amen.*

# TRUST

*Trust the Lord with all your heart, and don't depend on your own understanding. Remember the Lord in all you do, and he will give you success.*

Proverbs 3:5–6 NCV

**Trust** is a tough word. It's tough because many of us have become wary about where to place our trust. The weather station wants us to trust their forecasts. Your insurance carrier wants you to trust that they will be there to help if your house gets flooded or your car is damaged. Your employer wants you to trust that your job is secure and that your advancement in the company is important to everyone. Trust is key.

But there are no real guarantees. When you most need someone to be there for you, they may walk out. When you are in greatest need of your health insurance, or your car insurance, they may deny your claim. So where do you go? Whom can you trust?

Recall the wisdom of Solomon. The smartest person who ever lived suggested that there is one place to put your trust—and it's not in yourself or in the way you understand the world around you. It is not in government or institutions or other people. Trust the Lord with all your heart. When you have conviction about something, then your heart affirms your thoughts. When you remember the Lord in all you do, He is close to you, and can help you no matter what crisis may come.

Today is your day to practice trust. You can trust He'll be with you through the storms of life. Trust in the Lord with all your heart.

*Lord, I am not ever sure who I can **trust** as I look at other people. I'm not even sure I can trust myself. Help me to always trust You. Amen.*

# VIEW

*If Abraham was made right by the things he did, he had a reason to brag. But this is not God's view, because the Scripture says, "Abraham believed God, and God accepted Abraham's faith, and that faith made him right with God."*
Romans 4:2–3 NCV

Most of us have a personal world view. We tend to see things through the lens of our culture and our lifestyle. We manage our expectations by the way things have gone in the past and the ways we believe they will be in the future. What if we were to look at the world with more spiritual eyes? Would we discover that we have totally missed God's view of our personal situation?

In Romans, we read that Abraham could have bragged about his connection to God. He could have, but he didn't. He could have imagined that God thought He was more worthy than others, which made God choose to work with him. It appears that Abraham did the one thing that worked with God's view of him. Abraham believed God. He believed that God would do what He said He would do. He believed that God could turn him into a leader of thousands of people. He believed that God would give him a baby in his old age. He believed that God was with him every step of the way. He believed God and so God accepted Abraham's faith.

God's view then was built on the fact that He found Abraham to be a man of great faith. His view, His opinion, His connection to Abraham was built on their relationship. God had a favorable understanding of Abraham because they knew each other well and walked together every day. People of great faith are still changing the world. They create the possibility for others to know God and have more faith as well.

As you do your work today, imagine what view God might have of you. Is it built on your relationship with Him? Would you be considered right with God because of your great faith? May all that you are and all that you do please God. He sees you right where you are.

*Lord, I pray that Your view of me is built on our relationship so I can continue to walk with You and build my faith. Help me to do all I can to align my life with Your intentions wherever I may be. Amen.*

# WEAKNESS

*Concerning this thing I pleaded with the Lord three times that it might depart from me. And He said to me, "My grace is sufficient for you, for My strength is made perfect in **weakness**."*     2 Corinthians 12:8–9 NKJV

When you feel faint and feeble, suffering from emotional or physical **weakness**, you wonder how you will survive. After all, sometimes life requires all the strength you can muster. Weakness doesn't help you make the world better. In such a vulnerable state, it's easy to understand why you might pray for God to intercede, to take away some of your burdens and come to your aid. God hears your prayers, and at times, God will do just that. He will send Providential help your way and turn things around.

At times, though, God takes a less direct approach because He wants to heal your relationship with Him. He may see when you're weak or you feel vulnerable, but He also knows that when you are feeble, not operating at your peak level, you are more attuned to Him. You are more open to His guidance because you want things to change as quickly as possible. He does too, but for now, He wants to strengthen your weakness by directing you back to Him. He wants you to live in His grace and listen for His voice.

It may feel like the lights are flickering and everything is growing dim, but that's when God comes in and lifts you up, carrying you in His mighty arms. He strengthens your shaky knees and your fainting heart. He is there and all He asks of you is that you relax, rest in that uncertain, weakened state and know that He is strong. Curl up in His Presence and He will be with you today.

*Lord, it is hard to feel overwhelmed by **weakness**, where I feel so vulnerable. I don't know if I can stand much more. I pray that You will hold me up with Your strong right hand, and I thank You for sustaining me now. Amen.*

# WONDERFULLY

*I will praise You, for I am fearfully and **wonderfully** made;*
*Marvelous are Your works, And that my soul knows very well.*

Psalm 139:14 NKJV

Do you have any handmade treasures? Perhaps you have a quilt from your great-grandmother that was painstakingly created, lovingly put together so that every stitch was perfect. Maybe your father made a beautiful chest out of stained and polished wood, and you delight in having it in your home. These things are **wonderfully** made so that every detail is extraordinary.

That's how God made you. Every aspect of your being was known to Him before you were ever born. He knew you then and He knows you now. He delights in His handiwork when you do the things that please Him and when you show your love and gratitude for all He has done.

You are wonderfully, delightfully, brilliantly, perfectly made, and even your soul knows the truth of it. God created the person you are with utter perfection. He has great purpose for your life, and the more you draw close to Him, the more He can help you discover His intentions.

Peek in your mirror today and say aloud, "I am wonderfully made. God made me perfectly." Say it three times, and then as you go about the day, give God the glory for all that He has done in your life. Imagine that every person you know is perfectly and wonderfully made.

*Lord, please help me to always realize that You have made me*
***wonderfully** well and that You have a great purpose for my life. I*
*praise You and thank You for all You have done. Amen.*

# YOURSELF

*The whole law is made complete in this one command: "Love your neighbor as you love **yourself**."*
Galatians 5:14 NCV

DIY projects are all the rage. Partly because you can save money but also because you take great pride in being able to "Do it **yourself**." It's fun to be a creative person whether you're building a flower box or making your own greeting cards. God must have placed a little creative genius in each of us.

God loves the things you can do for yourself, but He doesn't want it to stop there. He wants you to share those things that bring you great joy. When you do that, then the joy can be spread around. Before you know it, the whole neighborhood is a brighter, happier place. How do you know that?

The writer of Galatians rephrased something that Jesus often reminded us to do as well. "Love your neighbor as you love yourself." Maybe part of loving your neighbor is sharing the blessings you've been given. If the power goes out but you have a generator for your house, you can cook meals for the people around you. If you hear of a shut-in who needs help getting a prescription filled, maybe you do that and share your homemade cookies too. You've learned how to do a lot of unique and special things, and sometimes the best DIY project is simply helping the person next door to have a better day. It doesn't take a lot to show a little love.

Remind yourself about the little things that make your day special and then take a moment to offer that kind of help to someone else. No doubt, you will have fun simply loving your neighbor as you love yourself. It is one of love's greatest laws! Have a great day!

*Lord, I pray that I will take to heart the message "Love your neighbor as you love **yourself**." Help me to love others in this way, because I know that even little things can make a difference. Amen.*

# FORGIVE

*"Lord, when my fellow believer sins against me, how many times must I forgive him? Should I forgive him as many as seven times?" Jesus answered, "I tell you, you must forgive him more than seven times. You must forgive him even if he wrongs you seventy times seven."*

Matthew 18:21–22 NCV

Wait a minute! Does this mean if someone does something that feels like a slight, like an intentional act that hurts you, you need to **forgive** them, not just once, but 490 times? Exactly!

You probably don't have a chart that tells you how many times you've forgiven someone who hurt you. In fact, you may feel that what happened was so wrong that you stopped counting at number one. You stopped counting and you stopped forgiving in the same moment. Certainly, human beings are accountable for many horrendous acts, sometimes repeating them numerous times. Someone in your life may have hurt you more times than you can count.

What does it mean, then, to move past the hurt, to move past the event that caused you sorrow and get to the place where your heart is willing to forgive? Perhaps the best example is to look at your relationship with God. Would you say that you have offended God by your actions at least once? Twice? Maybe even 490 times? The fact is that God's love is so enormous that He does not count your offenses. He does not keep a chart of the wrongs you have done because once you have asked Him to forgive you, He forgives, once and for all. He does not hold a grudge and He remembers your sin no more. Imagine that. He doesn't think about what you did to slight Him ever again.

When you let go of your past hurts, the offenses that have weighed you down for years, you don't have to replay them in your mind anymore. You can give yourself permission to move beyond what was and discover more of what God has for you. The offense will not go away, the offender will not be absolved, but you will be free to start again. Perhaps it's time simply to forgive others as God has forgiven you, not for the other person, but for yourself.

*Father, please* **forgive** *me for the many ways I have disappointed You. Help me to forgive others in the same way. Amen.*

# ASKS

*For everyone who **asks** receives, and everyone who searches finds, and for everyone who knocks, the door will be opened. Is there anyone among you who, if your child asks for a fish, will give a snake instead of a fish?*

Luke 11:1–11 NRSV

When you **ask** for a glass of water at a restaurant, you fully expect the server to comply. If you ask your spouse to pick up lettuce at the store, you expect to find lettuce in the grocery bag. When you ask for something, your hope and expectation is that your needs will be met.

So what about the person who asks something of God? What about you? What can you expect? Luke gives you a portion of the answer. He writes that when you ask God for something, He hears you, in the same way that a Father hears the requests of His child. He hears with a heart that is open to giving what He can to His beloved.

That means when you ask for anything, you can expect an answer from God, the Father, because He loves you as His child. You can expect that God will see your situation and do what He knows is best. He receives you with open arms. He comes to the door when you knock and He understands what you need.

You may wonder if you ask enough, or maybe you feel like you ask for too much. In that case, look at the example of Jesus. He asked God for everything He needed. God does what He knows will help you grow and come to know Him in ways that will strengthen your sense of being part of His family. He wants to build the father and child relationship you share. Even when you don't understand God's response to your requests, keep on asking because you can be sure He is working on the problems you've shared, and He always answers with love.

*Lord, I know that You hear me when I **ask** You for something. Help me to understand when Your responses are not clear to my heart. Amen.*

# EXPERIENCE

*I am praying that you will put into action the generosity that comes from your faith as you understand and **experience** all the good things we have in Christ.*
Philemon 6 NLT

**Experience** is often touted as being the best teacher. It is the thing that guides our future choices, the thing that gives us an understanding of life itself. So what about our experience with God? How do we learn more about what God expects from us, or what we can expect from Him?

Part of the answer comes from our willingness to spend time with God. The more we listen for His voice or sit in His Presence, the more we understand what He wants from us. The more experience we have with the words of Christ, the more we ask ourselves, "What would Jesus do?" in any situation.

If you are seeking a richer prayer life, then you have to strive for a deeper prayer experience. You must spend time in prayer and ask for guidance that will help you grow as a prayer warrior. If you are seeking to know what your life purpose is about, then you must be willing to get to know God in new ways. Call on the power of His Holy Spirit and seek answers to what God wants you to do. Spending time in God's Word, time in prayer, and time with other believers will help you experience God in new and refreshing ways.

Your experience will then lead you to new actions. You will desire to share more of what God has done in your life. You will want others to know that God is real, and with every retelling of His stories in your life experience, your faith will grow. Today may you experience God in a refreshing new way.

*Lord, I am longing for a new **experience** of You. I ask that You direct my steps so that I grow in faith and understanding of Your love for me. Amen.*

# COMMIT

*Commit your way to the Lord, trust in him and he will do this:*
*He will make your righteous reward shine like the dawn, your vindication*
*    like the noonday sun.*                                    Psalm 37:5–6 NIV

Perhaps you're wondering why life is simply not going along the way you hoped it would. Maybe it seems like you face one crisis after another. With each morning sunrise, you feel farther and farther away from your goals. Nothing seems to be happening in your favor. What is going on?

One possibility may be that you have to **commit** your life direction to God. You have to lean on Him and trust Him for your hopes and dreams. When you take your concerns or your goals or your plans to God, then you continue to build your relationship with Him. You include Him on the things that are most important to you. The psalmist wants us to understand that we have to make that kind of commitment every day and we have to do it with complete trust. When you trust God and spend time in prayer, seeking His help, then He is there for you. He will turn His face toward you and send the light of His love in your direction.

The psalmist wrote this Scripture to remind us that God wants to share in a relationship with us. He wants us to rely on Him and to believe that He alone can take care of our needs. He wants to know that we long to hear His voice about the things that really matter to us. If you've been waiting for God to show up in your life, take the time right now to re-commit your life to Him. Let God know that you don't want to walk another step without His help. Let Him know that you trust His guidance. When you do, you'll see His hand at work in your life from sunrise to sunset.

Trust and commitment may not be standards of the world, but they are still God's standards because He has not changed. He knows you need Him.

*Lord, I ask You to be with me today and guide my steps. I **commit** myself to You and I trust in You for all that I need now. Amen.*

# CROSSROADS

*Stand at the crossroads and look; ask for the ancient paths, ask where the good way is, and walk in it, and you will find rest for your souls.*

Jeremiah 6:16 NIV

When Robert Frost stood at the **crossroads** in his famous poem "The Road Not Taken," he decided that he'd walk a new path. He didn't want to take the one that most people were on. He wanted to go on the path that was less familiar. As a Christian, you're on the path that is not quite so well worn as the one that much of the world may take. You're on the path that the ancients took, the one that the patriarchs paved for you. You're on the path that seeks God in a way that will provide rest for your soul. You're on the path of life.

If you're at the crossroads, wondering whether it's worth it to take that path, look at what the Scriptures share from those who went before you. Study the Psalms and the stories in Acts of the new believers in Christ and what guided their hearts and minds.

The world offers you a lot of choices. Some of them are refreshing and interesting and may make sense for you. Other choices are ones that God wants you to consider, perhaps choices you never even imagined would be put before you. When you're seeking God's direction for your life, make sure you examine the path that may not be as clear, but just may be the one that is illuminated by God Himself for the good of your soul.

May God bless your choices when you stand at the crossroads.

*Lord, be with me as I make choices today. Whenever I am in doubt, or whenever I stand at the crossroads, help me to choose the way You would have me go. Amen.*

# BURDENS

*Carry each other's **burdens**, and in this way you will fulfill the law of Christ.*

Galatians 6:2 NIV

John Baillie offered this prayer to God: "Give me a stout heart to bear my own **burdens**. Give me a willing heart to bear the burdens of others. Give me a believing heart to cast all burdens upon Thee, O Lord."

Burdens come in all shapes and sizes. Sometimes they are physical ones where you are trying to lift an object that simply weighs too much for you to carry it on your own. Sometimes they are problems that weigh on your heart and mind. When they are your personal burdens, you probably do your best to carry them with as positive a spirit as you can muster.

Sometimes you carry the burdens of people you love. You pray for healing for a good friend, or buy the groceries for someone struggling with a job loss, or share in the burden of grief when someone else is suffering over the loss of a loved one.

Remember that you don't have to carry the burdens that come your way by yourself, because whether they are personal or connected to someone else you care about, you simply can't bear the weight of them. You have one choice. You must believe with all your heart that when you cast the burden on Christ, He will bear you up and help you keep going. Burdens that are cast upon the Lord are ones that you do not take back. You leave them in His loving hands, trusting that He will indeed take care of the needs they represent.

Today, remember that you do not have to bear the burdens of your own life, or those of others. Just believe with all your heart that Jesus will carry those burdens for you.

*Lord, it isn't easy to bear my own **burdens** or those of others. Help me to trust in You for all that weighs on my heart today. Amen.*

# DONE

*"His master replied, 'Well **done**, good and faithful servant! You have been faithful with a few things; I will put you in charge of many things. Come and share your master's happiness!'"*  Matthew 25:23 NIV

Nothing gives any of us quite the same satisfaction as the simple act of marking an item off our to-do list. We have a lot to do and we like to know we are making progress. When something is **done**, over, finished, we can do a little happy dance.

Completing a task, getting something done, may not always be the end of your project, though. Sometimes it's just the beginning, just a step you had to complete in order to go further. Sometimes being faithful to the first step is what gives you the ability to move on to a bigger step.

Getting things done has become an increasing burden in our culture because we are so used to multitasking, doing numerous things at once to keep up with everything. We seldom have the luxury of focusing on just one job. Perhaps the reminder to us here is simply to celebrate the steps that move us on to the next opportunity. When we get one thing done, it means we can do another. It means we can take the time to do something else. We can be faithful servants.

The longer you walk the path with God, the more you will recognize those moments when He is well satisfied with your work for Him. The more you stay connected to Him each day, the more you can celebrate the joy of the work you do together. Imagine today that He sees you hard at work and stands ready to give you His praise. "Well done, good and faithful servant!"

*Lord, please help me to keep doing each task You have given me until I have **done** it in the best ways possible. Help me to serve You faithfully wherever I am today. Amen.*

# GRIEVE

*"They are blessed who realize their spiritual poverty, for the kingdom of heaven belongs to them. They are blessed who grieve, for God will comfort them."*
Matthew 5:3–4 NCV

Jesus often reminded those around Him of life's blessings. Going through Matthew 5, you might imagine the gift that comes with being pure of heart or the blessing of being a worker for peace. But it's a bit more difficult to understand the blessing of those times that cause you to **grieve**. After all, the grief you feel comes from a significant loss. You grieve the loss of people you love, or you grieve the loss of your childhood home, or your family pet. You grieve and God comforts you. Perhaps the blessing that Jesus shared is twofold.

When you suffer a loss, you are saddened by a depth of feeling that comes straight from the heart. Since God is love, He knows how hard it is when the light of love is extinguished. He tries to comfort you in the process of mourning. He also tries to help you see how important it is that you are moved by love so much that everything about it matters. Perhaps grief is one of the truest emotions because it speaks to the depths of your love like nothing else can.

When Jesus lost his friend Lazarus, He wept. He suffered because He loved His friend. He knows what it is like for a heart to be broken and so He offers comfort.

You may not have realized the gift of grief, but God knows that your heart cannot break unless it is fully aware of how much it has loved. Your heart can then be comforted by only one thing—more love, God's love. May God comfort your heart anytime you have cause to grieve.

*Lord, thank You for drawing near to me when my heart is broken. Help me to mend from those things that truly cause me to grieve. Amen.*

# PLANTED

*Those who are **planted** in the house of the Lord shall flourish in the courts of our God.*
*They shall still bear fruit in old age; They shall be fresh and flourishing,*

Psalm 92:13–14 NKJV

Whether you're planting vegetables or planting a new church, or moving to the other end of town, you're doing the same thing. You're putting down new roots. You're looking for new ways to flourish.

The psalmist says we want to be **planted** in the house of the Lord. Where is the house of the Lord? In Old Testament times, it was a real place, physical buildings that God asked His followers to build. It was a place of refuge where God's name could be honored. Today, we might imagine that many of our churches represent places to be called the "house of the Lord." These are the places we invite God in and where we can worship Him and be nurtured by His Spirit and by His Word. But the most important way to be planted in the house of the Lord is by inviting God into your heart, into the sanctuary of your very being.

Jesus said that He was in the Father and the Father was in Him. What that suggests is that they were always connected to each other. He also said that He was in us and that we are in Him. We have created spaces for each other and we are connected all the time. Our faith takes root in ways that replenish us in hard times and bring us warmth and comfort even into old age. We can be planted in the house of the Lord wherever we go, because we carry God's Spirit within us.

*Lord, I know that I am rooted in You and Your grace. Help me to stay **planted** in Your house all the days of my life. Amen.*

# HOPE

*Be of good courage, And He shall strengthen your heart,*
*All you who **hope** in the Lord.*                    Psalm 31:24 NKJV

Human beings thrive on **hope**. We hope for good news. We hope for better days ahead. We hope that God forgives us. We hope even when hope seems to have no basis in our reality.

Hope is expectant. It is a kind of strength that moves us toward belief and trust. It imagines that tomorrow will bring the sunshine and it anticipates that the good will flourish and that God will redeem His people. Hope takes courage, and it serves us best as we trust God to honor the hope we have in Him.

When you think back over your life, you can identify instances where your hopes and dreams came true. You lifted the desires of your heart up to Heaven and God heard your prayers. He granted you the opportunities for your hope, your courage, and your confidence to come to fruition.

Take time today to treasure those moments. Remember what God has done already to help make your life richer and more fulfilling. As you recount the times that He showed up just for you, your hope will be renewed once more. Your heart will be strengthened, and your prayers will never be limited. God is with you now and always. You can continue to hope in the Lord.

*Lord, help me when I lose **hope** in the future, or in the things I most desire. Help me to trust in You, believing in my heart that You are the greatest hope I could ever have. Amen.*

121

# LAUGH

*Abraham was a hundred years old when his son Isaac was born. Sarah said, God has blessed me with laughter and all who get the news will **laugh** with me!*                                   Genesis 21:5–6 MSG

Have you ever noticed that when you're tired and overwhelmed at the same time, you get a little punchy? The slightest thing can make you **laugh**, simply because you're trying not to cry. That may be what happened to Sarah when she laughed over the thought of having a baby at her advanced age. She may have simply been simultaneously stressed and relieved. After all, God had finally answered her prayer. We all need stress relief. We need ways to cope with the circumstances we face, whether they are good or bad. One of the ways we might do that is by giving ourselves permission to have fun, to laugh at ourselves, or to recognize life's absurdities. Laughter can help keep things in perspective. You get to laugh, tease, giggle, play, and enjoy your life even when everything seems a bit crazy.

In Genesis, it says Abraham and Sarah had a pretty good laugh over the fact that they would be having a baby. After all, Abraham was already a hundred years old and Sarah was ninety. They were well past the traditional childbearing years, and though they had prayed for a baby for a long time, they finally gave up. They imagined that God was not going to answer their prayer. You can probably see why it caused them to laugh out loud. How could it be? How could they bring a new baby into the world? They were excited, shocked, relieved, and stressed beyond measure.

God heard their laughter and had them name the baby Isaac, which means laughter. Sometimes you need to just give in to unimaginable circumstances and simply laugh too. Step back from those things that feel out of control. Chances are good that you won't be having any new babies at an advanced age, but no doubt God knows other ways to cause you to laugh. He wants you to live abundantly and well.

*Lord, please help me to remember not to take everything quite so seriously. Give me opportunities to **laugh** in good, healthy fun. Amen.*

# SURELY

*Surely you know. Surely you have heard. The Lord is the God who lives forever, who created all the world. He does not become tired or need to rest. No one can understand how great his wisdom is.* Isaiah 40:28 NCV

The word **surely** appears nearly three hundred times in some Bible translations. It is a word that brings emphasis to an important piece of information. Often it is stated as a strong conviction, as in, "as surely as the Lord lives," and then is followed by what will happen. "Surely" brings the certainty and the confirmation to the point being made.

In the Scripture from Isaiah, we can almost feel the pleading tone of his voice. "Surely you know. Surely you have heard." He makes his comment without any doubt as if there is no possibility that you would not have heard or you would not know.

In our present-day mindset, there are many things that are said glibly or even falsely. We talk about fake news and information that circulates on the Internet with very little to back it up. We operate on half-truths and weak promises. Few things are said with authority and certainty and assurance.

Our hope, then, is in remembering the One who lives forever and who created the world. He does not lie, or grow weary, or speak in ways that are meant to mislead us. He is surely the One we need to know. He is surely the One we need to listen to at all times. Surely, He knows you and gives you grace and mercy each day.

*Lord, I know that You alone speak truth. I understand that as **surely** as You live, I will live, and that You draw near to all of us when we seek Your voice. Amen.*

# TOWARD

*If your people spread their hands in prayer **toward** this Temple, then hear their prayers from your home in heaven. Forgive and treat each person as he should be treated because you know what is in a person's heart.*

2 Chronicles 6:29–30 NCV

Solomon's prayer is an awesome request that God would acknowledge the prayers of each person who reaches **toward** Heaven. What does it mean to us to reach toward, in the direction, up to Heaven?

Anything we do that deepens our faith, renewing our hearts for a more intimate relationship with our Savior, is a definite reach toward Heaven. After all, moving toward God is a matter of the heart.

Think of the other things in your life that you might gravitate toward. Perhaps you move toward your friends when they need you. You seek to be helpful to them in ways that ease their cares or simply bring them joy. You might move toward getting a better education. You do that because you believe in your heart that you can become more than you are today.

As you move toward a deeper faith and reach your hands toward God, just remember that He already knows your heart. He already is open to hearing your prayers. It's a good day to lean in His direction then and offer Him unending praise for all He has done in your life, and to seek His guidance for those steps you have not yet taken in your relationships or in your career. Reach up toward God and you can be certain that He will act swiftly to reach down and grab your hand. He will lift you up with love.

*Lord, I do seek Your guidance for the next steps in my life and I reach **toward** You on behalf of everyone I love. I pray that You will bend down and touch each of our lives with Your grace and mercy. Amen.*

# CLOUD

*When the **cloud** rose from the Holy Tent, the Israelites would begin to travel, but as long as the cloud stayed on the Holy Tent, they did not travel. They stayed in that place until the cloud rose. So the cloud of the Lord was over the Holy Tent during the day, and there was a fire in the cloud at night. So all the Israelites could see the cloud while they traveled.*

Exodus 40:36–38 NCV

When we were kids, we imagined shapes and pictures in the **clouds**, like birds, animals, or angels. It was a calming distraction as we watched the clouds go by.

As interesting to us as clouds in nature might be, imagine what it was like for the children of Israel to have clouds that were intentional and directed their steps. The cloud would rest on the Holy Tent, the place where God resided. When the cloud was still, no one moved. When the cloud rose to go, they packed up and went with it. At night, the cloud appeared to have a fire inside it as it lit the way.

This story is a mystery. It's hard to imagine a cloud simply resting on a spot, then guiding us all day, shining a light through it at night, so that we could keep walking even in the dark. This was a cloud with a Divine mission. It was a cloud that was Holy.

Of course, the cloud was a gift. It shaded the desert walkers by day and lit up the sky for them at night as they traveled. As you go about your day, take a moment to consider the clouds in the sky. See them as one more opportunity to recognize that God is always in our midst, not hidden by the clouds, but residing within, around, and through them. He will guide you wherever you need to go.

*Dear Father, as I see the mighty works of Your hands, I am in awe. You guide us today with other versions of that **cloud** the Israelites could see because You want us to know You are near. Guide my steps today. Amen.*

# WISH

*I said, "I **wish** I had wings like a dove. Then I would fly away and rest.*
*I would wander far away and stay in the desert.*
*I would hurry to my place of escape, far away from the wind and storm."*

Psalm 55:6–8 NCV

Probably most of us have made the same **wish** as the writer of this Psalm. Life becomes overwhelming with financial distress or family matters or health issues, and the best idea we can think of is the one that simply says, "I wish I could run away."

The psalmist wanted to go to the desert, someplace where he could be alone and not worry about all the troubles that were brewing in the cities and the towns. He simply wanted to get as far away from trouble as he could.

We can understand the problem. We are continually bombarded with the news of the world and so we're faced with every disaster, every battleground, and every sad story that comes across the Internet or across the news and we wonder what is happening to the world. We wish we could figure out the mess and do something about it, but the job is too big for us, so we wish to simply get away from all the chaos and find a place of peace.

There is good news: Jesus offers us the gift of peace when we turn to Him. We can run to Him anytime we choose and seek His arms like an oasis in the desert. We can reach up and reach out to Him for comfort and He is there. You don't need to wish that Jesus would be near; simply pray, and ask Him to come close to you today and peace will fill your soul.

*Lord, thank You for hearing me every time I **wish** for a way of escape. Instead, please guide me to Your living waters of peace and joy. Amen.*

# SUSTAIN

*Restore to me the joy of your salvation and grant me a willing spirit, to*
**sustain** *me.* Psalm 51:12 NIV

Some days it feels like you have reached your physical, emotional, and spiritual limit. You cannot take on one more challenge. You can't go the extra mile for someone else, because you are simply spent. Everywhere you look, it feels like your life is simply out of control. You aren't even sure what can **sustain** you, grant you relief, and give you a secure place to stand. You know you need a willing spirit, a real desire, and help from God to keep you going.

You're not alone. That may not give you cause to feel more cheerful, but perhaps realizing that you do have a Source, a place to turn even yet, can be helpful. The psalmist cried out to God. He didn't want anything but a reminder that God was with him and that He had reason to still rejoice.

Restore my joy, he says. Renew my spirit, he pleads. Remind me that You save me and that in itself is worthy of joy. These thoughts are not foreign to us when we are going through difficult times. We want to be sustained. We want someone to hold us up and give us enough energy to keep going. We want to know that we can survive the mess and the chaos and rise to another day.

Christ hears those prayers. He knows the troubles you are experiencing, and He walks with you to carry the weight of what you must bear. Let God's loving Spirit sustain you, hold you, and give you strength today.

*Lord, please help me today to get through the obstacles, the things that weigh me down so that I can hardly bear them. Sustain me by Your loving hand. Amen.*

# ROOTS

*But blessed are those who trust in the Lord and have made the Lord their hope and confidence. They are like trees planted along a riverbank, with roots that reach deep into the water. Such trees are not bothered by the heat or worried by long months of drought. Their leaves stay green, and they never stop producing fruit.* Jeremiah 17: 7–8 NLT

Many of us enjoy researching our family genealogies so that we can dig deeper into our **roots** and understand more about where we came from and even why we do what we do. Maybe we come from a long line of farmers, but we live in the city. Our love for animals and growing a garden reminds us of our connection to those who came before us.

Our roots are more than just origin and ancestry. Our roots go back much farther than that. Through faith in God and belief in Jesus, we have become rooted into a tree that is so deep nothing can shake it, nothing can cause it to be broken. Jeremiah reminds us that our roots, our ancestry, our origins are built on the trust, hope, and confidence that we have in God. Our roots may be touched by long months of drought, times when we were not as trusting or as certain in the things we believe, and yet they sustained us. Those roots are deeper than our passing fancy, or our worried minds, or our current circumstances.

God does not change, and He alone shares everything we go through, keeping us solidly connected to Him so that we can continue to bear fruit no matter what else is going on in our lives. Be confident in the roots you've established with the One who knows your every need.

*Lord, thank You for keeping me securely rooted in Your love and mercy. Grant that I will be continually aware of the **roots** I have in You. Amen.*

# CALM

*But I am **calm** and quiet, like a baby with its mother.*
*I am at peace, like a baby with its mother.*                    Psalm 131:2 NCV

It's hard to imagine a better image than the one the psalmist chose to share about what peace and **calm** and quiet can feel like. Picture that tiny baby drifting quietly to sleep, not a care in the world, just gently at rest in its mother's arms. What could be better than that?

When we're not babies anymore, we trade that comfortable, loving, quiet, trusting space for the chaos of the world. What helps us to stay calm then?

We may have to grow up and grow away from our mothers, but we do not have to grow away from that understanding that our Father takes over when we go off into the world. Our Heavenly Father is the One who can help us find peace and remain calm because He is always there, close beside us, ready to help carry the load or strengthen our weary lives.

If you sense that you have wandered too far, perhaps forgetting that you have loving support available to you at all times, you might consider this picture and hold it in your mind. Picture a loving Father holding you close, calming your fears, supporting your steps wherever you go. God is ready to calm and quiet your nerves, remove your worries, and like a mother, simply cradle you in His arms.

*Lord, I long for that sense of **calm** that I know only You can really give me. Help me to relax today and rest in Your tender embrace. I pray for all those who need Your amazing peace. Amen.*

# BEAUTY

*It is not fancy hair, gold jewelry, or fine clothes that should make you beautiful. No, your **beauty** should come from within you—the beauty of a gentle and quiet spirit that will never be destroyed and is very precious to God.*

1 Peter 3:3–4 NCV

**Beauty** may well exist in the eye of the beholder, as an adage says, but the writer of 1 Peter seems to have an even better definition. Beauty, as it turns out, may have nothing at all to do with outside appearances. It emanates from within and is a precious and gentle spirit that is given to you from God. In that light, your heart makes you beautiful!

We identify things that have radiance and give us pause as we consider their design or texture, the landscape or the color palette. We're amazed when we view canyons and mountain peaks, or simple rosebuds that seem to exist in utter perfection. Beauty is all around us, a gift of the creation, and the handiwork of God, and when your spirit is connected to the Creator, you recognize the beauty of nature, as well as the beauty that exists within the people all around you.

You are beautiful! Your beauty comes from the very essence of the Spirit of Christ that lives within you, causing you to embrace others with kindness, forgive those who offend you, and help people in need. God has given you a gentle and quiet spirit so that you can share the light of His love with everyone else. He sees how precious you are.

Today, remind yourself about who you really are. Take a moment and peek in the mirror and thank God that He made you an incredible beauty.

*Lord, it's hard for me to call myself beautiful, but I know You think I am. You have a way of encouraging the love in our hearts so that we are able to see the **beauty** in each other. Remind me to see the beauty in each person I meet today. Amen.*

# NOTHING

*Let **nothing** move you. Always give yourselves fully to the work of the Lord,
because you know that your labor in the Lord is not in vain.*

1 Corinthians 15:58 NIV

Let **nothing** move you! That's a bold statement. That statement means that
you will do anything in your power to go forward, to keep working, to
keep trying. You will not let obstacles deter you and you will not let time or
circumstances stop you from accomplishing your goal. Nothing will stop
you. That makes this a big word because it doesn't allow for any excuses.

Nothing only means zero when you're working on certain kinds of
math equations. It may be something you say to others, as in, "Think
nothing of it," if you've done a good deed or you've been slighted somehow. If you are really working so hard for the kingdom of God that you are
willing to stop at nothing, or let nothing move you away from your task,
then you are moving toward doing a big job. You are doing life-long work.

Think of the Scripture that says, "All things are possible with God."
Now say it in another form, "Nothing is impossible with God." We're
reminded that if nothing is impossible, then there are no obstacles, no
mountains too big to climb, no miracles that can't happen. We're able to
understand that if nothing stands in the way, then opportunities are all
around. All things become possible, according to God's plan and direction for your life.

Remember today that nothing can get in the way of the work you are
doing for the Lord. He knows your heart and He makes all things possible.
Nothing can stop His Divine intentions for your life.

*Lord, please help me to understand that **nothing** is more important
than making myself available to You and all that You make possible.
Amen.*

131

# WAS

*In the beginning there **was** the Word. The Word was with God, and the Word was God. He was with God in the beginning. All things were made by him, and nothing was made without him. In him there was life, and that life was the light of all people.*                    John 1:1–4 NCV

You may think back from time to time about your youth, where you lived, how you grew up, remembering all that **was**. You can picture the house you lived in and the neighborhood. You might remember who was living next door and the park that was down the street. You may have assorted memories from those days. That was your story back then. That story helped to make you who you are today. It can be helpful in the present moment to look back at what happened before, to understand all that was.

Perhaps you've always appreciated history because it gives you a better understanding of the present. You like to see more clearly why decisions were made or why laws were written. In a way, that is what John is trying to do.

He is looking back at the beginning of all things and he is sharing a mystery. He wants us to get a picture of the relationship of God and the Word, that is, of God and Jesus. He tells us that, together, they made everything. If we can get our arms around that information, then we might better understand our heritage and why God tried to give us rules to live by.

Because He was, we are. Today, reflect on the very essence of who God is, the Word, the Light, the Redeemer, the Creator. He created this moment in time knowing the day would come when you would breathe His Spirit into all that you do. The Word was with God, and the Word was God. What He was and what He is—these are the keys to your existence. Give God thanks and praise for the light He bestows on you.

*Lord, there are parts of Your mystery that I truly don't understand. I thank You and praise You, though, for all that **was** and all that will be in Your mercy and grace. Amen.*

# GENTLE

*Accept my teachings and learn from me, because I am **gentle** and humble in spirit, and you will find rest for your lives.*        Matthew 11:29 NCV

When you think about the things that are **gentle**, you may think of soft, warm breezes on a spring day, or your grandmother's smile, or the kindness of your friend. You know what gentle means and how much you appreciate that quality in others.

It's amazing to think of Jesus as gentle. He is the King of the universe, the most powerful force in all existence, and yet he describes himself as gentle and humble.

Sometimes we make the mistake of thinking that a gentle person, a kind person, a person who puts others first and watches tenderly over those around them, is not a powerful person. Perhaps the opposite is true. Perhaps a gentle soul commands the universe in some ways because that person already knows that they can rest, cradled in the arms of God, anytime they need strength and renewal. Perhaps the gentle person doesn't need to prove their power to anyone and so that increases the power they actually have available to them.

As you reflect on what it means to be gentle and humble in spirit today, ask God to help you see the strength you can receive every day by resting in Him. May God bless your gentle heart and mind today and give you peace in your life.

*Lord, I thank You for the **gentle** people who are around me and I ask that You help me be more like them, resting in Your strength and kindness each day. Amen.*

# CUP

*Lord, you alone are my portion and my **cup**; you make my lot secure.*

Psalm 16:5 NIV

It appears that the psalmist had more than his favorite **cup** of tea in mind when he declared that the Lord was his portion and his cup. Putting aside your favorite beverage mug, we can see that the image of the cup holds more than water. You may recall that Jesus prayed that God might take "this cup" away from him if God was willing, and then in the next breath, He agreed that he was willing to drink from this cup according to God's will and plan.

In Psalm 23, we read that the psalmist's cup overflows with blessings and God's goodness. God is our portion, our cup, the One who makes us secure in this life and the next. When we take communion and break bread and drink from the cup, we are sharing in the life, death, and resurrection of Jesus. We are saying that we are willing to drink from the same cup, taking on whatever God wills for our lives. And our cup does overflow with blessings.

Today, as you sip your early morning coffee, perhaps you could consider the cup you hold. Notice its design and its ability to securely deliver its contents with ease. Imagine then that you are holding the cup of God's blessings. Drink from it and enjoy what He wants you to have today, knowing that He is your portion, that He is your provider, and that He is the One who makes your life secure. Offer Him your thanks and praise for all He is doing to sweeten your life with simple joys.

*Lord, help me to remember You today with every **cup** I raise to my lips, acknowledging that You are the One who provides for all my needs. Amen.*

# OVERCOME

*"I have told you these things, so that in me you may have peace. In this world you will have trouble. But take heart! I have **overcome** the world."*

John 16:33 NIV

Your plate is full. You are managing everything you can, and it doesn't feel like you have room or energy to take on one more issue. You wonder how you will move forward because you are overwhelmed with life. Stress is a fact of life for all of us, but sometimes it seems to get so big, you simply want to run away. You have no sense of peace because your mind is racing at hundreds of miles per hour trying to come up with answers, solutions to all that weighs you down.

You may be overwhelmed, but the good news is this: You won't be over-powered, you won't be **overcome**, because you are on God's radar and He is watching over everything you are doing. He sees you. He knows what you are dealing with, and He wants to remind you to take heart because He is with you. Jesus has already overcome the world, meaning that He has redeemed us and can help manage the chaos.

It may not look very easy from where you stand. It may not even look easy to Jesus, but He knows the outcome. He knows the result is that He is there with you, and with His help and His power and His love, you will not be overcome. You will stand firm and you will find peace. You may struggle with peace in this world, but you will surely find it in the next. If you have more than you can handle on your plate today, put down your fork and spoon and move it away from you. Hand it all over to the only One who can take care of things. He has already overcome the world and He knows what you need!

*Lord, please help me today to stand in Your grace and to receive Your guidance for all the chaos around me. Only with You can I hope to **overcome** all these difficulties. Amen.*

# PICTURE

*The law is only an unclear **picture** of the good things coming in the future; it is not the real thing.*
                                                        Hebrews 10:1 NIV

Consider the finest photograph, drawing, or oil painting you've ever seen of the Taj Mahal or the Grand Canyon. It might make you long to be there. It might give you hope of possibility or a desire for your chance to visit the site, but it's just an image, it's not the real thing.

At best, a **picture** is simply a representation of something. It brings an image to light that we can carry with us in our hearts and minds. It can be impressive and beautiful, but it can never truly show us the real thing.

The Scripture from Hebrews, though, reminds believers of the picture they may have had about God based on the law. He says your picture is no longer accurate. In fact, it only gives an unclear view or image of the future. The law, then, is not all there is because with Jesus comes a new reality, a new picture.

This reminder is for you as well because you can only see part of the picture. The image of all that God has done to redeem you may be a bit fuzzy. You may not recognize the real picture until you're called home again. Let your personal image of Jesus bring you peace and fill your mind with everlasting hope. You may be seeing only a shadow, a portion, or through a glass darkly for now. Someday you will see the real picture and the real future.

*Lord, thank You for a glimpse of You that we can carry with us each day. I pray that a **picture** of You will become more real to me and those I love with every breath I take. Amen.*

# PUBLISH

*Sing to God, everyone and everything! Get out his salvation news every day! Publish his glory among the godless nations, his wonders to all races and religions. And why? Because God is great—well worth praising!*

1 Chronicles 16:23–24 MSG

When we **publish** something—a news article, a book, or some other printed material—we do it because we have something that we believe is worth sharing. We want other people to know something that we have discovered. We're energized and excited about all we have to share.

Imagine what the writer of Chronicles was really saying. He was joyful. No, he was ecstatic! He was beside himself with the goodness of God and he wanted to shout it from the rooftops. He was driven by love. He had an awesome story to tell.

Don't you love the idea of that? Does it resonate with you that, as Christians, we have even more stories to tell? We can publish, circulate, send out the news of our salvation through Christ for everyone to hear. We have every reason to celebrate.

The writer in this Scripture even answers his own question. He says, "Why should we publish this news?" "Why should we be getting the word out?" Oh, because "God is great." He is worthy of our praise.

Chances are you have a lot of reasons to sing God's praises and even a strong desire to tell others about God's work in your life. Go ahead, then, publish what God has done!

*Father in Heaven, You are amazing! If I could write and **publish** the things You have done in my life, it would take volumes of books. Thank You for Your steadfast love. Amen.*

# RELAX

*The Lord watches over the foolish; when I was helpless, he saved me. I said to myself, "**Relax**, because the Lord takes care of you."*

Psalm 116:6–7 NCV

**Relax!** Now there's a word that is easier said than done! You know what it's like when every nerve ending is on edge, when every fiber of your being is somehow tied in a knot. That's the way you feel when worry takes over, when rational thought and positive choices leave the room. You're tangled up and all you can imagine is that the worst possible things are heading your way.

The psalmist must have had that dilemma as well. He looked at what was around him and part of him was foolish enough to simply let worry take over. He could feel his pulse rising and his heart rate accelerating. He imagined that all was lost.

You may know people who actually spend a good deal of their lives in that negative space. All they can think about is how gloomy life is. Everything is horrible. Everything makes them nervous. They simply cannot help thinking the worst about whatever is going on in their lives. Maybe you're like that some days yourself. If so, here's the thing you need to remember: "Relax, because the Lord takes care of you."

Can you say that right now? Stand in front of a mirror and simply say out loud, "Relax, because the Lord takes care of you!" If you're struggling with it, that's okay, just practice. Stand there until you really mean it. Stand there until the Spirit of God embraces your heart and mind and reminds you that you are not alone and that God watches over you every moment. Worry is foolish. Trust gives you strength. Relax!

*Lord, I know that I can get pretty wound up at times. Help me to **relax** and remember when I am worrying needlessly that You are there, that You see me, and that You take care of me. Amen.*

# RUSH

*Then the Spirit of the Lord will **rush** upon you with power. You will prophesy with these prophets, and you will be changed into a different man.*

1 Samuel 10:6 NCV

It appears that the Spirit of the Lord is not slow. He doesn't walk over to someone, chat a while, and then decide if He's there to help. He doesn't linger on the sidelines before He comes to your aid. No, He is in a **rush**. He comes quickly and powerfully and nothing stops His movement. He changes your life!

The Scripture here talks about a time when Saul was filled with the Spirit of the Lord. He began to prophesy and He became a different man. Whatever Saul was thinking he was going to do that day was rerouted. Changed! He walked a new path.

We think about rushing here and there to get our various tasks done through the day. We imagine that we must step lively to get it all accomplished, and no matter how busy we are, we can't complete everything, even when we rush as quickly as possible.

Perhaps a closer analogy to what happens when the Spirit of the Lord rushes upon anyone is the way it feels when your heart flutters quickly and causes your face to get all rosy. Think of how it feels when you get a sudden rush of emotion that changes your perception or even causes you to cry or laugh aloud. Are you open to it? Are you ready to be changed? Are you willing to become different? If so, may the Spirit of the Lord rush upon you with great power today.

*Lord, I know that I'm a bit sluggish when it comes to inviting You into my life each day. I pray that You would fill me with Your Spirit so that I might **rush** to do Your will in ways I've never imagined. Amen.*

# SMILE

*Happiness makes a person smile, but sadness can break a person's spirit.*
Proverbs 15:13 NCV

Have you ever stopped to consider what a **smile** does for you? There may be many things to ponder, but one of them is that when you smile, it means you are lit up from within. It means you feel generous and warm and that hope guides you wherever you are. You have embraced life and have something to give. You offer your smile, that little personal beam of light and electricity, and it connects you immediately to others and they are instantly invited into your circle.

There is unspoken joy that permeates the place where you are. All of this happens from one simple, yet incredible asset God has given you. He gave you a face, with a smile that can light the world around you. He gave you a simple way to communicate your personal joy.

Genuine, heartfelt, love-filled smiles make a difference, and it's a difference you can create regardless of your bank account, your job title, or your cultural background. A smile comes in every language, is useful to every age group, and requires no particular training. Even more, it means the same thing to every person who encounters it. It means joy is ready to be shared.

You have lots of reasons to smile and so today it might be good to thank God for all that He has done to lighten your load, or stand by you in the tough times. No matter what your circumstances are, He sees you and He works to help you through whatever is going on. His desire is that you would always have reason to smile, to be happy. May His love renew your spirit and give you continual opportunities to smile.

*Lord, thank You for the simple gift of a smile. I know how much I appreciate people who welcome me with the warmth a smile always brings. Amen.*

# STORY

*The heavens declare the glory of God, and the skies announce what his*
*hands have made.*
*Day after day they tell the **story**; night after night they tell it again.*
*They have no speech or words; they have no voice to be heard.*
*But their message goes out through all the world.* Psalm 19:1–4 NCV

God is a **story** teller. He's a dynamic author, setting the scenes, creating the landscapes of time in ways that defy imagination. We see His work and even get a glimpse of what He's trying to say as we take note of a glorious sunrise or a twinkling night sky. He made sure all of us could read His story anyplace we happen to be.

Your life is a story. You have ancestry and roots. You have colorful characters and villains. You have saints and sinners. Every family has its share of the good ones and the more difficult ones. The question, then, is this: "What story do you want to tell?"

God already knows your story and He thinks it is brilliant, timeless, worthy of being shared. The more you can connect your story to His story, the greater your relationship with Him will be. He has a lot left to say, and some of His ideas need to be written by you. You're His example. You're His story outline, waiting to come to fruition. May the message He hopes to share through you go all over the world as you tell His story through love.

*Lord, thank You for sharing Your **story** with me. Help me to see You*
*and listen for Your voice everyplace I go. Amen.*

141

# VOICE

*In my trouble I called to the Lord; I cried out to my God. From his temple he heard my **voice**; my call for help reached his ears.* 2 Samuel 22:7 NCV

Your **voice** is powerful. It is unique to you. Jesus once said that His sheep hear His voice and they know to follow Him. It's true: sheep will only follow the literal voice of their shepherd. His voice is all they trust, all they know.

Many of us seek to listen for God's voice in our lives. We pray for His guidance and His direction for our big decisions. We pray that He will hear us when we need healing or support or help in any way. We want our voice to be heard by God because we pray for answers.

John the Baptist was called a voice crying in the wilderness, asking people to prepare the way for the Lord. You may be struggling to find your own voice, meaning you're looking to understand your life purpose or your unique stamp on the world. You have a voice that needs to be heard.

As you listen to the voices of others today or notice the words that come from your own mouth, imagine that each word you speak is powerful, creative, even transformative for your listeners. Imagine that God gave you a unique voice to meet the needs of those around you and to shine a light on His one true voice. Be glad that you are part of His flock and listen as He speaks to you today. When He calls, follow His lead, and all will be well. You can be sure that He is always listening for you to speak and that your unique voice will reach His ears.

*Lord, thank You for hearing my **voice**, especially when I need Your Presence. Help me to be a voice for good in the lives of those I love. Amen.*

# WAITS

*Be patient, then, brothers and sisters, until the Lord's coming. See how the farmer **waits** for the land to yield its valuable crop, patiently waiting for the autumn and spring rains. You, too, be patient and stand firm, because the Lord's coming is near.*

James 5:7–8 NIV

The person who **waits** for something, anything really, has a few choices to make. You can wait patiently as the farmer does, praying for the crops to come in. You can wait with worry. You've probably tried this and discovered that it is typically a big waste of your time.

You can be a person who waits with others, surrounding yourself with people who are invested in the outcome as much as you are. When you wait with others, you have continual support for the moments when doubt or fear may choose to strike.

You can be a person who waits in prayer and meditation. What this means is that you have something to turn to while you wait. You can seek God's embrace, His support, His voice to help you with the process.

Whichever way you choose to wait, the writer of this Scripture adds this dimension. He says to wait with patience and stand firm because the Lord is near. He doesn't say the Lord is on the way, or the Lord is thinking about showing up. He says the Lord is near...already, right now, closer than you think. Toss out worry. Focus on knowing that you can be patient and stand firm because right now, today, the Lord is near you. He waits with you.

*Lord, thank You for drawing near to me and supporting my heart and mind. Bless everyone who **waits** for something important in their lives today. Amen.*

# TRYING

*Am I now **trying** to win the approval of human beings, or of God? Or am I trying to please people? If I were still trying to please people, I would not be a servant of Christ.*                                        Galatians 1:10 NIV

**Trying** is one of those words that has a double meaning. When you're trying to achieve a goal or some type of special outcome, then you're making an effort. You're doing everything you can to make your dreams come true, and the people around you applaud the things you're doing. They know how hard you are trying.

The writer of Galatians is making a point that has to do with placing our efforts in the best possible light. He reminds us that we can do a lot of things to please people, but trying to please people is not a worthy goal. Gaining the approval of human beings won't do a lot to move your life forward.

Perhaps it helps to look at the list of things you're trying to do and see if you're trying to please God, please yourself, or please others. Galatians tells us that the writer wanted to please Christ, so trying to please others didn't matter to him anymore. We might apply that same measure to the things we are trying to do.

Our standard might be, if we're trying to do anything, we should be trying to please God. Only God can reward our work when we please Him. Keep trying. God loves to see all you are willing to do for Him.

*Lord, You know I am always hoping and **trying** to please You. Help me to do the things that make a difference to those closest to me. Amen.*

# TEST

*Dear friends, do not believe every spirit, but **test** the spirits to see whether they are from God, because many false prophets have gone out into the world. This is how you can recognize the Spirit of God: Every spirit that acknowledges that Jesus Christ has come in the flesh is from God.*

1 John 4:1–2 NIV

We're pretty familiar with the process of testing. We go to school and **test** our learning experience all the way to graduation. We go into the world and we begin to see that the tests haven't ended. We have to prove ourselves in our jobs or in other pursuits.

The writer of this Scripture suggests that we have to examine or "test" spiritual things as well. We must assess those who preach and teach and speak with authority. Voices everywhere claim to have some hold on the spiritual realm, and some even proclaim that they have the way to Heaven figured out. All these voices can drown out the truth, and then we're not sure where things stand.

The good news is that our test method is straightforward. We seek the help of the Holy Spirit to show us whether those preachers and teachers and voices of authority recognize and openly confess Jesus as the Son of God. If they acknowledge that Jesus is the One who came to Earth, lived, preached, taught, died and was resurrected, and is living now, then they pass the test. Don't be afraid to test the ideas and the theology of those who proclaim truth. When you do, God will reveal that truth to you in no uncertain terms. You'll be able to discern those who pass the test.

*Lord, help me to be wise when I listen to those who claim to have all the answers, or who imagine that they have the secrets to You. Help me to **test** those ideas that are unclear to me and guide me to Your truth. Amen.*

# WHOLE

*God, whom I serve with my **whole** heart by telling the Good News about his Son, knows that I always mention you.* Romans 1:9 NCV

When was the last time you did something with your **whole** heart? Anything you do with your whole heart means that you are totally engaged with it. You are completely absorbed, you're one hundred percent in, and nothing can change your mind. When you offer your help to someone and you do it with your whole heart, it makes a difference. It means that you're on top of the game and you believe in what you are doing. You're committed!

Many of us do a lot of things in a halfhearted way. We clean the house, or we do our job, or we make our way to church, partly because we want to do those things and partly because we feel an obligation to do them. Doing something with a sense of obligation is not an effort of your heart as much as an effort of your conscience or your mind. You could even say that you don't put your heart into those activities at all.

In contrast, remember the first time you fell in love. You probably put your whole heart into your new relationship. You wanted to be fully engaged, involved in every possible way, and you were ready to jump in with both feet. Take that idea and imagine that you want to fully, wholly, totally engage with the work of God. You want to tell others about what God has done for you with passion and commitment. That's the picture God wants you to have as you promise to serve Him with your whole, entire, complete, generous heart. Give Him everything you've got today!

*Lord, I know that I do a lot of things somewhat mindlessly, not even totally awake to the task at hand. Help me to serve You now with my **whole** heart. Amen.*

# WRITE

*Go now, **write** it before them on a tablet, and inscribe it in a book, so that it may be for the time to come as a witness forever.*   Isaiah 30:8 NRSV

We **write** for a lot of reasons. You may write reminders to yourself for things you have to do. You may write a note, encouraging someone through a hard time or wishing them well on a new venture. You write out of obligation, you write for pleasure, and you write simply because you are task oriented. The best thing, though, is when you take the time to write from the heart.

Some people write their own marriage vows. These vows may stand the test of time because the people who wrote them make the effort to live them every day. They may write their wedding date in special places, engraved on the inside of their wedding bands or set into a plaque that hangs on the wall. They create lasting tributes to an event guided by love.

God wrote the Ten Commandments on tablets of stone. He did this in front of Moses, His witness, and He wanted Moses to share those words, those exact words with His people. God could have simply spoken those ideas to Moses, but He wrote with His own finger, and His words are known by most of us even today. They stand as a witness forever.

Words have impact that can exist through generations. Write down the words from Scripture or from your own heart that are deeply meaningful to you. The power of those words might just light up your day when you see them again.

*Lord, I'm so grateful that You inspired so many people to **write** their thoughts throughout the generations. I pray that I might write about Your love and share that with those around me. Amen.*

# EVERYTHING

*The Lord is my shepherd; I have **everything** I need.*        Psalm 23:1 NCV

One of the most potent phrases in Scripture comes from the Twenty-third Psalm. It is a simple statement of fact that rests on knowing "The Lord is my shepherd." It goes on to remind us that when we have the Lord as our Shepherd, we have **everything** we need. We don't have some things, or a few things, or most things, but everything! We have everything we need.

Keep in mind that there is a significant difference between the things you need and the things you want. God, the Lord and Shepherd, tends to your needs and provides everything. Perhaps you are going through some trials in your life now and you're not so sure this statement is true. After all, you've been praying for a partner, or a new job, or the opportunity to rise in your career. You may feel like you don't yet have everything you need.

"Everything" may seem like a relative term. After all, someone with great material wealth may have everything on one hand, but suffer from illness or spiritual poverty on the other. Someone with no worldly possessions may feel completely blessed because they have close family and friends. Each of us might define "everything" rather differently. When the rich young ruler came to Jesus and asked Him what he would need to do to be one of Jesus' followers, Jesus asked him some tough questions. The man told Jesus he already did all the things that Jesus requested. Finally, Jesus said, then all you have to do is give it all up. The young ruler walked sadly away. He did not want to give up everything in this world simply to gain Jesus in the next.

The psalmist is looking at the work of what a good Shepherd does. The good Shepherd provides for every need of his flock. He watches over all they do. The sheep are totally in the Shepherd's care. The sheep have everything.

Sometimes it's good to look at what you have and give the Shepherd praise for all the ways He takes care of you. He sees you and He knows all the places where He will lead you into new blessings. When you look to Him, His heart is open to you and He wants to always give you everything you need.

*Lord, I know that I sometimes don't give You the credit for everything that I enjoy in my life. Help me to seek Your face any time I feel I need help. Thank You for giving me **everything** I need today. Amen.*

# FAIR

*God's word is true, and everything he does is right.*
*He loves what is right and fair; the Lord's love fills the earth.*

Psalm 33:4–5 NCV

We often hear the statement that life just isn't **fair**. In fact, most of us have plenty of stories about situations where we weren't treated fairly. When those things happen, we walk away somewhat wounded and wonder if there's anyone or anything that we can trust.

The psalmist tells us that God's word is true and everything He does is right. That means that He is true to His word one hundred percent of the time. He remembers His promises and He provides for your needs. He sees you and loves you unconditionally. He is fair to you in every way because He cannot be anything less. He can only be truth and love and righteousness. His Spirit is everywhere, and He fills the Earth with His love. That means you can find Him wherever you go, and you can count on Him to treat you with dignity and kindness.

Since that is the way God treats you, all the time, never changing, never doing less than His best to take care of you and to treat you right, He loves it when you do the same for others. Today, wherever you are, see if there is anyone near you that is not being treated fairly. See if there is anything you can do to change the situation or make it better. If you cannot do anything, then turn the circumstance over to God and ask Him to cover it with grace and love.

The world is not fair. Life is not fair. But God is fair, just, and reasonable! He fills your life with His love, and all you have to do is receive it.

*Lord, thank You for watching over the injustices in the world and*
*helping to transform our hearts so that we speak truth and love.*
*Thank You for being more than fair to me. Amen.*

# FULFILL

*God is not human, that he should lie, not a human being, that he should change his mind. Does he speak and then not act? Does he promise and not fulfill?*

Numbers 23:19–20 NIV

The writer of Numbers reminds us of one important fact. God is God, and we're not. He doesn't say it glibly, though. He says it as a pronouncement, a statement of fact. He reminds us that since God is not human, He doesn't change His mind, or speak and then not **fulfill** His promises. He always knows the next step, and He knows it for you and for your family and your community and for every social construct that exists in our universe. God will fulfill His plans.

If you're not certain about this point, you can go back in your Bible and read the stories of Noah or of Abraham, or Moses and David. The Patriarchs knew God. They walked with Him on a daily basis, talked with Him, and received their marching orders from Him. When they needed help, they called out to Him, knowing He could hear their voices, trusting that He would come to their aid, and believing that they needed Him more than they needed anything this Earth could offer. They knew only God could fulfill their hopes and dreams and put their plans into effect.

You have the same opportunity. God has not changed. He hears your voice when you call, and all you have to do is trust in Him, believe Him, and recognize the direction and the call He has on your life. He will fulfill His work in you. He counts on you to seek Him for each important step. Spend time with Him today and give Him a chance to offer you His love and grace and direction.

*Lord, I know that only You can truly **fulfill** Your good and perfect work in me. Help me to always seek Your guidance for all that I do. Amen.*

# GIFT

*For the wages of sin is death, but the **gift** of God is eternal life in Christ*
*Jesus our Lord.*                                        Romans 6:23 NIV

Think about your favorite **gift**, the one that delighted your heart when you
received it, like nothing else could do. Hold that thought.

A gift, a present, something you receive from the generosity of someone
else, is special because of its incredible value. Oh, not the value of the gift
itself, but the value of the relationship that you share with the giver. The
joy you feel is because the gift represents how much that person cares for
you. The gift represents the love you share.

Now if you look at the gift that God gave you when He washed away
your sins, not just washed them, but eliminated them, and then you add
to that the gift of His Son, the Only name under Heaven by which you
receive eternal life, you might realize that this gift is worth more than any
other. This gift is the ultimate love, given from the heart of the One who
designed you and everything else in the universe. He looked into your
heart and He saw that you were ready to receive Him, ready to embrace
the amazing and powerful gift of His love.

The one who generously desires to give a gift delights in the thought of
how much it will mean to the recipient. The right moment arrives, the gift
is offered, and then only one thing stands in the way. The recipient must
accept the gift, and receive the gift with the same love through which it
was given. Once received, the gift lasts forever. The giver and the receiver
celebrate the moment for they have sealed their love for all time. That's
the gift God gives you, the one that makes you His child, fully loved, fully
redeemed, fully blessed each day.

*Lord, thank You for offering me the gift of eternal life. Let me be*
*worthy of Your precious gift by shining a light on Your love for others*
*to see. Amen.*

# FREE

*"Then you will know the truth, and the truth will make you free."*
John 8:32 NCV

Have you ever been caught in a lie? Perhaps it wasn't a big lie, conceived to do harm to someone else, but still a lie that made you feel slightly uncomfortable. You knew that in some small way, you were hiding the truth of a matter, or you were sharing something that you hadn't verified.

In the Old Testament, God shared some of the things that He didn't like. He didn't like a scale that was not properly balanced, one that gave the owner more than the owner should have received. The scale was a lie. He didn't like people bearing false witness, that is, making up stories about others for personal gain. Looking at the Ten Commandments, you can easily see that God considered lies to be the worst kind of deceit, the total opposite of love.

It's easy to see, then, why the truth sets you **free**. Telling the truth means that you don't have to cover up anything. You don't have to suffer guilt or shame or any of the other insidious forms of the traps that lies present. The good news is that God has been trying to help us learn His truth since the very beginning.

Jesus is the supreme example of truth, the one who literally can set you free. He forgives all your mistakes and lies and damaging things that may keep you feeling trapped and unable to move forward. You are free. You are God's beautiful child, and He wants you to live in truth and love every day of your life. He wants you to know that the only way to experience being free is when your heart is set free in Him. Truth lights up your life.

*Lord, I thank You with all my heart for setting me free. I know that nothing is more important than doing everything I can in truth and integrity. Amen.*

# ARMOR

*The hour has already come for you to wake up from your slumber, because our salvation is nearer now than when we first believed. The night is nearly over; the day is almost here. So let us put aside the deeds of darkness and put on the armor of light.*                          Romans 13:11–12 NIV

It's interesting to try to imagine the **armor** of light. Typically, we picture armor as the heavy chain mail of the knights of old, the armor worn by kings and those who went to battle in the days of the Patriarchs. Armor was always depicted as heavy and more like a modern-day army tank than a vision of light as seen here in Romans.

In our current entertainment culture, we've seen the lightsaber as depicted in the *Star Wars* movies. That saber was a helpful protector of the one who carried it. It was a piece of his armor. It may be interpreted as "light" armor.

The writer of Romans reminds us of the Light of God. His armor guards us no matter what is going on in the darkness. Nothing compares to the power of those who are wrapped in this Light, who have the light of Christ as their shield. The light is the protector. The light is the strength that sustains us because salvation is near. The Light then is the new suit of armor.

Open up the shades, awaken to the world around you, knowing that when you go about your work today, you have your armor in place. You have the Light of the world going before you and living within you to save you, guide you, and protect your heart, your mind, and your spirit. Your strength depends on standing firm in the light wherever you are.

*Lord, I have not really thought about the Light of Your love being the strength of my soul and spirit, the **armor** that protects me even now. Thank You for waking me up to see Your light. Amen.*

# CALLING

*Then Eli realized the Lord was **calling** the boy. So he told Samuel, "Go to bed. If he calls you again, say, 'Speak, Lord. I am your servant and I am listening.'" So Samuel went and lay down in bed. The Lord came and stood there and called as he had before, "Samuel, Samuel!" Samuel said, "Speak, Lord. I am your servant and I am listening."* 1 Samuel 3:8–10 NCV

Samuel didn't know the Lord when God first **called** him. He was only a boy, just a servant of Eli. God had to call him three times because Samuel kept running into Eli's room, thinking that his master was calling him. As Eli figured out what was going on, he gave Samuel the instructions to wait for the Lord to speak, and then to answer His call. Samuel had to let the Lord know he was listening.

Perhaps it's fair to note then that God does not always have a relationship established with someone He calls. You may not have known God when you first heard His voice. You may not have yet understood His purpose for your life and His desire to build a relationship. Maybe you, too, were only a child when you first realized God was near. The wonder of this is that God continues to call His children even into our day. He doesn't always wait for us to seek Him, but He always waits for us to be willing to receive His call.

You may have a specific calling in your life and you may be doing everything you can to fulfill that call, to achieve your purpose. Whatever your vocation, though, you have work and a purpose for your life given to you from the One who knows you and who loved you from the day you were born. You have a choice. Only you can determine if you will answer when you hear God calling your name. May you respond as Samuel did, "Speak, Lord, I am your servant and I am listening."

*Lord, thank You for **calling** me to serve You. I pray that I will continue to listen for Your voice in every part of my life. Amen.*

# GOOD

*We know that in everything God works for the **good** of those who love him.*
*They are the people he called, because that was his plan.*

Romans 8:28 NCV

God is **good**, and He defines what the word "good" really means. He works for your good every moment of your life. He wants you to know of His steadfast love, and His desire for you is to reach your potential physically, spiritually, and emotionally.

It's possible that, as human beings, we don't truly understand how good God really is. After all, He created the ground we walk on, gave us the breath of life, provides for our daily needs, and keeps the planet from moving off course. His goodness sustains the life of every living soul.

The next time you wonder if God will answer your prayers, remember that He is with you and He is able to do even more than you may ask or think. More than you ask! More than you think! Is there anything that is too big or too hard to take before God? When you need an answer, or you need comfort from a frazzled day and a world that is too chaotic, then come to the only One who can make a difference, the One who seeks only your good. Out of His extraordinary generosity, He will open the way for you because of your faith in Christ. He works everything for your Earthly and eternal good according to His plan for you. Now that's about as good as it gets!

*Lord, I come to you with the things that are too big for me to handle.*
*I believe You are **good** and able to take care of all my needs. Bless all*
*those who seek Your face today. Amen.*

# CREATE

*Create in me a clean heart, O God,*
*And renew a steadfast spirit within me.*          Psalm 51:10 NKJV

Sometimes we forget that God is our Creator and He can use His power to **create** any time He chooses. The same God who formed the universe and set the planets in motion and started the Earth spinning is the same God who created you. He's the same Being who saw that goodness and beauty and kindness and love were things that human beings were capable of sharing. He blessed the work of His hands and He went so far as to put His Spirit within us.

When you stop to imagine what it really means that God can create a new heart within you, you might find that you tremble in awe. The world wants to sell you ideas that carry a host of attitudes, behaviors, and human drama, some of them good and some of them downright evil. Fortunately, your Creator made it possible for you to choose. He made you with a clean heart so that you could decide between good and evil and seek His help with the direction you wanted to go.

You're a good person. You try to do the right thing and you often help those around you. You recognize most people are just like you, hoping to live happy lives, hoping to raise good children, and seeking to understand what life is about. You seek God with all your heart because you also know that when you fail, or when you do an unkind thing, or when you drop the ball on being there for your neighbor, you can turn to Him for help. You know that this Creator can reshape your heart. He can mold you to be more like Him. He can create a clean heart within you. We all have sinned, fallen short of what God expects and so He gives us a clean heart out of His love and mercy.

*Lord, thank You for all that You have **created** in me. Help me to*
*strive to be more of what You designed me to be each day. Amen.*

# FIND

*"Keep on asking, and you will receive what you ask for. Keep on seeking,
and you will find. Keep on knocking, and the door will be opened to you."*

Matthew 7:7 NLT

We may see an acronym in this passage from Matthew: ASK (Ask, Seek, Knock). It helps us see that we may not be as persistent as this Scripture reminds us we could be.

How often do we ask for God's help? How far will we look to find answers to our concerns? How loudly will we knock so the door will be opened?

You may ask God for something, and when you don't receive it, you may assume that it wasn't part of God's plan for you. That could certainly be true, but perhaps the essence of this Scripture is about trust. You have to trust that when you ask God to hear you, He will listen. With that trust, you can imagine the One who loves you is leaning in to hear your every word. You have to know that as God listens, He immediately begins to help you find the answers you need because He wants to help you. And finally, you have to believe that when you knock on His door, He answers. He opens the door and lets you in to talk further. Jesus said that God always wants to give you good things. It's up to you to knock on His door, though.

If there is something you hope to find, perhaps your life purpose, or the best place to live where you can do your work, or a stronger relationship with the Lord, then you need to keep on looking. When you want answers like these, you can't look halfheartedly. You must be sincere, intentional, and truly seek to find His answer, because no other answer will suffice.

*Lord, I feel like I come to You often with my requests, and yet I
realize that I may not be persistent in seeking Your help with the
desires of my heart. Help me to truly find You and Your will for me
today. Amen.*

157

# IS

*The Son reflects the glory of God and shows exactly what God is like. He holds everything together with his powerful word.*　　Hebrews 1:3 NCV

This little word **is** casts a significant presence into any sentence. It is the action. It declares that something is happening right now. It says, a thing is current, not yesterday, not will be in the future, but now. When we use this word in reference to God, it becomes even more powerful.

Begin with the simple phrase "God is." Those two words don't ask you to define what God is; they simply tell you in no uncertain terms that God is, that God exists, that God is very present at this moment!

When we suggest that God is love, we define more clearly one of God's attributes. It doesn't mean that He used to be love, and He's not any longer. It doesn't mean that He will be love once you get to Heaven. It means that you can embrace His love because it is ongoing, consistent, and steadfast. God is love!

Consider the words that you might use to describe who God is. Perhaps you define God as the Creator, or as the Father, or as the One who redeems you. These ideas are key to the person of God. They are aspects of His being. When you accept that God is, and ever shall be, you get to know Him and you become clearer about Him every day of your life.

The important thing to remember, especially when you're stressed or overwhelmed with life itself, is that you can look up, reach out, seek to find the One who is, the One who knows you just as you are today. Because God is with you always, you can count on Him. God is there for you!

*Lord, thank You for being the Living God, the Creator, the One Who always will Be. No matter what I go through in life, knowing You are the great I AM, the One Who Is, makes all the difference because my hope is in You. Amen.*

# LIFE

*Be careful what you think,*
*because your thoughts run your life.*                    Proverbs 4:23 NCV

Your thoughts run your life! Wow! That's a somewhat scary statement because it puts you squarely on the hot seat as the one responsible for your attitudes, your philosophies and ideologies, and your management of life. You build your responses to life, to creating a living, making choices, according to your own thoughts and ideas. Your actions are based on what you hold to be life's truths, and what you believe to be true is what you think about.

In church circles, we often talk about "who" is on the throne of your life? Is it you? Or is it God? If you are at the center of your thoughts, then you have every reason for concern, because you have put all possibility and all responsibility on your shoulders. If God is at the center of your thoughts, your heart, and your actions, then you have given Him the controls. You have said, "I want to follow you."

Since you have only one life, one chance to become the person you most hope will please God, then your thoughts need to be aligned with His thoughts. Your thoughts, placed squarely in God's hands, move your life forward in significant ways. Otherwise, unguarded thoughts will run you ragged, bouncing you from one place to another, until you hardly know how you got there.

It's your life and your choice. Protect your heart, your thoughts, and your life by putting everything you are in God's hands.

*Lord, I know that I often have thoughts that cause worry and stress.*
*Please guard my life and my thoughts today. Amen.*

# YEAST

*He told them still another parable: "The kingdom of heaven is like **yeast***
*that a woman took and mixed into about sixty pounds of flour until it*
*worked all through the dough."*                    Matthew 13:33 NIV

If you're a bread baker, you know what **yeast** does to cause the dough to rise, giving it lightness and breathing air into the loaves you are making. Yeast is the agent that makes all the difference because it permeates every part of the dough. It makes light, airy, delicious bread possible.

Jesus told us that the kingdom of Heaven was like yeast. In His example, where the woman puts the yeast into sixty pounds of flour, we can only imagine He wants to impress on us that many, many loaves of bread are made from this Heavenly yeast so that even a little of it will make a difference. Perhaps when we add a desire, a focus, a connection to the kingdom of Heaven to daily life, it fills our souls. It permeates every aspect of our being so that we become more filled with God's Spirit.

Jesus said that the kingdom of God is within you. You have greater possibilities because of all that God can do with you. Your heart is filled to overflowing, getting bigger as you work with the people around you. You have been filled with the yeast of God's love and nothing can change that. Once the yeast is added to the flour and the dough, you can't take it out again. Once God's Spirit was poured into your heart, everything changed, and it permeates every choice, every decision you make.

*Lord, I haven't really thought of Your Spirit as a kind of **yeast** that*
*fills my heart and soul, but I like the idea of that. Thank You for*
*helping me to be a little more like You each day. Amen.*

# REMEMBER

*Remember my words with your whole being. Write them down and tie
them to your hands as a sign; tie them on your foreheads to remind you.*
Deuteronomy 11:18 NCV

We celebrate significant holidays each year to **remember** the meaning of
a specific event. Some of those events, like Christmas and Easter, remind
us of the things that God has done to show us He knows we're here and
that we need Him. Other events celebrate milestones in history or cultural
developments. We also mark other festive occasions like birthdays and
weddings because we want to remember the special blessing that happened in our lives.

Our memories may serve us well and offer us delightful moments to
recall, but the writer of Deuteronomy has something even more important
in mind. He wants to be sure that people continue to follow God's ways
and listen to His commands. Moses charged the people of his day to find
ways to remember and recognize the importance of what He was saying.
He wanted them to remember His words with their whole hearts, minds,
and souls.

Imagine what this means. You remember something, not just with your
head, but with your heart, and not just with your heart, but with your
hands and your vision and your hearing. Everything about you, every one
of your senses, is attuned to those important words. Make a sign and tie
the sign to your hands. Make a headband and put the words on it.

God wants each of us to remember what He has done. He wants us to
recognize His hand in the events of our lives so that we are aware of our
blessings and can offer thanks and praise. Make a list and write down the
things God has done for you lately. Once you have that list, share it with
someone you love.

*Lord, thank You for the amazing things You have done in my life.
Help me to honor You and **remember** You with love. Amen.*

# MIND

*Do not conform to the pattern of this world, but be transformed by the renewing of your **mind**. Then you will be able to test and approve what God's will is—his good, pleasing and perfect will.*     Romans 12:1–2 NIV

It is the stories in our heads that guide our choices and decisions on any given day. If we're stuck in yesterday's problems, we'll bring them right into today and pile more issues on top of them. Then we pack them up and take them into the following day as well. We do the things we have a **mind** to do. Sometimes that works well for us. Other times, we need to change our minds.

This Scripture from Romans offers us insight into what we must be aware of about the ways we think. We need to watch that we do not conform to the world. We don't want to follow the whims of politics or cultural philosophies or anything else that distracts us from believing in God. Sure, there are ways we must conform to the rules of the road and other commonsense guides, but those things do not damage the spirit. The work we have before us all the time is to watch out for those ideas we might unintentionally buy into because of peer pressures or cultural influences. God calls us then to renew our minds and be transformed by His Spirit. He wants us to be intentional about the things we're willing to allow into our minds.

Why? Because the things you put into your mind affect your heart. God wants your heart to be right with Him, and so He wants you to be totally aware of how your mind works. The job of a Christian is to seek to know the mind of God and to love God with your heart, soul, and mind. Keep your heart and mind on Christ Jesus today.

*Lord, thank You for giving me a strong heart and a willing **mind** to serve You. Help me to stay close to You each day. Amen.*

# PITIES

*As a father **pities** his children, so the Lord pities His children. God knows our frame; He remembers that we are dust.* Psalm 103:13–14 NRSV

We don't always take it positively when we think that someone **pities** us. We assume that they think we are weak or unable to manage life. It may even wound our egos a bit to imagine ourselves as the subject of someone's pity.

But actually, "pities" is an active, caring, compassionate word. It speaks to the nature of God and His protective and nurturing Spirit that He sometimes looks at us as lost and broken people that simply do not understand who they are and what they were meant to be.

The word "pities" conveys the very essence of the way God sees us and the relationship we have with Him. He is a Heavenly parent looking at his Earthly children, remembering that He created them from dust, and yet seeking to reach out to us, and help us when we are downtrodden. God cares and empathizes with our feelings and our circumstances and has sympathy for all that we are.

His love and His compassion for us give Him perfect insight into our needs and desires. Imagine how you feel if one of your children abandons your values and goes off to live in a self-destructive way in the world. You might feel like there isn't much you can do about the situation, but your heart and mind agonize over it. Your love for your child continues to cause you to grieve over what you know might be a very difficult outcome for them. Your heart pities them and hopes for better things.

When God pities you, it is as a Father who wants more for you than you even want for yourself. God's heart is full of compassion and love for you because He knows everything about you. You can rejoice in His pity and His love today.

*Lord, thank You for Your willingness to watch over me, even as a Father who **pities** His child. Help me to feel worthy of Your love and grace all the days of my life. Amen.*

# IN

*On that day you will know that I am in my Father, and that you are in me
and I am in you.*                                                    John 14:20 NCV

When we're young, we like to be considered part of the in-crowd. We want
to feel like we have the approval of our peers and that we have achieved
the kind of popularity that makes people want to be with us. We imagine
that it is cool to be "**in**."

As we grow older, we prefer to be in the company of people who encourage us or laugh with us. We like to know that when we're in trouble, or
when we're celebrating the good things in life, there are people who want
to share in our success and our sorrow. No matter what is going on in our
lives, we appreciate the people who are in this dance of life with us.

When we look at this Scripture from John, though, we understand the
word "in" a bit differently. Perhaps the best opportunity for us to be on
the inside is when we look at where we are with Jesus. Since Jesus is in the
Father, His strength, His divinity, His holiness, and His love of humanity
are gifts that they share. God loves you and strengthens you through your
faith in Christ Jesus. They are One.

You share a similar relationship with Jesus. He is in you and He will
reside with you until you rest in Heaven. He has a place for you because
you can be wherever He is. You can be there because you were made One
with Christ through faith and baptism. You are in Him. He is in you.
Nothing can separate the two of you ever again.

May Jesus be in your heart and in your actions in all you do today.

*Lord, thank You for putting a portion of Yourself within me. Help me
to rejoice in all we may share today. Amen.*

# DUST

*Where the Lord goes, there are whirlwinds and storms,*
*and the clouds are the dust beneath his feet.*　　　　Nahum 1:3 NCV

**Dust** is everywhere. It floats around and lands on your desktop, your windowsill, or wherever it pleases. You do your best to manage its presence as it congregates on your ceiling fan and dresser tops. It doesn't seem to ever go away, no matter how much you pledge to take care of it. It's continually in the air, even when you can't quite see it. Sometimes when the sun filters through your window just so, the fine dust particles are illuminated, and you realize they are present, and that you are always breathing them in.

In light of the dust swirling around us all the time, it's interesting in this text from Nahum to think of the dust as a metaphor for God's presence. If we choose to look up at the passing clouds and remind ourselves that they are made of dust, we can imagine that God himself is walking by. He is in the whirlwinds and the storms and the clouds. He's in all things and makes Himself known to us. He's even in the places where we can't quite imagine Him to be.

Every time you run your finger through the dust on your table, or on your shoes after you've taken a walk outside, remind yourself that something as simple as dust can be a way to embrace God's Presence. You can use it as a reminder that He is never far from you and that you don't have to see Him to know that He is really there. He walks near you and He walks on the clouds and they are the dust beneath His feet. May you see Him everyplace you go today.

*Lord, thank You for this simple reminder of Your presence in my life.*
*I know that You swirl around me like precious **dust** all through the*
*day if I only have eyes to see you. Amen.*

# SEAL

*Place me like a **seal** over your heart,*
*like a seal on your arm.*

Song of Songs 8:6 NIV

When a document is important, perhaps even legal in its intent, it is often signed in front of a notary and sealed with a stamp. In the days of the Patriarchs, any document with the **seal** of the king's ring was deemed to be of the highest authority.

Imagine, along with the lovers in the Song of Songs, that God has placed you like a seal over His heart or carried you like a seal on His arm. It would show His authority and His kindness in choosing you. It would document His intentions to keep you close to Him all the days of your life. The seal will never be broken by Him.

What people or ideas would you be willing to carry like a seal over your heart or on your arm? Your list may include your spouse and your children, perhaps some other family and friends. Primarily, though, as you read in 2 Corinthians 1:22, you have been sealed by the love of Christ and sealed by Him, so you can carry Him over your heart and on your arm. You carry His image within your spirit, and you have agreed to do so in front of a cloud of witnesses. Your seal is eternal.

Today, as you consider those things that are of the utmost importance to you, remember, as it says in Ephesians 4:30, you were sealed by the Lord the day you accepted His gift of salvation and that gift is meant to sustain you through everything you experience. You are so important to God that He not only delivered you, but sealed you with His mark of eternal grace and love.

*Lord God, I know that I don't always even recognize the importance of Your hand on my life, but I thank You for placing me like a **seal** over Your heart. I praise You for Your incredible kindness and love. Amen.*

# TURN

*For the Lord will again rejoice over you for good as He rejoiced over your fathers, if you obey the voice of the Lord your God, to keep His commandments and His statutes which are written in this Book of the Law, and if you **turn** to the Lord your God with all your heart and with all your soul.*                    Deuteronomy 30:10 NKJV

You can wait your **turn**. You can turn up at a special event or at church, or you can do what might be considered a U-turn as you look at this Scripture from Deuteronomy 30.

When you turn around, or take a U-turn, you're making a decision that indicates you're pretty sure you were going the wrong way. You need to make a course adjustment. Sometimes, you need to make a significant turn in your attitude, or in your willingness to consider other opinions, or simply in your desire to listen to someone else. You may need to do an "about-face" in your walk with the Lord, spending more time studying His word, or listening for His voice. The good news is that when you turn in His direction, He'll be there for you.

In this case from Deuteronomy, God is putting in a request. He is saying that He will be there for you, and He will cheer you on, and He will help you if you are simply willing to turn to Him with your heart and soul. He's not looking for you to make a quick turn to the right or the left. He wants you to turn straight toward Him, praising His name as you go. When you do, your life will surely take a turn for the better.

*Lord, thank You for all You do to help me with the choices I make each day. Help me to **turn** toward You with my whole heart. Amen.*

# TEACH

*You will **teach** me how to live a holy life. Being with you will fill me with joy;*
*at your right hand I will find pleasure forever.*          Psalm 16:11 NCV

You may wonder at times how you can ever be considered holy. You know that God wants you to be holy, but it seems impossible or at least improbable that you could reach His standards. Of course, you headed in the right direction the day you accepted Christ because He resides within you, and He's the holy part of you. In fact, you need Christ in your heart before you can even seek to be holy before the Lord.

What else do you need, though, to even attempt to become a more holy person? The psalmist gives us a clue when he says, "You will **teach** me how to live a holy life." That statement implies that you weren't born holy, nor should you necessarily know how to be holy, but there's good news. You're teachable!

God will teach you how to live a holy life. Like anything else you have to learn in this life, the lessons may not always be easy. You may discover that you're not necessarily a good student because you can be hardheaded and imagine that you can handle things independently. Your ways of doing things don't frustrate God, though. He knows you have a lot to learn and He never stops being willing to be your teacher.

As you go about your life today, look at those areas you might yet need to surrender to God so that you are ready for "teachable moments." Look to discover what God wants to teach you, not simply to make you a better person, but to give you the desire to be more aware of what it means to be holy. As you look to God to teach you, He will clarify, shape, and impart to you what you need to live in a way that is more holy, and perhaps even more wholly His.

*Lord, I pray that You would **teach** me how to be more holy, so that I*
*can shine for You. Take away my stubborn heart and replace it with*
*one that is ready to learn all You want me to know today. Amen.*

# TODAY

*God again set a certain day, calling it "**Today.**" This he did when a long time later he spoke through David, as in the passage already quoted: "Today, if you hear his voice, do not harden your hearts."*

Hebrews 4:7 NIV

Many of us wake up to a new day, run the current to-do list through our minds, and feel behind before we even get out of bed. We worry about the things we didn't do yesterday and what we need to do tomorrow, along with the concerns of **today**.

Since God is always present, meaning He's not just in your yesterdays or your tomorrows, but He is with you right now at this very moment, then today becomes important. Today becomes the only day you really have to worry about, or perhaps not worry about, but operate within.

One of the most popular verses from the Psalms is 118:24, which reminds us that, "This is the day the Lord has made. Let us rejoice and be glad today."

If you could only have today, then, God is asking you to be open to Him, to listen for His voice, and to soften your heart toward Him and all that He wants you to do. He wants you to take today seriously, trusting in His plans for your life and believing that He works things out for your good. When you do those things, you will find yourself humming His praise, knowing that as you step out into the world, there is every reason for you to be glad today, right now. Incline your heart and your ear to the One who makes all the difference.

*Lord, I thank You for giving me another day to start again, to seek Your face, and become a better listener. Soften my heart toward You today. Amen.*

# WHATEVER

*Finally, brothers and sisters, **whatever** is true, whatever is noble, whatever is right, whatever is pure, whatever is lovely, whatever is admirable—if anything is excellent or praiseworthy—think about such things.*

Philippians 4:8 NIV

Some people experience life as a **whatever** kind of world. That means that when something comes up that they don't really agree with, they just shrug as though there is nothing they can really do about it anyway, so they just proclaim, "Whatever!" It's somewhat of a resignation, somewhat apathetic, somewhat pathetic. It means they haven't really learned to engage with life in a way that will help them enjoy the things that are good.

The writer of Philippians, though, used this word several times as one that would be inclusive, intentional, directed. He wanted us to think about whatever we could that would make a difference in our attitudes and our ability to give God the praise.

Consider writing those things down in your journal, so that when you're having a day that requires an attitude adjustment, you can review your list and remind yourself that there are many things to call excellent and praiseworthy. If you need help starting your list, begin with the fact that you are a child of God, and that God has blessed you with family and friends and a set of skills to do certain things well. You are unique in His sight. God has not changed. He has not become apathetic to your life. He knows what matters to you. He wants you to spend more time thinking about the good things, and moving past the negative things. The next time someone you know just shrugs their shoulders and responds to life in that halfhearted "whatever" way, remind them that there's another side of the coin. Think about whatever is noble and true and pure. It makes an incredible difference.

*Lord, thank You for giving us so many good things to consider. Help us to know that **whatever** we think about can change the way we see the day. Amen.*

# ONE

*Adam was like the **One** who was coming in the future. But God's free gift is not like Adam's sin. Many people died because of the sin of that one man. But the grace from God was much greater; many people received God's gift of life by the grace of the one man, Jesus Christ.*    Romans 5:14–15 NKJV

Sometimes we wonder if **one** person can make a difference. We look at the chaos of the world, the needs of people crying for help, and we get frustrated because we can barely take care of ourselves, much less the rest of the world. When we feel like that, we're apt to simply do nothing because we feel so powerless to effect any real change.

That attitude is reasonable and yet it is not the only truth. You are only one, but you are one who can make a difference. You are one with the power of God within you, ready to bring light to those in the darkness. You are more than a candle in the wind. You are a child of God with a purpose.

When you read through the Scripture in Romans 5, you realize that Adam may indeed have been the cause of the downfall of humanity. He was only one man and yet human beings have needed redemption ever since. God knew that. He sent Jesus and gave His Only Son as a gift to redeem those who were under the curse of Adam's sin. Jesus is one, in fact The One, and with Him, we can do more than we ever could imagine.

If you wonder what you can do as one person, check within yourself for the grace and mercy and power of God that lights up your heart. Then, wherever you are today, share that light.

*Lord, thank You for being the **One** who redeems us all with your incredible love. Guide me when You want me to be one voice for You. Amen.*

# ALL

*The Lord will keep **all** his promises; he is loyal to all he has made.*
*The Lord helps those who have been defeated and takes care of those who*
*are in trouble. All living things look to you for food, and you give it to*
*them at the right time.* Psalm 145:14–15 NCV

It is no wonder that David was a man after God's own heart, because David gave **all** of his heart to God. He surrendered to Him because he believed in God's promises. David was the shepherd king, and he realized that whether he was a shepherd boy watching over flocks, or the king watching over his people, God was in charge. God was watching over everyone and everything because only God keeps all of His promises.

David didn't write this Psalm by saying that God keeps a few of His promises, or most of His promises. He didn't say that God was loyal to the good guys or the ministers or the angels. He was very clear that God keeps every promise, all the time and for all time. Not only that—God keeps those promises for every creature that He made.

You may wonder whether God keeps His promises to you. You may question whether He is still loyal to His followers and there can be no other answer than this. The Lord helps everyone who seeks Him. He blesses those who have been or who feel defeated by the ups and downs of life. He takes care of those who are in pain or in poverty or in trouble. He knows what you need. He knows how to feed your spirit, and if you turn to him today, He will help you discover that He is near you.

God is good all the time. He sees you and the things you need clearly, every day, all your life through. You simply must surrender all you are to His care and keeping.

*Lord, help me to give You my **all**, my best, my true and devout heart.*
*I thank You for knowing my needs and keeping me safe at all times.*
*Amen.*

# BREAD

*"I am the **bread** of life. Whoever comes to me will never go hungry, and whoever believes in me will never be thirsty."*          John 6:35 NIV

Sometimes life leaves you hungry. You feel famished because you have meager provisions. You are hungry for a better life, a new way to look at the world. You are starved for affection or truth or spiritual renewal. And when you're starving, you would give anything for a piece of **bread**!

Do you remember the story of Jacob and Esau? Esau was famished. He had worked all day outside, hunting and taking care of things, and when he came home, Jacob had just made dinner: a big pot of stew, and likely bread as well. Esau was so hungry that he would have given anything for a meal, and that's exactly what he did. He gave Jacob his birthright, his family inheritance, for a bowl of stew.

Jesus offers one solution to this problem. He reminds us to come to Him, feast on Him, go to His word, and pray with all our hearts and minds, because then He can feed us. He is the bread of life, and with Him, you will never be hungry. He says just to come and to believe and you will be satisfied. May your heart and soul be satisfied by the bread of Christ today.

*Lord, thank You for taking care of the things that overwhelm me and leave me feeling deprived or starved. I know that You alone are my living **Bread**. Amen.*

# WORKS

*And we know that in all things God **works** for the good of those who love him, who have been called according to his purpose.*    Romans 8:28 NIV

God **works**! No matter how you look at this simple statement, you can take it personally. If you take it to mean that God works on your behalf, that He does all that He can to be sure you have what you need, then you are correct. If you take it to mean that God never rests, that He neither slumbers or sleeps, then you'd be right again.

Perhaps you see it another way. Perhaps you recognize that no matter what your situation is, God works to improve it, repair it, and give you peace in your soul about it. God works.

If you think of God as "the works," meaning that He is the whole thing, all encompassing, totally the answer, that He gives you everything and then some, you are still right. God gives you the works so that you can live the best possible life. He doesn't withhold anything from you and He doesn't even wait sometimes for you to ask for what you need. He simply gives you what works, what He knows you need, and then continues to work for your good all the time.

Yes, God works for those who love Him and are called according to His purpose. He does that because He can do no less. He wants your life to have everything that works best for you, and so with steadfast, tireless, endless love, He pours His love on you. He gives the works . . . mercy, grace, peace, and love.

It's your day to remind others that you know for sure, that God works.

*Lord, thank You for knowing what **works** best for me and doing everything You can to provide for me and for the people I love. Amen.*

# JUMPED

*Taking him by the right hand, he helped him up, and instantly the man's feet and ankles became strong. He **jumped** to his feet and began to walk. Then he went with them into the temple courts, walking and jumping, and praising God*

Acts 3:7–8 NIV

If you've ever injured your knee or your leg and found it difficult, perhaps even impossible, to walk, you might wince at the very thought of what is described in this section of Acts. Here's a guy who has been lame, with feet and ankles that were so weak he couldn't stand up, and yet we read that the instant he was healed, he **jumped** to his feet and began to walk. He didn't take a tentative step to see if he was healed. He didn't hold on to the wall and check to be sure that he wouldn't simply fall over once he had been helped to his feet. No! He did something remarkable. He jumped.

Most of the time when you haven't had the use of an arm or a leg, you know that even when it gets better, it takes time for it to be strong again. You take baby steps or you move very carefully. The healing may have happened, but you have to work with your limbs to get them back in shape.

Isn't it amazing, then, that this man who had been lame since birth, who had been carried into the temple every day of his life so that he could beg for money and food, suddenly stands on his feet, walks, and jumps? He leaps into the air and you can only imagine the utter joy that he must be experiencing. He had never walked before and now he could jump. Even more than that, Peter didn't ask the man to share his faith first, he simply offered him the gift of Jesus and the healing took place.

Take a look at your life. Perhaps you have areas that need some kind of healing, or burdens that you would simply like to have lifted off your shoulders, so you can feel whole and healthy again. You, too, might just be willing to jump for joy!

*Lord, it's hard to understand how Your healing power works, but I believe that it does. I believe that You can come to any of us and help us **jump**, walk, and run in Your glory. Amen.*

# HUMAN

*Steep your life in God-reality, God-initiative, God-provisions. Don't worry about missing out. You'll find all your everyday **human** concerns will be met.*
Matthew 6:33 MSG

Often it appears that people would be content to live in a virtual reality world. We love to watch television shows that dramatize the beauty, the wealth, the failings, the strength, or any other combination of factors that make us **human**. We watch, but we watch a controlled environment, often staged, seldom with any sense of reality at all.

We have a tendency then to disconnect with our neighbors and others because we can hide behind computer screens, keep a safe distance, turn our heads the other way, and literally skip human interactions. Instagram and Facebook help us skip this as well—we're being at best safely social. Yes, the world is smaller in the sense that we could possibly learn more about each other, recognize our common bonds, and be gentle with our humanness, but our attention to virtual reality has caused us to miss each other. Matthew says that we should steep our lives in God-reality. We should look to see what God is doing and what God provides. Why? Because then we will realize the truth of life. We will recognize all that God is doing to intervene in the lives of humans—all over the planet.

As humans, we must engage each other, help each other, and make the path of life easier for each other. We need to live in a reality that gives us a greater sense of community. Look out for the good of those around you wherever you are today.

*Lord, thank You for watching over every **human** being. Help us to come together in love to honor the work of Your hands. Amen.*

# COME

*All that the Father gives Me will **come** to Me, and the one who comes to Me
I will by no means cast out. For I have come down from heaven, not to do
My own will, but the will of Him who sent Me.* John 6:37–38 NKJV

How many times have you been asked a question like, "Where are you
from?" or "Where were you born?" Where we **come** from often helps people to identify our characteristics and our mannerisms. We discover differences and commonalities based on the land of our families.

Jesus said that He came from Heaven and He was literally born of the
Spirit of God. Those are pretty strong credentials. He came for a specific
purpose, and it wasn't even His purpose; it was His Father's purpose.
Knowing where Jesus comes from then adds validity to all the claims He
made about Himself.

Oftentimes, our credibility comes from family heritage too. However,
some of us prefer to think we can make choices as we wish, and that we
aren't typically tied to the rules of our family. We live our lives according
to our own plans and ideas and not much is based on where we come
from.

Jesus knew His heritage and the work He was called to do. Jesus came
from Heaven so that we can choose Him and come to Him, so that we can
one day go back to Heaven, where He already is. We celebrate that He has
come to us every Christmas. We honor that He has come and gone every
Easter. We know that His coming and going are eternal events that affect
all of humanity. Draw near to Him today because He still looks for people
to come to share in His saving grace.

*Lord, thank You for **coming** to save us. Remind me wherever I may
go today that You are with me and that You will never cast me aside.
Amen.*

# KINDNESS

*He has been very kind and patient, waiting for you to change, but you think nothing of his **kindness**. Perhaps you do not understand that God is kind to you so you will change your hearts and lives.*
Romans 2:4 NCV

You may remember that **kindness** is listed among the characteristics of the fruit of the Spirit. It's an attribute that most of us appreciate in others. We are drawn to people with kind hearts who make it clear that you matter to them. How does that idea equate, then, to the kindness of God?

The writer of Romans says that God has been very kind and patient. That means He is willing to be compassionate and sympathetic with the circumstances and the situations that you deal with each day. He sees what you need, and He waits to see what you will do. He waits for your prayer or request for Him to help you with any specific event. He waits with patient kindness because He wants to give you a chance to make good choices on your own. He wants to see if you are willing to live heart first.

Imagine what it means for you then to receive God's kindness today. To understand what God has done on your behalf or to discover the ways He has given you favor, you have to be in tune with Him. You must be able to recognize His hand on your life. When you do, it's easier to understand what His Presence means to you.

You are kind to those around you. You are polite and nice and helpful. You are a good-hearted person. If you can look at that and understand what it means for you to be kind, then you will have a glimpse, just a hint, of what it means for God to show His kindness to you.

*Lord, You have shown me so much **kindness** over my life and I confess that I did not always feel I deserved it. Thank You for being kind enough to help me change my heart to become more like You. Amen.*

# BRAVE

*Watch, stand fast in the faith, be **brave**, be strong. Let all that you do be done with love.* 1 Corinthians 16:13–14 NKJV

Typically, when we think of someone as being **brave**, we think of military service members, those in law enforcement, or firefighters. It takes a brave person to stand up to danger in the world every day.

You may not realize it, but you are brave too. It takes courage for any of us to live in the world, protect our children, and spread love and kindness. Those things take faith and strength, but being brave is even more than that.

You must be brave enough to love at all times. That means you have to love your neighbor as yourself and love God with all your heart, and not just on the days when you're feeling pretty good about those things. You must do so every day, every time, every chance you get. You must be so strong in your faith that you can stand up to anything with love. When you can do that, the world opens to you. It invites you in to every possible setting because it needs what you have to offer. It needs to know how you can be so brave and so loving.

Of course, you know the answer. You have chosen to allow God's grace and mercy and Spirit to flow through your veins and through your soul, strengthening your heart muscles in ways that few people do. You are brave enough to love! May God strengthen and renew every step you bravely take today.

*Lord, help me to be **brave** in You. Help me to do everything I can with a spirit of love today. Amen.*

# NATURAL

*If there is a **natural** body, there is also a spiritual body. So it is written: "The first man Adam became a living being"; the last Adam, a life-giving spirit. The spiritual did not come first, but the natural, and after that the spiritual.*
1 Corinthians 15:44 NCV

We live most of our days doing things that are **natural** for human beings to do. We set a typical daily routine, do work that we prepared ourselves to do, care for our families, go to church, and do the best we can to make each day count. Perhaps this natural tendency we have is part of the reason we have difficulty with the spiritual or the supernatural.

Those things that are Divine, or of God, are supernatural. As the Corinthian writer put it, when God created Adam, He created a natural man. God breathed life into the man, but He was the beginning of the line. When Jesus came, He was different. He was the Son of God, He was God, and therefore, He was the spiritual man.

When God calls us to draw near to Him, He does so knowing that we are human, that we have natural bodies, and that we are not superheroes, not extraordinary in any way, but also designed for great purposes. Our faith in Jesus changes us. We not only maintain our natural selves, but we are inspired, literally we breathe in the Spirit of God through Christ. We are then able to have a clearer picture and a deeper understanding of the supernatural side of our nature.

We try so hard to give God human qualities, but we can overlook the importance of what it means for God to be a being beyond our finite comprehension, beyond our natural grasp. He's super and supernatural.

*Lord, I know I am an ordinary, **natural** person, but my spirit longs to know more of You. Thank You for drawing near to me today. Amen.*

# WONDERS

*Now Stephen, a man full of God's grace and power, performed great*
***wonders*** *and signs among the people.*

Acts 6:8 NKJV

It's hard to imagine what the writer of Acts considered to be great **wonders** and signs as Stephen witnessed to the people of his day. Surely, we would say that healing people of lifelong illnesses, helping the lame to walk and the deaf to hear, would all be wonders in any age and culture.

Perhaps we think of wonders like the great manmade architecture of the world; things like the great pyramids of Gaza or the Taj Mahal, or such God-made wonders as the Grand Canyon. We've all been blessed by the wonders and signs that God has given us of His Presence in our midst.

If you see the performance of the Cirque de Soleil, or an impressive magician, you might think they have performed wonders. You might remember the story of Moses standing before pharaoh turning his staff into a snake, and turning the water into blood. These were wonders.

So what does it mean to us that when we're full of grace and power from God, we, too, can perform wonders? You may recall that Jesus said we would be able to do even greater things than He had done as our faith grew. We might find that we speak and a whole crowd of people not only hear our words, but also draw closer to the Lord. We might find that our faith serves as a powerful example that causes others to want to strengthen their faith as well. Whatever work we do for God, the kind of work that turns one heart toward Him, is the kind of power He gives us to perform wonders.

*Lord, I know that I do not give You my whole heart so that You*
*can fill me up from head to toe and let me be a beacon to others. I*
*surrender all that I am to You today so that I, too, might perform*
***wonders*** *in Your name. Amen.*

# WORD

*For the **word** of God is alive and active. Sharper than any double-edged sword, it penetrates even to dividing soul and spirit, joints and marrow; it judges the thoughts and attitudes of the heart. Nothing in all creation is hidden from God's sight.*                                    Hebrews 4:11–13 NIV

The **Word** of God is not just an expression or an idea. It's not just the way God is thinking today. It's not just a simple matter at all. It's Divine!

The writer of Hebrews helps us understand the significance of the Word of God. Our first task is just realizing that God's Word is alive and active. It's a living thing. Whether you think of Jesus as the Word of God, or Scripture as the Word of God, the fact is that the Word of God is a living thing. It exists with a mission. It is intentional. It will act as a sword splitting thoughts and attitudes, defining matters of the heart, recognizing and judging good and evil no matter where it lives. The Word is eternal.

What does knowing the Word do for us then? It reminds us to give God thanks and praise for loving us so much that He knows how to help us when we make unwise choices, or when we have thoughts that don't please Him. It reveals God and shows us that He can strengthen us at any moment because His Word is part of us and He is alive and well. We can be grateful that God knows the difference in the things we do that make us feel guilty and sad, and the things we do that seek His grace and mercy. He can cut through the self-deceit and the things we hide even from ourselves.

God does all of that because He stands on His Word. He knows that you trust in His Word and so He helps you every day to define what that means for you. He wants you to give Him your whole heart because He will always care for you. You have His Word!

*Lord, help me to come to You when I have any concerns or doubts. I depend on Your **Word** every moment of my life. Amen.*

# ROOM

*When I call, give me answers. God, take my side! Once, in a tight place,*
*you gave me room; Now I'm in trouble again: grace me! hear me!*

Psalm 4:1 MSG

From your earliest days in the womb, you've been looking for growing **room**. You've wanted space where you could stretch your limbs and spread your wings and fly.

God knows you need to breathe. He knows that conflict and the pressures of everyday life can squeeze the energy out of you. Adversity can make you feel uncertain about your direction and drain all your confidence. You need more room!

If you meditate or pray, you may find it helpful to simply close your eyes and rest quietly in God's Presence. You can take this step almost anywhere you happen to be. Take a time-out! Give yourself a moment to breathe in the Spirit of the One who goes before you and behind you, above you and below you. He has endless room for you, infinite room for you, and He can carry you out of those tight places.

If you're in "trouble" again today, then you need space to think things through. You need to find room to consider your options and to hear God's voice for His intentions and direction. Go to Him; He always has room for you.

*Lord, I do feel somewhat boxed in at times and I know I need*
*Your help to give me **room** so that I can breathe in Your peace and*
*comfort. Be with me and those I love today. Amen.*

# JOURNEY

*Your life is a journey you must travel with a deep consciousness of God. It cost God plenty to get you out of that dead-end, empty-headed life you grew up in. He paid with Christ's sacred blood, you know.*  1 Peter 1:18 MSG

When you plan a trip, you usually look at where you'll start, where you'll end up, and how you'll get there in the best possible way. What makes your way the best is all about your intentions and your purpose. You may want to take a leisurely route that skips by the big heavy-traffic roadways and takes the slower, more scenic vistas. You may want to be sure to see the most amazing historic sites along your path, or the most incredible landscapes. You get to choose. It's your **journey**.

Your life is a journey also. You were born and you will die, so you know where you start and where you end. What you get to choose, though, is everything in between. You can choose to travel aimlessly with no designated points to stop along the way. You can just show up and see what happens. Or you can choose to set goals about when you'll complete one course of action and then take the next. You can even choose whether you'll go it alone or whether you'll invite God to go with you.

In this passage from 1 Peter, we are reminded that our journeys are not just about us. Our travel plans include God and we must consciously seek His Presence every step of the way. When we go to Him for direction and guidance, He offers us the adventure of a lifetime.

Travel in the daily Presence of God, and you'll discover landscapes you never could have found on your own. Happy traveling!

*Lord, I know that I don't want to take this life journey, or even another step, without You. Help me to seek Your guidance for each place I go from here. Amen.*

# LAMBS

*When they finished eating, Jesus said to Simon Peter, "Simon son of John, do you love me more than these?" He answered, "Yes, Lord, you know that I love you." Jesus said, "Feed my lambs."*                    John 21:15 NCV

When shepherds refer to their baby sheep, they call them **lambs**. The lambs are innocent and tender. They are still learning how to listen for the shepherd's voice. They follow the example of the older, more mature ewes but they are easily led astray. They need continual guidance in order to grow up and be strong. If they tumble over on their backs, they can't get up on their own. They need the shepherd to pay constant attention to their needs.

Jesus was asking a very big favor in this Scripture from John. The fact is that not only did He ask it of Simon Peter as the ministry of Jesus began to take hold, but He also asks it today, right now. He asks each person who follows in His steps if they are willing to help. He asks you. Are you willing to feed my lambs?

You're not a shepherd. You don't have a flock that may wander over the hillside and get attacked by wolves. But you can choose to feed the hearts and minds and spirits of those in your sphere of influence. They heed your voice. They recognize your call to do good.

Whether you feed one lamb or thousands, you know the work is at hand. The Shepherd has need of you and He continues to call His followers so that they can help Him bring others into the fold. "Feed my lambs," He says. What do you say?

*Lord, I know that I can do more to help feed the spirits of those near me. Grant me the wisdom to do Your bidding to feed Your lambs. Amen.*

# BREATH

*The God who made the whole world and everything in it is the Lord of the land and the sky. He does not live in temples built by human hands. This God is the One who gives life, **breath**, and everything else to people. He does not need any help from them; he has everything he needs.*

Acts 17:24–25 NCV

It's interesting that when you're anxious or feeling stifled by the world, it helps to simply stop and take a deep **breath**. We even sometimes call it a cleansing breath. We try to take in more oxygen so that our brains work more efficiently, and we are more at peace. This option was designed just for you by your Creator. And the One who gave you breath works continually to help you fill your lungs with His life and Spirit.

You exist at the pleasure and purpose of God. He doesn't need your help to get anything accomplished, but He will allow you to share in His work. All you have to do is remain close enough to Him to breathe His Spirit into your heart and mind and soul and then you can fulfill His purpose.

You need air! When you feel like you are being smothered in a world that doesn't always give you space or energize your spirit so your heart and mind work at their peak, then you need breathing room. Don't wait until you're gasping for air to draw close to God. Simply take a deep breath, call on His name, read His Word, and fill your lungs with peace. When you do, oxygen will flow, His Spirit will flow through you, and you will be energized with every breath you take.

*Lord, I am so grateful for Your Presence and the blessing of Your Spiritual **breath** into my heart and lungs. Help me to stay close to You always. Amen.*

# ENVY

*Love is patient, love is kind. It does not **envy**, it does not boast, it is not proud.*                                    1 Corinthians 13:4 NIV

Envy evokes a somewhat sickly pale green image that doesn't really flatter anyone. To become green with **envy**, jealousy, or covetousness doesn't put any of us in a good light.

It's interesting that as the writer to the Corinthians imagined what real, unconditional, authentic love was all about, he included "does not envy."

Perhaps envy doesn't strike you as something you've needed to worry about. After all, you're not jealous because your friends have a beach house and you don't, or because they have a kid going to Harvard and your kid doesn't know what they even want to do with their life. But chances are good it still strikes your emotions each time you see their posts on social media.

If love does not envy, then it means that love doesn't wish to have someone else's beautiful home. Love does not feel slightly jealous when every head turns because a handsome man or a beautiful woman has entered the room. Love is not always comparing itself to others. Love is delighted with what it already has because it feels blessed by God's generosity.

God wants you to act in every way possible with love. When you do, He can change those green shadows into glorious and beautiful light. In fact, you will radiate with great joy.

*Lord, help me not to **envy** others even in the smallest ways. Let me recognize the beauty in everything You have done for me today. Amen.*

# FOLLOW

*As Jesus was walking beside the Sea of Galilee, he saw two brothers, Simon called Peter and his brother Andrew. They were casting a net into the lake, for they were fishermen. "Come, follow me," Jesus said, "and I will send you out to fish for people." At once they left their nets and followed him.*

Matthew 4:18–20 NIV

When you were young, you may have played a little game called "**Follow the leader.**" When you followed the leader, you did everything you could to mirror what the leader was doing. If the leader raised his hand, you raised your hand. If the leader hopped on one foot, you hopped on one foot. It was a fun game and usually made everyone smile as the leader thought of silly things to do so everyone would follow.

We also use the word "follow" as a sign that we are interested in the material that someone presents on social media. We "follow" them so that we can keep up with what they are doing and feel the connection of belonging to a group that finds that person interesting.

Jesus was busy gathering followers for only one reason: to teach them how to bring others into God's kingdom. He wasn't trying to win a popularity contest or trying to show the world how important He was. He was simply a leader, trying to show the way for people to be saved.

Jesus called you to follow Him and you've been shining His light ever since, showing people what it means to walk in His footsteps each day. Fortunately, Jesus leaves a pretty easy trail, and anyone who wants to follow along can do so. All you have to do is imitate the leader.

*Lord, thank You for asking me to **follow** You. It is my joy and privilege, and I pray that I will help others have a greater desire to follow You as well. Amen.*

# BLOT

*Have mercy on me, O God, according to your unfailing love; according to your great compassion **blot** out my transgressions.*        Psalm 51:1 NIV

If you spill coffee on your favorite shirt and it leaves a stain, you probably think quickly about what you can do to **blot** it out. How can you get that stain out before it sets in? That stain can ruin your favorite shirt forever.

In like manner, what do you do about those stains that may have appeared on your heart and mind and spirit? What do you do to keep those spots from showing? You may recall that when Adam and Eve stained their lives, the first thing they wanted to do was hide. But no one can hide from God.

It's interesting that the word "blot" can refer to the spot itself, or it can also refer to its removal. It can be the way we get rid of the stain. We blot it out. The psalmist knew that He had some spots—some unclean, stained areas of his heart—that needed to be made white again, made whole again, made clean. He wanted God to blot out his transgressions, his failures, his stains.

You may have a few blots to deal with, and if you do, God only asks that you come to Him for help. If you need any stain removal, seek God's help and grace. He alone can make you spotless again. When He does, you will find that you look great in anything you might wear.

*Lord, thank You for Your mercy and Your willingness to **blot** out my sins and my flaws. Create in me a clean heart today. Amen.*

# LESSON

*"Now learn this **lesson** from the fig tree: As soon as its twigs get tender and its leaves come out, you know that summer is near. Even so, when you see all these things, you know that it is near, right at the door."*

Matthew 24:32 NIV

Learning a **lesson** can be a complex thing, especially if it involves something you had to learn the hard way, as in, "I hope you've learned your lesson." You may have heard that as a kid, and it was never an easy moment. It usually meant that you had made a poor choice or that you didn't understand the consequences of something.

In the case of the fig tree, Jesus was trying to use a concrete example to help his listeners understand something valuable. He was giving them an object lesson. He gave them a simple way to understand a sign that God was doing something important. When they saw the leaves come out, they knew that summer was coming soon. In other words, Jesus wanted them to be watchful, aware of the times and the seasons, so that they were prepared for the work God was doing around them.

In other places in Scripture, we are given object lessons and examples and even warnings about what to look for in the times to come. God wants us to be alert and prepared. He wants us to recognize His hand at work.

Perhaps the lesson for any of us is simply to watch and observe what is going on in the world and in the neighborhoods where we live. God is teaching us, preparing us for what is to come. This might be a good time to brush up on your knowledge of the signs of the times. If you need to study a bit, your Teacher will help you anytime you ask. This is an ongoing lesson until the Lord returns.

*Lord, I know that I have not understood every **lesson**, every sign You've given me to help me prepare for Your return. Thank You for giving me remedial help. Amen.*

# CAMPS

*This poor man called, and the Lord heard him and saved him from all his troubles.*
*The angel of the Lord **camps** around those who fear God, and he saves them.*                                        Psalm 34:6–7 NCV

One of the gifts of Scripture is how colorful and picturesque it is. You may not have thought about the angel of the Lord setting up a tent somewhere close to you, but apparently that's what happens. The angel **camps** near you and is ready at any time to save you.

How can you know that to be true? One way perhaps is to realize that the day you put a stake in the ground to give your life to Jesus came with quite a few benefits. It came with a gift of salvation, but it also came with a helper.

In the days of the Patriarchs, the places where camps were set up were chosen very carefully. They had to be aware of wild animals that roamed through the darkness. They had to be near a source of water to care for the people and the livestock. They had to set up a worship center to honor God. These camps were often their base of operations for many months.

It's a wonderful thought to imagine that God, or one of His angels, is camping near you wherever you are. He provides security, warding off evil and predators that you may not have even known were there. He hears your cries when you're in trouble and instantly helps you, running to save you as quickly as possible. He watches over you day and night, making sure that you have all that you need. Give God thanks and praise today for providing you with such a close companion, someone to watch out for your heart and soul.

*Lord, I know that Your angel **camps** close to me, and I thank You for Your protection. Hear my cries today for those I love who are in need and watch over them. Amen.*

# AGAINST

*Look out for those who cause people to be **against** each other and who upset other people's faith. They are against the true teaching you learned, so stay away from them.* Romans 16:16–17 NIV

This Scripture from Romans comes as a bit of a warning. It says, "Look out!" for people who stir up discontent and intentionally provoke people to choose sides **against** each other.

That scenario happens all the time. Sometimes it happens in families. Sometimes it happens with your team at work, and it goes on and on. The caution here, though, in this warning note is to especially be on the lookout for people who undermine your faith. They come at you with ideas and theories and philosophies that sound good on the surface, but which are designed to take you away from your faith in Christ. The intention is not to help you grow and learn and think more clearly. The intention is a total deception. It is a plan to cause you to take a stand against all the things you've learned, all that you believe in.

The good news is that they can't harm you if you don't let them. They can't get through the armor of God, the Scriptures that you've memorized, and the hymns that come to your mind at the name of Jesus. They can't snatch you out of God's hand no matter what they do. So don't try to disarm them. Don't try to teach them a lesson. Do the thing that is the most protective for you. Simply walk away. May God bless you and keep you wherever you are today.

*Lord, thank You for protecting me **against** the forces of evil that are in the world. I praise Your Holy name. Amen.*

# HOME

*So we are always confident, knowing that while we are at home in the body we are absent from the Lord. For we walk by faith, not by sight.*

2 Peter 5:6 NCV

By now you're probably right at **home** with that person you see in the mirror each morning when you rise. After all, you've been walking around in that body now for a few years and you have become fond of it. You've gotten comfortable with who you are and adjusted to the home you've made together.

The word "home" conjures up a lot of different images. Your body is your home, and so is the place where you live. You may have a home church.

If you're a sports fan, then you may have a favorite home team, or you may appreciate buying produce from a local farmer because you know it's home grown. The word "home" usually gives you a sense that you're in a safe place, one where you are welcome and invited to be part of all that happens. You might say that the state or country where you live is your home.

So where is your true home? The answer is that it is not in your body. It is not in your neighborhood or your church or even on the planet. Your home is in Heaven. You're just a visitor here with a pass to explore this life. When your adventure is over, you'll go back home, to your real home, with your real Father in Heaven.

*Lord, thank You for providing us with a home where our address will never change. Bless all those who come home to You today. Amen.*

# EASY

*But the wisdom that comes from God is first of all pure, then peaceful, gentle, and **easy** to please. This wisdom is always ready to help those who are troubled and to do good for others.* James 3:17 NCV

Perhaps some of the best prayers that any of us offer up to God are prayers for wisdom. We want to get wise counsel before we proceed with an idea or a plan of action. We want to be sure that God is with us and that He will lead the way. We seek His help so that even if what we have to do isn't **easy**, it will be placed squarely in God's hand.

When we're troubled, or when we are uncertain about what may be ahead of us on any given day, we know that the pure and gentle reasoning of the Lord will help us do the right things. When God makes things easy for us, it simply means that He takes away the chaos, the complexity that can be overwhelming, and He causes our hearts and minds to be peaceful. He sets us at ease so we can calmly deal with our circumstances. He knows what we need.

Most of us would like things to be easy. We'd like to move all the obstacles out of our way and have smooth sailing at least for a little while. For whatever reason, though, the world we live in spins in total chaos and our personal lives can start churning right along with it. So what do we do? We go to God. We ask for His pure, uncluttered, easy-to-understand, gentle hand on our lives. We ask for His will to be done so that we can go on and do the good that He would have us do for those around us. May God's easy, peaceful, stress-free form of wisdom come your way today.

*Lord, help me to breathe in Your **easy**, gentle Presence. Grant me the wisdom that only You can give to help me accomplish the work You'd have me do today. Amen.*

# OBEY

*So go and make followers of all people in the world. Baptize them in the name of the Father and the Son and the Holy Spirit. Teach them to **obey** everything that I have taught you, and I will be with you always, even until the end of this age.*         Matthew 28:19–20 NCV

**Obey** is one of those words that makes people recoil. After all, it carries a sense that you are being ordered to do something, and if you don't follow the orders, you'll face the consequences. It's one thing to be obedient, as a servant might be, but that may not be exactly the posture that Jesus was taking here.

When you want your kids to respect the rules of the house, you want that to happen as a protection for them, as a way for them to understand the boundaries so they know how to make good choices. You want them to adhere to the rules because you love them, and you know that rule-following can sustain their sense of security and add to their well-being. God wants the same for you. He shows you the boundaries, so you can operate freely within those guidelines. When you do, your relationship grows, and you know that you can count on each other always.

The intention of this command comes from a voice of love, a voice of compassion. It is from the One who is worthy to be obeyed and who will be with you always, even to the end of time.

*Lord, thank You for calling me into Your spirit and for baptizing me with love. Help me to **obey** Your wisdom and counsel so that I can be a blessing to others. Amen.*

# MIRACLES

*Your ways, God, are holy. What god is as great as our God?*
*You are the God who performs **miracles**; you display your power among the*
*    peoples.* Psalm 77:13–14 NIV

St. Augustine said that he never had trouble believing in **miracles** because he had undergone the miracle of the change of his own heart. When we start there, recognizing all that God had to do to bring us aboard, to get us to accept His love and mercy, it does indeed make it easier to recognize that miracles happen every day because God's power is unlimited.

Perhaps you already see your life as a miracle, but if you don't, you should! After all, as independent, brilliant, and self-sufficient as you may be, you probably didn't get where you are today totally on your own. Usually, a little walk down memory lane will remind you of the people who somehow were there for you when you most needed them. You had teachers who saw your potential and encouraged you, or close friends who helped you stay on the path to become what you wanted to be in the world. We see God's Divine handiwork in the lives and stories of those who went before us, reminding us that we do not walk this Earth alone.

Numerous miracles take place in the Old and the New Testaments. According to the psalmist, God is in the miracles business. Always has been. Always will be. May you be a witness wherever you are to all that He has done.

*Lord, thank You for the **miracles** You've performed in my life, ones*
*that I have not always understood but now embrace. You have*
*blessed me beyond measure. Amen.*

# LOAD

*Jesus replied, "And you experts in the law, woe to you, because you **load** people down with burdens they can hardly carry, and you yourselves will not lift one finger to help them."*　　　　　　　　　　Luke 11:46 NIV

Need to take a **load** off? Chances are good that you're carrying a whole lot more on your shoulders than you intended. For whatever reason, we all tend to pile things on top of the pile of things that already weigh us down.

Jesus rebuked the Pharisees because they were hard on the people of their day. They scolded people who slipped up in the slightest ways and didn't do anything to help them. Jesus understood that the people were weighed down with burdens, with loads they simply could not carry, and He drew attention to that fact. Later on, He tells us that when we walk with Him, we can cast our burdens onto His shoulders and He will help us carry them. This is in stark contrast to the leaders of His day.

In our day, there are still taskmasters who make it difficult for people to get their work done. Your boss may be someone who seems to never let up, never giving you a break or a moment's peace, because no matter what you do, it is never enough. There's always something more you have to do and it needed to be done yesterday. Your load becomes unbearable.

The point to consider is: How can you lighten the load? One answer is to simply put it down. Lay it at the feet of Jesus and ask for His help. Look at your to-do list and erase one thing that is not really urgent. Breathe! Give yourself a chance to take in God's Divine presence so He can help you adjust the load you bear.

*Lord, thank You for being willing to help me bear the **load** I have now. Help me to bless others and carry burdens for them anytime I can. Amen.*

# PLACE

*You are my hiding **place**. You protect me from my troubles*
*and fill me with songs of salvation.*                    Psalm 32:6–7 NCV

When you were a kid, did you have a special **place** you could go when you simply needed to have time alone or think for yourself? Maybe you enjoyed taking walks along the beachfront, or you enjoyed hiking somewhere special. Maybe you simply had a tree house, or a backyard fort, and it felt good because it was your place. You could even put up a sign and keep everybody else out.

We still enjoy a place to run to when life gets tricky or chaos abounds. We may think a trip to the mountains could cure what ails us or an ocean cruise will soothe our souls. Sometimes an avenue of escape, a hiding place, is exactly what we need to balance out the rest of life.

Remember that God promises to be your hiding place. He can hold on to you when things are rocky. He can lift you up when you can't take another step on your own. He can quiet your fears when your heart is racing. He will protect you like a mother bird under His incredible wings.

It's okay to run away, to go to that place, either physical or mental, that gives you a few moments of tranquility. Next time you go, though, besides packing the things you need for your hike or your beach trip, pack your Bible so you and God can spend time together. He's always ready to let you hide out with Him. He will protect you and strengthen you and fill you with songs of joy by the time you leave His side.

*Lord, I know that finding a good **place** to hide is not always easy, so*
*I am glad that I can come to You and You'll keep me safely at Your*
*side. Amen.*

# DARKNESS

*My enemies are chasing me; they crushed me to the ground. They made me live in **darkness** like those long dead. I am afraid; my courage is gone.*

Psalm 143:3–4 NCV

It's natural to be somewhat afraid of the dark. After all, you can't see what is going on around you. The shadows seem bigger and the sounds seem scarier. When the **darkness** surrounds you, it's easy to feel vulnerable, and it can steal your courage away.

It's interesting that as close as David felt to God, His Creator and Redeemer, He, too, felt a bit afraid in the dark. We can understand his fear because we all have moments when a moonless night or a dimly lit room can give us the shivers.

The thing to remember is that God sees you just as clearly in the darkness as He does in the light. If you need His arm of protection, He's there. If you need a place of refuge or solace, He hears your prayers and He never leaves your side. Imagine that He is your floodlight, a beacon that lights up the sky and the room you're in and the heart that suffers in doubt. God is light and nothing can change that. His light came on inside you the moment you handed your life over to Christ. You're on His radar day and night, darkness and light, and so you have nothing to fear. Hold on to your courage. You may not even need a flashlight to help you see further.

*Lord, I do become wary when I must walk anywhere that feels overcome by the **darkness**. Walk with me every step of the way and keep me strong and brave in Your light. Amen.*

# LETTER

*Do we need letters of introduction to you or from you, like some other people? You yourselves are our **letter**, written on our hearts, known and read by everyone.* 2 Corinthians 3:1–2 NCV

Have you ever written a love **letter**? You know, it's that note where you simply can't find the words to truly express how you feel. You think about each word, each sentence, hoping that it will somehow convey the things your heart wants to say. That may be a bit of what we see here in this Scripture. It's a testimony to the joy that has been shared by everyone.

Jesus is God's love letter to humanity. Because of His sacrifice and His teachings, because of the very way He lived His life, we have examples of God's love. Jesus lived a heart-shaped life, and His thoughts and actions came together in a way that time can never change. He is loved by millions, and His love for each person is unconditional.

You are somebody's love letter. You are their example of what it means to be a believer. When you share your smile and your heart, your kind words and your actions share the story of God's love.

Continue today to be God's love letter. Show others what it means to be caring and giving and selfless. Be God's light in the world, sweetened by heart-shaped grace and mercy.

*Lord, thank You for being my love **letter**. Thank You for helping me to write my story in ways that please You so that I can share Your love with others. Amen.*

# ENEMIES

*But love your **enemies**, do good to them, and lend to them without hoping to get anything back. Then you will have a great reward, and you will be children of the Most High God, because he is kind even to people who are ungrateful and full of sin.* Luke 6:35 NCV

Chances are that you never consciously set out to create **enemies**. You didn't wake up one morning and decide that you had just had it with friends, and from now on, you would just make enemies. But do you have a few people who have fallen through the cracks of your life because you have a strained relationship—a friendship that became something else?

If you have any person that comes to mind, God wants you to rethink your actions and your possibilities. What can you do to change enemies into friends, and why would you want to?

At one time, you and God were enemies. You had not yet chosen to hold Him close to you, to make Jesus a part of your life, and so you had no way to get back to Heaven.

Even though you may have chosen to do that for a while, God continued to love you. He loves His enemies into friends. He wants you to do the same thing. He wants you to see that whatever slight or injury or hard-hearted experience you may have with that person on your enemy list, He's been there too. His answer is love. Love your enemies and He will reward you with an even greater understanding of His love for you. Be kind and good to those around you today.

*Lord, I may not have **enemies**, but I may have people in my life that I don't nurture very often or even lift up in prayer. Help me to do a better job. Amen.*

# SMALL

*"Truly I tell you, if you have faith as **small** as a mustard seed, you can say to this mountain, 'Move from here to there,' and it will move. Nothing will be impossible for you."*  Matthew 17:20–21 NIV

How would you define your faith today? Would you say your faith is fragile, or limited, in need of repair or maybe just the opposite? Maybe you can truly define your faith as enormous, grandiose, large because everything you do in life is built around it.

It's not only the size of a person's faith that is being considered here, though. It's actually more significant than that. This is not just about big or **small** faith: it's about the power behind that faith, because no matter how much faith we might think we have, God can use us to do amazing things. Nothing is impossible for God when it is our faith that connects us to whatever we want to do. The shepherd boy, David, and the king named Saul are good examples. Saul was the great king but he did not trust in the power of God to take on the giant problem of Goliath. He could not go out and face the mountain, the giant Philistine, because he did not believe that, with God's help, he could defeat the giant. Saul put David in his armor, but the weight of it was too much for David. David said, "I don't need this armor. I have God and that's enough for me." In other words, David had big faith. He was ready to move mountains and slay giants because he trusted that God could do anything.

You may not need to slay any giants today, but you may still need to move some people toward better decisions, or influence the direction of those around you. You can do it. You don't need Saul's armor either. You simply need the armor of God and big faith. If your God is too small, seek His help so that you can recognize that He truly means it when He declares that, with Him, everything is possible.

*Lord, I pray that You will help me grow beyond my **small** faith and give me giant faith, Goliath faith, as I meet the world head-on today. Amen.*

# HIRED

*A **hired** hand will run when he sees a wolf coming. He will abandon the sheep because they don't belong to him and he isn't their shepherd. And so the wolf attacks them and scatters the flock. The hired hand runs away because he's working only for the money and doesn't really care about the sheep.* John 10:12–13 NLT

If you've been **hired** to do a job for someone else, you may be dedicated, talented, and motivated, but chances are, you won't be invested quite the same way as the person who owns the company. After all, they have put everything they have into their effort to succeed and they don't ever see losing as an option.

This example from John talks about a hired hand who runs away when a wolf comes to attack the sheep. He is okay about taking care of the sheep and doing his duties when things are calm and no danger lurks, but he's not especially interested in facing wolves to get the job done. After all, he's not being paid enough to lose his life for the sheep.

Jesus wasn't a work-for-hire shepherd. He didn't come to take care of things as long as the going didn't get tough. He came as the Son of the Owner, taking full responsibility for every sheep. Jesus faced the wolves and He faced the cross because He loved the sheep and wouldn't leave them. He was more than a hired hand.

Perhaps the lesson, then, is to check our motivations for the things we do. When we ascribe ownership to something, it means we are in it for the long haul and nothing will scare us off or make us run. When we work for God, we're never hired hands. We're sons and daughters doing all we can to please Him.

*Lord, help me always to be mindful of doing great work for You. When troubles come, I ask that You keep me strong and fortify me to follow through on all You have **hired** me to do. Amen.*

# SING

*He has given me a new song to **sing**, a hymn of praise to our God.*
*Many will see what he has done and be amazed. They will put their trust in*
*the Lord.*          Psalm 40:3 NLT

What makes you feel like singing? Maybe your favorite song comes on the radio and you're ready to belt it out with gusto. After all, you're in the car and no one can hear you anyway. Perhaps you're at church and the hymns you love are being featured in the service and so you **sing** at the top of your lungs. It feels great!

The fact is that most of us feel like singing when something wonderful happens. We just received good news, or we're finally in the relationship we waited years to find. When we are happy, our hearts are full of joy, and it's easy to understand why music fills the soul.

If we look at all God has done in our lives, providing for our daily needs, granting us good health and people who love us, it should make us feel like singing. After all, when we think about the list of reasons we have to give Him thanks and praise, it is virtually without end. All that we are and all that we will ever be are in His hands.

Whether you're a crooner or a little bit country, lift your voice in praise to the One who is worthy of your trust, the One who knows you and watches out for you every moment of the day. So go ahead, put your whole heart into it, and sing!

*Lord, You put a song in my heart, and I am grateful for the gifts*
*beyond measure that You have given me and the people I love. I **sing***
*Your praises every chance I get. Amen.*

# LIGHT

*And people don't hide a **light** under a bowl. They put it on a lampstand so the light shines for all the people in the house. In the same way, you should be a light for other people. Live so that they will see the good things you do and will praise your Father in heaven.*     Matthew 5:15–17 NCV

As human beings, we're drawn to the **light**. We feel more comfortable in a well-lit room and less vulnerable on a well-lighted highway. We like to see where we're going and we like knowing that others can see us coming as well. Light helps us trust our surroundings.

On its own merit, the world is dark. God set the sun to rule the day and the moon to rule the night, but it often feels that people are out of balance and that some prefer to live in the shadows, hiding out from the light of God's grace and mercy.

As a believer, then, your job is to do everything you can to turn up the light. Your job is to shine like the noonday sun. People will be drawn to you because of the irresistible nature of God. They see you, but they know that God's presence, His light, lives within you.

Every time you offer your smile, your kind words, your thoughtful encouragement and love to others, your light is shining for all to see. You become a beacon of possibility and you point them toward your Father in Heaven. Keep on beaming. The world needs you today.

*Lord, thank You for allowing me to share Your **light** with others. Help me to be willing to do all I can to shine for You. Amen.*

# TIRED

*We must not become **tired** of doing good. We will receive our harvest*
*of eternal life at the right time if we do not give up. When we have the*
*opportunity to help anyone, we should do it.* Galatians 6:9–10 NCV

**Tired**, worn-out, weary, somewhat burned out…that feeling that you simply can't keep doing what you're doing. Have you been there? It's no surprise if you have the feeling that there's more to cope with from day to day than you might wish. After all, you deserve a break, but the people you give to far outnumber the ones who seem to have a burning desire to give right back to you. Equal opportunity giving doesn't seem to be alive and well.

When you're giving, giving, giving, it wears thin after a while. You might be tempted to close the door, take down the good-neighbor shingle, and simply hide out. After all, there are others who can do what you do. Right?

God respects your feelings of getting worn out, not only from giving to others, but simply from the work involved in taking care of those around you. He knows that you are tired sometimes and that you, too, need rest. The idea here is that our best selves are the ones that serve others. We're at the top of our game when we are aware of doing all we can to embrace opportunities to help those in need. Those are the true measures of success, the real opportunities for you to shine, and guess what? Your opportunities are everywhere.

Dig in. Do what you can. Everything you do for others makes a difference in the kingdom of God, and God sees your heart and all you do. He will restore your energy and provide for your needs.

*Lord, I feel a bit worn out and **tired**, and I wonder why there aren't more people doing all the good they can. Help me to keep doing my best for the good of Your kingdom here on Earth and for my life with You in eternity. Amen.*

# CHANCE

*I have seen something else under the sun: The race is not to the swift or the battle to the strong, nor does food come to the wise or wealth to the brilliant or favor to the learned; but time and **chance** happen to them all.*

Ecclesiastes 9:11 NIV

**Chance** is an interesting word because you may not really believe in the concept. After all, when God is an integral part of your life, He orchestrates your days and knows exactly what you need. He doesn't rely on coincidence or fate. He's invested in you, and together you're doing all you can to create a meaningful life.

The wisdom writer of Ecclesiastes, though, sees things from a different perspective. He realizes that there really is no such thing as "black and white." It doesn't naturally follow that a good person gets all the breaks in life. A smart person may or may not succeed, and a person with incredible talent may waste it and throw it away. He says that time and chance happen to the best people and the worst people.

You can determine how you wish to interpret the idea of chance as discussed in Ecclesiastes, but consider your own life. Would you throw every situation and circumstance into a bucket and imagine even for a moment that the perfect opportunities that have happened in your life all came simply by chance? As a believer, you recognize and embrace the Presence and the guidance of God. You know that only He could have created some of the experiences you've known. You have witnessed His love and His protection firsthand.

Some say that the planet we live on is the result of randomness and chance. Others say that everything known to human beings was totally designed for our good. No matter what you believe, God sees you and He won't ever take a chance on losing you.

*Lord, thank You for my relationship with You, which is built on faith and not on **chance**. Help me to trust in You no matter what things look like all around me. Amen.*

# BLIND

*He replied, "Every plant that my heavenly Father has not planted will be pulled up by the roots. Leave them; they are **blind** guides. If the blind lead the blind, both will fall into a pit."*　　　　Matthew 15:13–14 NCV

Have you ever been somewhat mesmerized by someone, perhaps even becoming **blind** to their actual character? The salesperson who knew exactly what you needed to hear the last time you bought a car may have fallen into that camp. After all, you bought the car and hoped you could trust in the process. Your favorite actor or singer may be part of that group, someone you admire and want to believe in, trusting that who you think they are is really accurate.

In this Scripture, though, Jesus is suggesting that it's important to know those who truly are "planted" by God in the sense that God is using them to guide you on your path to Him, compared to those who simply blind you to the truth.

Maybe you imagine that you're too smart for that. You're not easily swayed and no one can "pull a fast one" on you, but no matter how careful you are, it pays to be discerning. It is important to stay so close to God that nothing can come between you. You don't want to be blind-sided by others. You don't want to follow the wrong leader.

How can you protect yourself? You can seek God's help in prayer so that He shows you the people He has put in your path. You can search the Scriptures, especially when you don't feel totally certain about someone. You want your eyes to be open so that you are alert and ready to keep walking with the Lord as He bids you to follow. When you stick close behind Him, you won't ever fall into a pit.

*Lord, please help me to have my eyes wide open to those who would try to be **blind** leaders. Protect me and keep me on Your path alone. Amen.*

# FORWARD

*You should live holy lives and serve God, as you wait for and look **forward***
*to the coming of the day of God.*                    2 Peter 3:11–12 NCV

Think about the things you genuinely look **forward** to. Perhaps you love Christmas, and the delight of the season inspires your heart and soul. Maybe you look forward to going to the beach each summer or a special event with your family. Whatever it is, anticipation brings the excitement that motivates you to prepare for the event itself.

The enthusiasm you may have for those things pales in comparison to your heart's delight in waiting for the return of Jesus. Part of you may find it scary. Part of you may find it awesome. The writer of 2 Peter simply wants to remind you that the best way to look forward to this incredible event is to live as close to God as you can. Live a holy life. Live in anticipation that His return is now imminent, and you will share in the joy and the glory.

If you're uncertain about what you might do to live a life that is holy, consider that each thing you do to serve God and to serve others uplifts your soul and causes you to recognize what it means to be holy. Each thing you do with love causes your heart to be refreshed and renewed and brings glory to your Father in Heaven. That's part of the very definition of being holy.

As you look forward to all you have to do today, and as you anticipate the special events that bring joy to your life, remember to continue to do things that cause your spirit to rejoice. Your Savior is coming one day soon!

*Lord, thank You for giving me so many delightful things to look*
***forward** to each day of my life. I anticipate Your coming with great*
*joy. Amen.*

# STONES

*Some of the Pharisees in the crowd said to Jesus, "Teacher, rebuke your disciples!" "I tell you," he replied, "if they keep quiet, the stones will cry out."*

Luke 19:39–40 NIV

We don't often get pictures in Scripture of anthropomorphized objects, but Jesus is making a significant point here. He reminds the Pharisees that there's something greater going on with the work His disciples are doing than the Pharisees can comprehend. They are limited by human reasoning and hearing and seeing, and so they expect everyone to do as they do. The concept that the **stones** around them might cry out, talk, or otherwise praise God is way beyond their thinking.

The point for us, though, is that when God is doing something, when He is acting in a way that serves His children to help them come to know Him better, He will use anything at His disposal to get the job done. As far as planet Earth is concerned, anything and everything is at His disposal. He can make the rocks speak for Him if He needs them to do so. God's power is unlimited.

Those who assume that they are in authority and that they have power are sometimes surprised to discover that they clearly have none. They aren't even needed in the scheme of things, and their words are useless.

When God uses the stones to talk, or a donkey to speak, He is simply showing His hand. He is reminding us that there is nothing He can't do if He chooses. The laws of nature obey Him. It's not the other way around.

As you go into the world today, look around. Remind yourself that no one is in control of your neighborhood but God Himself. No one has even a portion of His power unless He gives it to them. Speak out for Him wherever you happen to be. He is with you.

*Lord, thank You for using **stones**, donkeys, and even me to do small things for You. I pray You will help everyone I love to know You and speak up for You. Amen.*

# SAFE

*We know that anyone born of God does not continue to sin; the One who was born of God keeps them **safe**, and the evil one cannot harm them.*

1 John 5:18 NIV

Isn't it a wonderful thought to realize that God keeps your soul **safe**? That means He protects you and watches out for you. It means that your soul is securely placed in His hands and nothing can change that. You are so attached to Him that life or death or angels or demons or anything else you might wonder about can never come between you. Nothing can separate you from God. You are safe for eternity.

You probably can't make that claim about most anything else in your life today. You may keep your money stored in the safe at the bank. You may keep your family secured at home with technology and guards. You may manage to keep your valuables in a safety-deposit box, but none of those safeguards are guaranteed. None of the measures of the world that feel safe today will do a thing for your safety in eternity. God secured your place, though. He invested in you, and He will be sure you're safe in His hands.

It's important to feel safe and secure. Part of that feeling comes from knowing where you stand, from knowing God is on your side and that He delivers on His promises. He will not let go of you so perhaps the best way to show your gratitude for His protection is to simply let others know what it is that gives you peace. When you're at peace, it means you have handed your insecurities and your worries over to God. You're safe and you know it, and nothing brings a more peaceful night's sleep than that.

Someone may rob the bank where you keep your money, but no one will ever steal you from the One who keeps you safe and secure today.

*Lord, it is scary in the world these days and safety is always an issue, a fear, almost anywhere we go. Thank You for keeping me **safe** for eternity. Amen.*

# WITH

*You, Lord, keep my lamp burning; my God turns my darkness into light.*
*With your help I can advance against a troop; with my God I can scale a*
*    wall.*                                            Psalm 18:28–29 NIV

**With** is a connector word. It reminds you that you're not alone. It sustains
you because you know that in anything you do and anywhere you go, God
is with you. "With" implies that you have help, that you are strengthened,
and that no matter what you have to do, you can do it as long as God is
with you.

The psalmist doesn't suggest that he can scale a wall on his own. He
doesn't imply that he can fight a battle or take on his adversary. He doesn't
say that maybe he could do it if he had to, or possibly he could climb the
wall of obstacles in front of him. He knows one thing. He can't do it alone.
He needs God's help, and with God at his side, he will do well.

Jesus told His disciples that those who were with Him were not against
Him. Even if they did things differently, Jesus could still appreciate them
because they were helping others get to know Him and that meant that
God was using them. They helped the cause of Jesus, and they were with
Him in the ministry.

Think of the people who are with you in your work and in your life.
These are the ones who stand by you and encourage you. They help you
to stay on the task at hand and remind you of all that you are meant to be.
They are with you. In a similar way, God is with you today. That gives you
every reason to smile wherever you go.

*Lord, thank You for being **with** me all the time. You know me better*
*than anyone else, and You know the best ways to work with me. Let*
*me live in Your grace and mercy today. Amen.*

# EFFORT

*Be completely humble and gentle; be patient, bearing with one another in love. Make every **effort** to keep the unity of the Spirit through the bond of peace.*                                                                Ephesians 4:2–3 NIV

**Effort** that is halfhearted misses the point. Effort that tries one day and gives up the next falls apart. Effort isn't wimpy. Effort is courageous and strong and determined. Effort is an overcomer. Effort is your friend.

Sometimes you may be tempted to take the easy path. After all, you don't know many people who really put themselves out there and try to make a difference. Why should you? Why should you be the one who is always patient or gentle or giving when others are being selfish? The answer is simple. God makes your effort worthwhile. He already knows how difficult it can be, but He rewards you instantly. He gives you His peace. He fills you with His Spirit so that you can share it with others. He enthuses you so that you can keep trying and keep giving.

God knows it takes a lot of effort to bear with others. They can be so crazy or so selfish or so arrogant. They can exhibit a lot of behaviors that simply make you want to walk away. They can push all the wrong buttons and exasperate everything you try to do for them to make things better and easier. This word, though, isn't about them. It's about you. God is asking you point-blank if you will expend the effort to keep others in the fold, to treat them with love. Will you be patient so that they can see the light of His love?

Your efforts will pay off because God will use every opportunity to help you as you patiently and humbly come before Him to help others. You can be sure He wildly applauds all your efforts right now.

*Lord, help me to graciously make the **effort** to help others even when they make it difficult for me. Grant me Your strength and love to carry on. Amen.*

# CHILD

*When I was a child, I talked like a child, I thought like a child, I reasoned like a child. When I became a man, I put the ways of childhood behind me.*
1 Corinthians 13:11 NCV

Life requires a balance between maturing wisely and not losing sight of your inner **child**. We certainly are aware that human beings struggle with that balance, and the examples around us abound. The beauty of truly growing in wisdom and maturity, though, is that we recognize the difference ourselves. We know when it's best to contemplate our actions seriously, be intentional about our decisions, and seek God's plans regarding all things. We know, but it's not always easy getting there.

On the other hand, it is good to know when to be playful and trusting, innocently putting your hand in God's hand and allowing Him to make all the choices, move you as He wants to move you, and guide you as only a Good Shepherd can do. Laughter makes room in your soul and gives you air. It does your heart and mind good.

As you live and work and move today, see if you can notice the moments, no matter what age you happen to be, where you honestly could say you looked for God's hand at work in your choices and decisions. Recall when you laughed out loud, knowing full well that your Heavenly Father embraced you. See how God helped you know the steps you needed to take to achieve an awesome balance of child and adult.

God will always see you as His child even when you've grown up and put your childhood behind you. You grow up in faith and love, but you remain a child of God forever.

*Lord, I am continually learning. Help me to be a **child** that always trusts in You and who knows to come to You for every important choice I make today. Amen.*

# WASHING

*He saved us through the **washing** that made us new people through the*
*Holy Spirit.*                                                   Titus 3:5–6 NCV

**Washing** yourself or anything else is about cleansing away the dirt, the odors, and the residue. Getting cleaned up feels good because you know you can start again fresh and new. In fact, no one will even know you had a little grime on your face from doing the gardening. You've come clean. Imagine what it would be like if the skin you're in didn't have a way to be made clean, soft, and glistening again. By now, you'd be quite a mess!

This verse in Titus says that when you came to faith in Jesus Christ, God did the washing for you. By the time He'd finished making you a new person, you were not only clean behind the ears, but shiny inside and out. He washed you, and then He gave you an amazing aura of light, a little extra polish in the form of the Holy Spirit, so that you shine with utter brilliance as you wear the Presence of God within you.

It's good to know that, at one point, you were all "washed up," meaning you were lost, just a person walking around in your own dust storm, but God changed your direction. He gave you a good washing and sent you on your way to shine your light for others to see. The soap in your shower may be 99 percent pure, but God has taken you a step beyond that. He cleaned you up 100 percent for eternity.

*Lord, thank You for taking me by the hand and then **washing** me so*
*I could be renewed in Your love and mercy. Amen.*

# PROGRAMS

*The world is full of so-called prayer warriors who are prayer-ignorant. They're full of formulas and **programs** and advice, peddling techniques for getting what you want from God. Don't fall for that nonsense. This is your Father you are dealing with, and he knows better than you what you need.*

Matthew 6:7–10 MSG

We're used to having **programs** that will help us lose weight, or initiatives that will strengthen our savings account, or help us set goals to get a job done. We have grown up with technology and there are always new programs being tested in the market. You may not have thought that prayer techniques were something you've been programmed to consider, but this version of Mathew 6 brings up an important point.

You can become so used to saying a certain prayer that you almost forget what it truly means. After all, you say it Sunday after Sunday. There are some who would even suggest that if you just pray the way they do, you'll find the dream job you've been looking for, financial benefits you didn't even think were possible, and the relationship that has eluded you for years. All you have to do is pray right.

Programs, exercises, things that stimulate your thinking are all good as far as they go, but when it comes to prayer, no one has a corner on the market. The people you may admire who seem to say the right things when they pray aloud in your group need to do just like you need to do: They have to pray from the heart. Your prayers are a matter of putting your heart before God and then resting in His hands as He determines the best course for you. No one knows you better than He does! After all, He designed the program for you.

*Lord, thank You for keeping prayer a matter of the heart, and not a matter of getting the right **programs** together. Thank You for all You do for me. Amen.*

# PART

*I hate what faithless people do; I will have no **part** in it. The perverse of heart shall be far from me; I will have nothing to do with what is evil.*

Psalm 101:3–4 NIV

You make choices every day. You decide whether you'll take **part** in a committee meeting, or whether you'll join a lunch group in your neighborhood. You determine what you want to do based on your interest and energy, and sometimes you choose not to take part for the same reasons.

Whether you're a social activist who takes part in demonstrations or parades either in support of something or against it, the psalmist is asking you to direct your attention to your reason for doing so. Your choice may be entirely humanitarian, because you're standing up for a friend or a cause, and that's a good thing.

Faithless people, however, are directed only toward themselves or their own goals, and do not consider the things of God first. It's important to know what motivates those who take part in a cause. You've probably witnessed people who only do damage to others, acting in ways that diminish people, depriving them of their humanity, and seeking to leave them powerless. Faithless acts are evil because they have nothing to do with the Spirit of God and what He wants for His children.

Sure, it's a bit of a tough call sometimes. You may not always be comfortable having to choose a side, but there's one thing you can do because you're a person of great faith. You can take your choice to God and seek His direction. He will guide you perfectly and bring peace to your spirit. You will always know when you should actively take part in the issues that surround you.

*Lord, thank You for helping me understand the activities You would have me take **part** in, as I make choices in my work and in my play today. Amen.*

# OLD

*Do not cast me away when I am **old**;*
*do not forsake me when my strength is gone.*           Psalm 71:9 NIV

No matter what age you happen to be, **old** is the person who is at least ten years older than you are. After all, you are not old!

It's interesting that even the writer of the Psalms had a concern about what would happen when he could no longer operate under his own strength. What would become of him when he was seemingly of no real use to God or to the world in general? Would God just throw him away? Would being old mean he no longer had value?

Culturally, we may have the same question. We see the elderly being abused or shut up in homes, alone and uncertain. We note that few people visit and that families just can't be bothered. We let it go until we get a bit older ourselves and suddenly everything about this becomes relevant.

Perhaps the thing to remember is that God is with you from your first breath to your last. He never forsakes you. He considers it an honor if you get to grow old. He looks to you to share the stories He's given you, the lessons you've learned, and the opportunities that are even now before you.

Perhaps it is important to redefine what is meant by old, and find the good news in being a person who knows more clearly who you are, and who recognizes the good choices from the bad ones and sees life from a wiser perspective. Perhaps old means you're wise and prayerful and filled with love, because your heart has had a chance to live and learn and love again.

*Lord, thank You for keeping me close to You no matter how **old** I grow to be. I know it is a privilege to live a long life, and I thank You for every breath I take. Amen.*

# DOOR

*"I am the **door**. If anyone enters by Me, he will be saved, and will go in and out and find pasture."*
John 10:9 NKJV

Your life is full of **doors**. Some of them open easily and you walk through them without much thought. Others are tougher to get through, and a few just seem to always be closed. Whatever the story is, when you go through a door, you enter into a different environment, a new arena. As you enter, you may not have a lot of control, or you may be a regular visitor to what goes on there. You bring something important and so the door is always open to you.

How do you imagine the door called Jesus? Is your door a solid, plain and simple, functional door? Is it elaborate, perhaps made of pure gold? Is there a window in the door so that Jesus can see who is coming? However you imagine Jesus as the door, one thing is certain: He opens the way for you to keep moving forward into green pastures, a more beautiful life. He gives you eternal gifts that will bring you peace and contentment. He is the threshold of a new life that you could never enter without Him. He's an elegant, simple, loving, awesome door that changes the life you have now and the one you will have in Heaven.

Today, as you go about your business, stop for a moment and think about the doors, the entryways, the thresholds that you cross, and take a moment to say a prayer of gratitude to the One who makes it possible for you to go in and go out as you wish, the One who always holds the door open for you. After all, Jesus said that He is the door. He didn't say He was like a door. He didn't say that He was one of many doors. He simply said, "I am the door." The door is clearly marked, and He's always waiting there for you and those you love.

*Lord, You are the **door** to all the best aspects of life here on Earth and certainly there in Heaven. Thank You for giving me an invitation to come to Your door and walk in. Amen.*

# DESERVES

*"But I, the Lord, look into a person's heart and test the mind. So I can decide what each one **deserves**; I can give each one the right payment for what he does."*                                    Jeremiah 17:10 NCV

You probably know people who imagine that they **deserve** special treatment because of their position in life or their status in the community. They may think that being the president or the pastor or the CEO means that everything is all about them. You may know people who are always kind to others, do what they can to lend a hand, and yet never seem to find time to take care of their own needs. People like that deserve a break. They deserve, have earned, merited favor.

The truth is, no one deserves more than what God agrees is right. Most of us love that we live under grace, because grace means we get to have good things even when we don't deserve them. Grace means that God protects, loves, and provides for us even though we haven't done anything to deserve it. In fact, unless we learn how to be Holy as God is Holy, then grace is our best shot, and we can be grateful that God doesn't actually give us what we deserve. He gives us what He wants us to have out of great love and forbearance.

Being the President of the United States or the Queen of England may come with some entitlement, but respect and grace come only to those who serve God with all their hearts and minds. People just like you.

*Lord, thank You for Your grace that gives me more than I **deserve** all the time. Amen.*

# FOOL

*Do not fool yourselves. If you think you are wise in this world, you should become a fool so that you can become truly wise, because the wisdom of this world is foolishness with God.* 1 Corinthians 3:18–19 NCV

You know what it's like when you simply try to **fool** yourself. You dupe yourself into thinking that you can break one of your bad habits, or that you can achieve a goal that is way outside the bounds of anything you have experience doing. You look at the "everybody's doing it" mentality of the world, and without really realizing it, you buy into it too. Everything seems okay until one day when you suddenly face yourself in the mirror and admit that you allowed yourself to be fooled. You were taken in, and none of your old thinking makes sense anymore.

The good news is this: Yes, you can be fooled sometimes. You can be drawn into the foolishness of the world because it all made sense to you, and then you can step away from it and seek your Father. You can go to Him and let Him know that you are grieving over your own craziness, your own lack of wisdom and integrity. You can share your heart and wipe your tears and He will hear you.

God accepts your sorrow and redeems you. He knows you are wiser now for the experience that you went through. He knows that you will be a better influence on those around you because you'll share the stories of His forgiveness with others. You will not allow the world to get into your head and destroy the wisdom that God has given you. You won't be duped again. You're stronger and wiser and you know what it means to surrender your heart to God. Take His hand today and let Him guide you anytime you find yourself on the slippery slopes of the world. Pray always for God's protection and favor.

*Lord, thank You for keeping me from being a fool in the ways of the world. Let me always come to You for guidance and wisdom. Amen.*

# STOP

*Job, listen to this: **Stop** and notice God's miracles.*
*Do you know how God controls the clouds and makes his lightning flash?*
*Do you know how the clouds hang in the sky?*　　　Job 37:14–16 NCV

**Stop!** Stop and notice God's miracles. Have you ever realized that maybe you needed simply to take a breath and look around and remind yourself of the amazing things God has done? And if you haven't, why not?

Every day, you wake up to God's hand at work. He has been up all night while you slept putting things in order just for you. Sure, He has a whole world to take care of, but you are not overlooked; you are not missed. He sees you and knows what you need. He provides for you personally because of His great love for you. All He wants sometimes is for you to reach up to Him in utter gratitude and let Him know that you see what He does. You notice the miracles that He creates every single day.

You had nothing to do with the ground you walk on. You have no control over the way the Earth spins on its axis or the way the mountains have been formed. You do not control the oxygen you breathe or the amount of rain that falls. The One who put the stars in the sky and hung the moon is still in control. He's still creating miracles.

All He wants is to know that His work is appreciated and noticed. He wants to feel your love and gratitude no matter what your life circumstances may be. Look up! Give God the glory for all He has done for you today.

*Lord, I know I need to **stop** right where I am today and thank You*
*for the gifts You've given me, gifts without number. I praise You for*
*Your unending and steadfast love. Amen.*

# UNITY

*Love is what holds you all together in perfect **unity**. Let the peace that Christ gives control your thinking, because you were all called together in one body to have peace.*                    Colossians 3:14–15 NCV

Love is what holds you together in perfect **unity**. Love is the key, and being in harmony, agreement, syncing your hearts and minds as one, those are the efforts that help you create a life of peace with those around you.

People of your inner circle may not always reflect harmony or oneness. They may pledge to have the same goals and ideals, but want to execute them quite differently. Chaos happens because those who hope to be in control of how and why and where things are done generally keep everything off balance to get their way. Unity is the last thing they really want.

When Jesus governs your thinking, He offers you peace from the tumult and the uproar and the chaos. He beckons you to come and rest, to sit at His feet and let Him handle the misfits, the ones who wish only to stir things up. Let Him guide you into all love, which is your calling.

You may think it isn't possible for you to have this kind of peace. Your team at work doesn't operate this way. Your family doesn't come together to work out issues. Everyone does what they think is right in their own eyes. These situations may indeed be your picture, but the choice is still yours. You can seek to cast your burdens on Jesus, and let Him help you discover a oneness of heart and spirit that brings you peace. After all, He is your teammate, and He is your Father. May you reside in total peace as you unite your heart to His today.

*Lord, thank You for holding me together in **unity** because of Your love. Help me to rest there and to find peace in Your Presence. Amen.*

# SAD

*So the king asked me, "Why does your face look so **sad** when you are not ill? This can be nothing but sadness of heart."*　　　Nehemiah 2:2 NIV

Have you ever stopped to think about the way your face reflects your heart? When your spirits are soaring, your eyes sparkle, your smile gets a little bigger, and even your posture signals your joy. Our natural expressions are very transparent. We actually have to learn to hide our feelings. We learn not to let our faces express our sadness or our joys.

When you're **sad**, gloomy, depressed, and downright mopey, you look it. Your body sags, and your face shares its misery. Nothing can hide the way your heart feels at that moment. The root of sadness is nearly always a heart matter. Sometimes it's about hurt feelings or issues of forgiveness. Other times, it's sadness over the treatment we see others are receiving that we find heartbreaking. Whatever the issue, some action usually helps make things better.

Whatever you face, the first action to take is to seek help. You can seek the help you need from professionals in counseling or ministry or simply from family and friends. You can seek help personally from God. You can ask that His face would shine upon you and comfort you and give you favor. When that happens, you have a place to go with the things that are weighing you down and causing the light to go out of your eyes.

Don't wait for someone to ask you what is wrong. Act—start unloading your burdens at the foot of the cross and seek Divine intervention. It won't be long before you're blessed with a happier countenance.

*Lord, I know that I bear the weight of things that make me **sad**. Today I commit to taking the first step toward healing, so that Your joy can live in my heart again. Amen.*

# REST

*"Come to me, all you who are weary and burdened, and I will give you rest. Take my yoke upon you and learn from me, for I am gentle and humble in heart, and you will find rest for your souls."*          Matthew 11:28–29 NIV

Need a break? You bet you do! It's not easy in this fast-paced, worry-worn, overextended world to feel like you can legitimately slow things down. After all, if you take time to relax, take a power nap, or **rest**, who will get your work done?

If the description of "weary and burdened" fits your life today, then look at what Jesus says. He wants you to know that you can come to Him. That means you don't have to carry those burdens around all by yourself. That means that He will lift them off your shoulders, reignite your spirit, and give you a refreshed heart and mind so that you can feel lighter. You can take a breather because He'll help you get things done.

The only thing you have to do is come to Him. Seek His gentle heart and learn what He would have you do when you feel like you simply can't handle any more. He wants you to know that you can put down those burdens, cast them on His shoulders, lay them at His feet, and He will be your main support. He will see that you feel rested right down to your toes and even farther than that. He wants you to have rest right down to your soul.

You can keep trying to tackle the top thing that sits on the pile of your burdens all by yourself, or you can simply stop the craziness and set things where they belong, set them right. Put them at the feet of the only One who can help you do that.

*Lord, thank You for offering me a rest. Help to lay my burdens down so that I can snuggle up by Your feet. Amen.*

# BIG

*"How can you say to your friend, 'Friend, let me take that little piece of dust out of your eye' when you cannot see that **big** piece of wood in your own eye!"*

Luke 6:42 NCV

This Scripture tells us that we can't simply point fingers at someone else. As the adage says, when we do, we discover that we have three fingers pointing right back at ourselves. Many of us are quick to notice the little things that others do that we would say are wrong or at least different from the way we would do them. We can imagine as we point those fingers that we're right in our assumptions, but we may find out later that we're wrong in a huge, immense, oversized, **big** way.

It's not easy to look squarely at our own faults. We are uncomfortable with the little things we do that might be annoying to someone else, or that may be thoughtless or self-centered. After all, it's okay for us to do those things, or at least that's what we tell ourselves.

What if we decided today to change all that in a big way? What if we simply choose to not judge anyone else's quirks and flaws and hope they might not judge ours either? It could make the people who live in your house a bit easier to take. It could make your friendships a little smoother. It could even improve the relationships you have at work.

If you think of all the times that God has not called you out on the carpet when you deserved it, all the times He simply let you learn and grow and live in His grace, you might see that doing the same for others is a big thing after all. Heap some loving grace on everyone you meet today.

*Lord, thank You for helping me to see the **big** picture here. I know that I have a lot of little quirks that other people put up with, so help me to do the same in return. Amen.*

# YES

*The Son of God, Jesus Christ, that Silas and Timothy and I preached to you, was not yes and no. In Christ it has always been yes. The yes to all of God's promises is in Christ, and through Christ we say yes to the glory of God.*

2 Corinthians 1:19–20 NCV

In this letter to the Corinthians, the writer is tackling one of those everyday issues that face us today as much as it did then.

Human beings aren't very good at keeping promises. We get married and break our vows. Even if we don't break them through adultery or divorce, we break them because we promised to honor our partner and we know we don't always do that. We promised to keep our partner number one, but then our job became so big and we were under so much pressure, we couldn't keep that promise either. We promised our family that we'd stop drinking or we'd stop smoking. We promised our kids that we wouldn't miss the school play or the football game. We promise and then we don't follow through. Our promise does not mean **yes**.

Fortunately for us, Jesus is a continual yes. He doesn't back down from what He agreed to do. If He says He'll forgive your sins, then He will. If He says that He is preparing a place for you in Heaven, then He is. He does not make promises that can be broken. His yes means yes, and His no means no.

Most of the time you operate with good intentions. That means you intend for your yes to be yes. Intentions are not real promises, though. From now on, let your yes be yes to God, to yourself, and to those you love.

*Lord, thank You for being a big yes in my life. Help me to mean what I say and to keep my promises to You and to my family. Amen.*

# RACE

*The sky is like a home for the sun. The sun comes out like a bridegroom*
*from his bedroom. It rejoices like an athlete eager to run a race.*

Psalm 19:4–5 NCV

This is such beautiful imagery of the incredible work of God. Imagine a crisp cool morning, a bright blue sky, and the sun rising to meet the day. It is a glorious sight, and everywhere you look, the Earth is aglow and alive with vibrant color. Though we take the sun for granted, it is a gift to us that continues to sustain our lives.

The psalmist goes further, though. He says the sun is like a bridegroom just coming out of his bedroom. He rejoices in the new day. After all, he's in love. He sees the world as the personification of love and he's eager to be part of it. He has so much energy and excitement because he knows that he's strong and he can take on the world. He's ready to join the **race**, and not only join in, but to win because he's an athlete and he's prepared for all that is ahead.

Think of it! The sun is a bridegroom, strong, athletic, ready to run the race. Sure, it's a twenty-four-hour race, but he's ready to take it on, ready to shine his light for all the world to see, because when he settles down again and rests his head in the arms of his bride, everything will be complete and happy.

Today, it's your turn. Be the sun. Be the bridegroom. Rejoice in all that is before you as you run the race, eagerly and joyfully, filled with love. God has prepared you for this day, and by evening, you can settle once again into the joy of your Creator's comforting arms.

*Lord, thank You for Your amazing creation. Help us to always*
*appreciate the beauty and warmth of the sun and to run the **race** of*
*life with joy. Amen.*

# GREATER

*God made a promise to Abraham. And as there is no one **greater** than God, he used himself when he swore to Abraham, saying, "I will surely bless you and give you many descendants." Abraham waited patiently for this to happen, and he received what God promised.*        Hebrews 6:13–15 NCV

When you put your hand on a Bible in the courtroom and swear to tell the truth, as symbolic as that action may appear, it has history that goes back to the ancients. In fact, when God made His promise to Abraham, He didn't have anyone else to swear by who was **greater** than He was. He had to swear by the only Being there was... the greater, the bigger, the most superior Being ever... Himself!

Abraham received God's promise and trusted it. If you know the story, you're aware that it took years for the couple to conceive; in fact, it must have seemed impossible because Sarah and Abraham were well past their child-bearing years before the promise came true. Isn't that just like God to demonstrate that He is not bound by time or physical nature? He created all things and can change situations as needed. Abraham was patient, which means he didn't give up; he simply kept waiting, trusting that God knew what He was doing.

Perhaps it's a good day to consider what you may be waiting for, what promise has not happened that you wonder about. The One who is greater than all things, beyond your imagination, the Designer of your heart and soul is still there. He knows what you need for the good of your spirit, and He keeps His promises. Sometimes, in spite of the odds, or despite how things appear, God reveals His plan and He gives you the desires of your heart. He knows you, and His love is more powerful than anything else on Earth. Nothing can be greater than that.

*Lord, You are **greater** than anything my mind can imagine, beyond my understanding, and I trust You to always keep Your promises. Help me to do the same. Amen.*

# STUBBORN

*"But no, my people wouldn't listen. Israel did not want me around.*
*So I let them follow their own **stubborn** desires, living according to their own*
*ideas. Oh, that my people would listen to me!"*     Psalm 81:11–13 NLT

Have you ever tried hard to help someone, give them thoughtful advice, console them when they were down on their luck, and yet for some reason they would not listen to you? They came to you for help, but when you gave it, they simply didn't want to go in that direction. You might have thought them to be **stubborn**, willful, unwilling to recognize what might be best for them.

In part, this is what God felt when His children simply wouldn't heed His counsel. They kept going their own way, getting into trouble, crying about their difficulties, and wondering why God didn't bail them out. The fact is that God wanted to bail them out, but they were always more interested in doing something else.

What about you? Does any of this resonate with you? As human beings, we often go to God, begging for His help, seeking His guidance, and striving to be more like Him. However, when His advice is not what we wanted to hear, we try again to go on our own, hoping we might find a way around the difficulty and not have to do the work God requires of us. We fail, though, because what God wants are soft hearts, not stubborn hearts. God wants children who will listen for His voice and then carry out the plans that He has. He wants us to come to Him and let Him help us, but unfortunately, we often turn the other way and get ourselves into deeper and deeper despair. It's disheartening for both of us. God grieves that we won't let Him help. We grieve because we don't want to do what God suggests.

If you're dealing with a stubborn heart, then stop everything right now, and go sit at the feet of Jesus. He will remind you who you are and soften your heart.

*Lord, I know that I can be **stubborn** and I'm so sorry. I regret it*
*every time when I don't listen to You. Please forgive me and help me*
*to do better. Amen.*

# QUIET

*Make it your goal to live a **quiet** life, minding your own business and
working with your hands, just as we instructed you before. Then people
who are not believers will respect the way you live, and you will not need to
depend on others.*                    1 Thessalonians 4:11–12 NLT

If we had a choice, many of us would opt for a *Little House on the Prairie*
kind of life, the one where we take care of most of our own needs, help our
neighbors as we can, and live **quiet**, considerate lives. As crowded and vio-
lent as the world can feel these days, that kind of life seems like a fantasy
never to be created again. Our personal sense of the "good old days" feels
like a standard we can somehow never reach.

Wherever we live, though, we have an option for minding our own
business and letting our neighbors know we're there for them, without
being busybodies. We can be kind and generous, and let the rest of the
world do whatever it is going to do because just adding to the noise of
the world simply makes no sense. Though our sense of privacy has been
eroded by social media, we can still strive to live meaningful, quiet, calm,
and peaceful lives.

Perhaps the benefits of a quiet life have eluded you. Maybe the noise of
the city or the demands of your job are appealing and feed your spirit. The
fact is that you can do all the things you do and still live a quiet, gentle,
humble, mind-your-own-business life. You don't have enough hours in a
day to get too involved with the little things that might be going on in the
neighborhood, or the daily office gossip that never seems to grind to a
halt. Using your time wisely and well means that you focus on the work of
your hands in ways that bring peace to your soul. Now settle in with some
tea and a good book.

*Lord, thank You for the **quiet** times, the ones that are not overblown
with the news headlines or the family issues of the moment. Help me
to rest in Your hands always. Amen.*

# SORROW

*See what this godly **sorrow** has produced in you: what earnestness, what eagerness to clear yourselves, what indignation, what alarm, what longing, what concern, what readiness to see justice done.*

2 Corinthians 7:11 NIV

You experience many **sorrows** as you go through life. It is part of the journey and no one escapes grief. The Scripture writer is reminding you here about "godly" sorrow. This is the sorrow that you feel because you know you cannot save yourself. You know the measure of your own sins and you recognize that, without Jesus and God's saving grace, you would have no hope. The positive side of taking a firm look at "godly" sorrow is that it may have incredible results in the choices you make from that moment on.

When you recognize what God has done for you and how you could best serve Him, it causes you to feel eager, earnest, steadfast, and ready to do His bidding. You're free of the weight of your sorrow and ready to move back to joy. Why?

You have opened your heart and your soul. You see the error of your ways and you long to do better. You want to surrender every concern, every stubborn thought or action, and ask God to renew your spirit. You want His justice to be done in your own life, so that you can recognize true justice in the world.

Give thanks when your heart grieves over your own wrongdoing, because it means you're ready to become more of what God designed you to be and you can hardly wait to get started. Godly sorrow is a gift to your heart, and it will serve you well.

*Lord, thank You for giving me a sense of the **sorrow** that my heart feels over each moment that I've disappointed You. Help me to surrender my thoughts and actions to You. Amen.*

# REASON

*"Come now, and let us **reason** together," says the Lord. "Though your sins are like scarlet, They shall be as white as snow."*　　　Isaiah 1:18 NKJV

Perhaps one of our best qualities as human beings is the one that allows us to be people who can **reason**. That means we're willing to hear both sides of a debate. We're aware there could be alternate views to the ones we hold. We want truth and justice to prevail, and we want to know that we have been cooperative in the process.

This Scripture from Isaiah is one of the most loving comments in the Bible. It comes straight from God's heart to yours. It suggests that the Creator of the Universe, the One who designed and delivered every shred of what we see around us, is asking for a chance to come together and discuss matters of concern. God is giving us an opportunity to share our humble opinions, a chance to hear Him out on His direction and guidance and then together come up with the solutions. He says that we can "reason" it out. We can figure it out together.

We know how sinful we are. We know that God made us and that He has the final say. Yet He presents us with this idea that we could simply share our concerns and talk them out, much like He did with the Patriarchs and with the prophets of old.

If you haven't considered this idea before, then take some time today and sit down one to one with your Creator. Bring your concerns to Him. Listen for His responses and see if you can work out all that troubles you in the most loving way possible, heart to heart and hand in hand. You have every reason to trust in Him.

*Lord, thank You for being willing to **reason** with me on things I may not understand fully. I seek Your guidance and wisdom for all that I do. Amen.*

# FUTURE

*"I have good plans for you, not plans to hurt you. I will give you hope and a good future. Then you will call my name. You will come to me and pray to me, and I will listen to you."* Jeremiah 29:11–12 NCV

This Scripture from Jeremiah is one of our favorite promises from God. It reminds us that whatever is going on around us, and whatever difficulties we may be dealing with, God may have other plans. God wants better things for us than we want for ourselves. He wants us to have a bright future, and He gives us a chance every morning to start again because He wipes the slate clean before we even rise from our slumbers.

When you begin the day with a sense of hope and a realization that you are not tackling the world all by yourself, and you're not stuck in yesterday, your future looks brighter. You don't have to bear all the burdens. You can cast some of those troubles off, because there are no plans to hurt you today. In fact, this is your day to shine and to do incredible things. Your future looks brighter and brighter by the minute.

If you've let the weight of the world depress your spirit, it's time to change course. Move closer to your Creator and listen for His voice. He's trying to reach out to you and to give you a sense of peace. He wants to deliver on the promises He has just for you, and all He needs is for you to turn to Him and ask for His help.

You don't know where you'll be five years from now. You don't know what you'll be doing tomorrow. You don't have to know, though, because God does, and if you stay close to Him, He will deliver on His promise to give you hope and a bright future. You can call on His name right now, because He's listening.

*Lord, thank You for paving the way for me to have a bright future. Help me to lean on You every step of the way so that I can receive Your promises. Amen.*

# NUMBER

*Teach us to **number** our days, that we may gain a heart of wisdom.*
                                                    Psalm 90:12 NIV

We assign a **number** to nearly everything. We have a street number and a phone number and a specific date to celebrate a birthday. We love to count things and so we continually look for numbers to help us track our progress. Our bank account has a number. At birth, we are assigned a social security number. So why have we set things up this way, only to forget one of the most significant numbers ever?

The psalmist reminds us that we are not going to live forever. We need to number our days, that is, be aware of our mortality, so that we live each day wisely and well. When we do, our hearts are open to God's leading. Our hands are prepared to work at the things He has called us to do. We have purpose and focus because we know we're finite and we don't have forever to get the job done.

Realizing that we are not in control of our own timing, that we have no idea whether we can be on the planet for five years or five minutes, means that we must be more intentional about the things we do each day. We must pick up the phone and connect with an old friend that we've been missing. We must be certain we tell the people we love how much they mean to us. We must get the jobs done that we know are ours to do.

We have a specified number of days and only God knows what they are. The upside of this is it gives you a desire to listen more intently for His voice, so that you can complete your mission here on planet Earth in a joyful and positive way. When you go home, then, He can embrace you and say as you come in His door, "Well done, my good and faithful servant." After all, for God, you are His Number One!

*Lord, thank You for teaching us to **number** our days so that we will do all we can to make each one count for the good of Your kingdom. Amen.*

# PLANS

*People may make **plans** in their minds, but the Lord decides what they will do.*                                        Proverbs 16:9 NCV

Some of us are planners. We get out our lists and we write down every nuance of what needs to be accomplished, by whom, and when. We are proud of the **plans** because we just know that putting everything in order means we'll get them done. It's a great theory!

Some of us fly by the seat of our pants and just hope for the best. We might realize that a project is due and we should be mapping out a plan for its execution, but other things get in the way and take priority so we just apply it to our chaos theory for how things work.

When your plans go awry, or you wonder why others are not sticking to your game plan, it can get frustrating. After all, you have thought this thing out and you know what works and so this plan is perfect.

How many times have you noticed that your plans, your life, your ideas, have not come to the place you thought they would? Perhaps you're missing a key part of the planning.

An idea may start with you, but if it's a God idea, then He will be the One to work it out. Begin your idea with God and try this. Don't tell Him the plan. Ask Him what the plan should be. Sit quietly and listen for His voice. When you seek His direction before you even take step one, you are almost assured success. God decides what to do, when to do it, and creates the plan. You're just His hands and feet to get it done. Planning takes a guide and there's no one better to guide you than your Creator.

*Lord, thank You for the **plans** that You have for my life. Help me to know what You would have me do, every step of the way. Amen.*

# ANGELS

*Are not all **angels** ministering spirits sent to serve those who will inherit salvation?*
Hebrews 1:14 NIV

It's good for us to consider the work of **angels** because they are great examples of what it means to serve God. Angels do God's bidding. They don't question His direction or His commands. They don't set aside time for God a few minutes each day and then go about their personal business. They serve the One who created them, and at His bidding, they serve human beings.

Often, when an angel appears in the Bible, the first thing that is said is something like, "Fear not!" Perhaps that message is relayed first because of the magnificent power and size and bearing of angels. They are God's messengers, and they come directly from the seat of Heaven.

Perhaps what we could learn from angels, then, is that we, too, could serve God with our whole heart, soul, and mind. We could be so intent on doing His bidding that others would stand back and let us pass through, knowing we were on a mission that would absolutely be accomplished. Perhaps, too, we could understand that we don't have to question every command of God, but we simply have to carry it out so that His purposes are fulfilled here on Earth.

We get to be a little bit of an angel when we serve each other with love. We can experience the desire of angels to accomplish the tasks we've been given each time we seek to honestly and intently hear God's voice and do His bidding.

Let us learn from the work of angels what it means to be a messenger, a ministering spirit that works for God with a devoted and loving heart. You can be sure that someone needs you to be a little bit of an angel.

*Lord, thank You for putting **angels** in our midst at times when we need their messages and their help. Bless the work of angels everywhere today. Amen.*

# SO

*For God so loved the world that he gave his one and only Son, that whoever believes in him shall not perish but have eternal life.*       John 3:16 NIV

"God **so** loved" is a powerful phrase. It doesn't simply say that God loved, or that God was working on a way to love, or that God was somewhat making an effort to love; it adds that little word "so" and gives it great emphasis and power. When we consider something to be so helpful or so wonderful or so amazing, we're adding to the impact of what that helpful or amazing thing was all about. "So" is a tiny word that packs a lot of gusto.

God so loved the world—that means you and your neighbor and the people in every town and country across the planet. He loved everything and everyone He made. He loved them so much that He did not want one of them to be lost and so He chose to provide a way back to Himself. He provided His Only Son, the one He loved so much, that He knew the plan could not fail.

Consider what it means to you when you tell someone, "I love you so much!" It means that you can't even express your love for them because you can't measure the height, or the depth, or the breadth of what you feel. It means that they are more important to you than anything you can imagine.

God so loved you. When you think about the unconditional love that God has for you, a love that goes deeper than anything you have ever experienced, you start to see the incredible gift of Calvary. You understand a little more clearly that God loved you, not just a little, not just somewhat, but so much, He sent you the gift of His Son.

*Lord, thank You for Your big love for me. I love You so much and I want to do my best every day to serve You and bless the work of Your kingdom. Amen.*

# BEYOND

*This command I give you today is not too hard for you; it is not **beyond** what you can do.*                    Deuteronomy 30:11 NCV

Sometimes when you start something new, it can feel like it's **beyond** your ability to do it. After all, you must stretch a bit farther than you've ever had to stretch before. Simply having to work harder to achieve a goal, though, doesn't mean it's beyond your grasp. In fact, if God calls you to do something, you might step back from it and imagine that you aren't equipped to handle it. The reason you feel that way is because you've either never done it before or you tried that once and it just didn't work.

We're quick to determine our limitations. But we have an unlimited God, and He doesn't look at us with the same lens that we look at ourselves. He sees our potential. He sees what we can do if we just had a little nudge, or a little training, or we simply just gave it a solid try. He sees us as having more power than we ever recognize we have.

Today, imagine what you could do if you went beyond your usual limits. What if you tried even harder to exercise, or to write that book you've always wanted to write? What if you stopped telling yourself that you can't do it and looked deeper within yourself to see what God already knows? You can do it! It is not beyond your ability or your physical strength. It's totally within your reach.

Whatever it is that you have set as just beyond your ability to achieve, take another look and listen to what God would say to you. He knows you and He knows you can do it!

*Lord, I know that I often start new things with the idea that it might be **beyond** me to accomplish them. Help me to reach up to You and seek Your face and Your encouragement when I think I've reached my limit. Amen.*

239

# BETTER

*And loving him with all passion and intelligence and energy, and loving others as well as you love yourself. Why, that's better than all offerings and sacrifices put together!* Mark 12:32–33 MSG

You make comparisons. You do it many times a day without even thinking. If you take one route to work, it's **better** and faster than if you take another. If you have the egg whites for breakfast, that's better than having the whole egg. You know that some things are simply better for you than other things.

In this gospel message, you're being given another opportunity to compare something that is good to something that is even better. We're talking about your energy and your passion and your motivation to love God and to take that love and use it in gentle and kind ways to serve others. The writer tells you that your zeal, your devotion, your intentional service to God are even better things than your volunteer work and the check you put into the collection plate on Sunday morning. Your dedication to learning more about God so that you can love Him better is literally one of the best things you can do for yourself.

Yes, it's good for you to tithe or give from your financial resources. It's good because it shapes your heart and sets your priorities. You may do those things out of obligation or because it's your habit, but you may not necessarily put your heart into it. That kind of giving doesn't ask you to show up to deliver your offering. Stepping into the world heart first, though, where you personally deliver your help, your compassion, and your empathy for others, is simply a better thing. Everything you do for the good of others reflects your love for God and even for yourself. So do the good things, but as often as possible, choose to do the better things. Show up in person and your heart will enjoy the journey from doing good to doing better to truly doing your best!

*Lord, I am learning more about You all the time. Help me to do those things that **better** serve You and the people I love. Amen.*

# INSIDE

*So we do not give up. Our physical body is becoming older and weaker, but our spirit **inside** us is made new every day.* 2 Corinthians 4:16 NCV

You may not think about it very often, but no matter what is happening to your physical body on the outside, your spiritual body on the **inside** is celebrating with youthful vigor. Your spirit is made new every morning and so you are filled up and over again with the power and energy of God. As soon as you step out of bed, you're energized by that amazing Spirit to face the day.

All you have to do is acknowledge the Spirit of God within you, seek God's guidance for your daily life, and live in a way that lets His light shine before others. If you're doing those things on a regular basis, you can be sure that Jesus is alive and well inside the temple of your body. He came in that day you asked Him to come into your heart and He's been there ever since.

Sometimes you need a reminder, though. You need to put a spotlight on that section of your body that holds your heart. Once you have the light on, pay attention to the things you've allowed to live in your heart. If you've crowded out that space with anxiety or anger or negative thinking, you might want to tidy things up. You might want to ask Jesus to become bigger so that you can have more of His grace and love and mercy, and less noise from those areas you've let in without even meaning to do so.

Perhaps a little daily peek inside your heart and a little chat with your Savior a few times a day will help you remember that He is always there giving you nourishment and renewing you heart and soul. Now that's worthy of praise and thanks.

*Lord, thank You for letting me know that You're living **inside** my heart. Help me always to stay totally connected to You. Amen.*

# SLOW

*The Lord is not **slow** in doing what he promised—the way some people understand slowness. But God is being patient with you.*

2 Peter 3:9 NCV

When you make a promise, or someone makes a promise to you, it sets a timeline in motion. You anticipate the promise being fulfilled and you try to wait patiently for it to happen. You know that it's important for the promise to be kept, but the process, the waiting, can seem deliberately **slow**, as though even time was against you.

If you're waiting for God to deliver on a promise to you, and you're wondering why it's taking so long, it might be good to take a little inventory about what's going on in your life that might inspire the delay. Perhaps God is patiently waiting for you to act on a portion of the promise. You may have a part to play in the way the prayer is answered because you asked God to give you time to work on it. Maybe He knows that when you receive His answer to your prayer, it will mean changes you're not quite ready to handle. He is giving you more time to receive His gifts.

Being slow, unhurried, tardy, or leisurely may cause you to wonder what to do next. Perhaps the best thing to do is seek God and ask what is causing the delay. When you do that, you might also ask what you can do to move things forward. One thing is sure. God keeps His promises and He will remember you when the time is right. Find comfort in His patience. As they say, the wheels of progress grind slowly. Keep praying!

*Lord, thank You for helping me to wait until You can deliver on Your promises. Even though it feels **slow** to me, I will trust that Your timing is perfect. Amen.*

# CLOSE

*This is the account of Noah and his family. Noah was a righteous man, the only blameless person living on earth at the time, and he walked in **close** fellowship with God.*

Genesis 6:9 NLT

You have a variety of relationships in your life. Some of them are important, but not particularly **close**. Some of them are long-distance friendships that are always there in the background should you have a chance to meet again. Some are simply people you say hello to on the way out of your building as you go to work, or they are people at church with whom you have a nodding acquaintance. It's safe to say you could put most of your relationships on a scale of close or not close and know exactly where they are.

So what about your relationship with God? How would you measure your level of closeness? Does it vary with your mood or the day of the week? Does it feel inclusive so that the two of you are very comfortable together, sharing the ups and downs of life every day?

The reference to Noah and his relationship with God is helpful because we can see that there was something very special going on between them. They had fellowship. They were close. They knew each other very well, and because of that, Noah knew what God expected of him. He knew what it meant to do the right thing, so he could be blameless before God. It's a picture of the relationship with God that most of us would envy.

You can have that kind of relationship as well. You can have intimate fellowship with God anytime you choose. He's ready to walk with you. He chooses to be close to you. He waits for you to invite Him into every aspect of your life.

*Lord, thank You for drawing me **close** to You and helping me to share in the gift of Your Presence day by day. I thank You for all the time we spend together. Amen.*

# REALITY

*My purpose in writing is simply this: that you who believe in God's Son will know beyond the shadow of a doubt that you have eternal life, the **reality** and not the illusion. And how bold and free we then become in his presence, freely asking according to his will, sure that he's listening.*

1 John 5:14–15 MSG

You may be a fan of **reality** TV. You know that stuff is neither real nor TV in the sense of having well-thought-out screenwriting. Culturally, we may be moving farther from reality than ever with our social media life on the Internet, where Photoshopped images appear on Instagram, or hyped-up contenders play on dating sites. It's a virtual reality world and we can get caught in its snare and deceived by its charms.

We used to believe that it was helpful for us to face reality. When we asked for God's help, it was in the spirit of truth, the spirit of trust that guided us. Apparently, there were questions from the masses in the days following Jesus' resurrection, where some were uncertain if eternal life was something they could truly believe in. They wanted to know if it was an illusion, or simply a hope, but not really a truth.

The writer of this Scripture answers by saying that eternal life not only is a reality, but is empowering. It is the reason that people are free to seek God's help, get His advice, and stand in His Presence. The reality is that God sees them and hears them and listens to their concerns. This is something that would hold up in a court of law because it goes beyond a shadow of a doubt. It's true; it's genuine and certain. They can count on this reality.

It's not always easy to know what is real and what isn't in a world where camera angles can manipulate the truth. All you must know, though, is that from any angle shining a light on eternal life, you can trust your eyes. It's all real.

*Lord, thank You for helping us know that You are certain and trustworthy and that eternal life is our **reality** when we believe in You. Amen.*

# NEWS

*The angel said to him, "I am Gabriel. I stand in the presence of God, and I have been sent to speak to you and to tell you this good **news**."*

Luke 1:19 NIV

These days it's difficult to put the two words "good" and "**news**" side by side. Good news doesn't seem to stream through the numerous devices we have at our disposal.

But in biblical times and still today, God tries to get us to hear the good news. He wants us never to forget that despite the mess the world gets itself into, He is still watching everything. He is still in control. Perhaps simply trusting that statement helps us to know that we can indeed receive good news into our hearts.

We can also spread the word. We can choose to play the angel and be people who are sent out to speak with others about the good news of God. We can be an ambassador of God's goodwill, His steadfast love, and His enduring kindness to human beings. We can go before God in our prayer time and in our study of His word and stand close to Him, seeking His guidance on how to create balance in the world; how to give people the good news.

You have a lot of things to do today, and each one is important, but see if you can find a moment to offer good news to someone. Extend a helping hand, offer a prayer, or make a connection. The world all around you is desperately waiting for something better; they are waiting for good news.

*Lord, help me to share Your good **news** in ways that will inspire others to be more aware of Your presence and Your mercy. Amen.*

# ALSO

*Future generations will **also** serve him. Our children will hear about the wonders of the Lord. His righteous acts will be told to those yet unborn. They will hear about everything he has done.* Psalm 22:30–31 NLT

**Also** is one of those nice words that means "you're included." It means you're not alone because you were expected and you're part of the story. When the psalmist talked about telling children about the things God has done, he was creating a legacy, because the children would then tell their own children somewhere down the road. Each generation would have a chance to speak of the wonders of the Lord. He didn't want them to think that God's wonders were only for that present moment.

As you look at your life and the story that you want to tell, there are probably parts of it that you would love to share with your children, your grandchildren, and perhaps generations after that. You'd like to leave a legacy. You'd like to know that your work and your life and the things you did would be remembered.

God has given you the opportunity to share His story with the people you love. He wants you to tell the story because He knows it does your heart good every time you share it. He also knows that with every telling of the story, it becomes more embedded in your heart and mind, and it is almost certain then that you will tell it to those who are near and dear to you.

Future generations will, likewise, share the stories that you have told about the wonders of the Lord. When you retell your stories, God blesses you over again, because He blesses your children also.

*Lord, thank You for blessing me, and **also** blessing those I love. Thank You for including each of us in Your plans and wonders. Amen.*

# TREASURE

*But store up for yourselves treasures in heaven, where moths and vermin do not destroy, and where thieves do not break in and steal. For where your **treasure** is, there your heart will be also.* Matthew 6:20–21 NIV

Most of us have a fondness for the things we select for our home, or for certain things we wear, but would we define those things as ones we **treasure**? What are the things that you would most regret if thieves took them from you?

The question posed here in Matthew is a good one because Jesus wants us to think about this matter very clearly. He wants us to differentiate between the things that we like and enjoy, and the things that truly mean something to our hearts. Things we appreciate may vary, but we probably only have a few real treasures, especially the kind that nothing can destroy.

God thinks of you as a treasure. You have accepted His love and His guidance. You come to Him when you're in trouble or have a specific need for direction. You come to Him when you don't know where else to turn. That kind of relationship is important and meaningful. It is a treasure.

Your treasures make your eyes sparkle when you talk about them. You may discover that your face softens and your heart races. Your treasures are about love and ideals and possibilities and about your reverence for your Father in Heaven. These treasures can never slip out of your hand, and no one can steal them from you. You know for a fact that where your treasure is, your heart follows. That's why God treasures you. You're always in His heart.

*Lord, I **treasure** our relationship and all that You do to shine a light on my life and help me make wise choices. Thank You for Your amazing love. Amen.*

# FAVOR

*For his anger lasts only a moment, but his **favor** lasts a lifetime; weeping may stay for the night, but rejoicing comes in the morning.*

Psalm 30:5 NIV

One of the most precious things about God is that He is willing to turn things around. He doesn't want us to hang our heads in shame and slink away, unsure how we can ever again please Him. He disciplines us as a loving Father, and then when we seek forgiveness, He offers us a way back to Himself. He lets us live in His grace and in His **favor**. His favor lasts a lifetime, your lifetime. It will never run out as long as you stay close to Him and seek His help when you regret your choices.

As human beings, we're always seeking affirmation and support and favor from our families or the people we work with. We hope that we can do the right things and that when we do, we'll be rewarded for our efforts. We hope that somehow, despite our behavior or the ways we disappoint each other, we can rise to the top again. We hope for that, and though we may get that result, it only truly happens with God. He may be angry with us, but He won't stay angry. He may be disappointed in our actions, but He won't keep us far from Him. He sees us weeping for the wrongs we do, and wraps His arms around us once again. That's what it means to live in His favor.

Think of the people in your midst who hope for a sign of your favor today. Open your heart to them and give them an opportunity to shine their own light and show the better sides of themselves. When you expect the best from others, you help them desire to be the best as well. Perhaps that's what God does. Perhaps He looks at us and, with each new morning, gives us a chance to rejoice in Him and do a better job. Why? Because we live in His favor.

*Lord, thank You for Your continual forgiveness. I pray that I may live my life in Your grace and **favor**. Amen.*

# FACE

*For now we see only a reflection as in a mirror; then we shall see face to face.*
*Now I know in part; then I shall know fully, even as I am fully known.*

1 Corinthians 13:12 NIV

One of the striking things about technology is that it opens up the world we communicate with from behind a screen and diminishes the world we communicate with **face** to face. We become increasingly more comfortable "talking" to others when we don't actually see them, and perhaps have never met them. For some people, if they cannot text or e-mail or post an Instagram, they can't communicate. They are not comfortable with one-on-one conversation.

As a person of prayer, you probably understand you can't see God's face, so coming before Him and imagining Him, or sensing His Presence, is the way He prefers to interact with you for now. Fortunately, He can see you. He can see your amazing face and the joy you express or the sadness you feel. He can shine His face upon you and let you know that He's there, and even more than that, He can see right through you, right through to your heart. He knows you well, so you don't have trouble talking with each other.

Your face reflects what is going on inside your heart and your head. Your face tells a story that others may either read well or misinterpret, depending on how willing you are to share what they see reflected there. You can create better communications, more intimate opportunities to be understood, if you are willing to put yourself out there and spend a little time with others, face to face. Conversation does not have to be a lost art. It's one that you can bring back into the heart of your life each day. Simply put down the device and get together one to one, and face to face. It will make your day!

*Lord, I thank You that I can come into Your Presence and that*
*someday we'll meet face to face. Remind me to connect more often*
*one to one with people I love. Amen.*

# RUBIES

*It is hard to find a good wife, because she is worth more than **rubies**.*
*Her husband trusts her completely. With her, he has everything he needs.*

Proverbs 31:10–11 NCV

**Rubies** are magnificent gemstones. They come in deep reds and incredible colors and are extremely valuable. Calling someone a diamond or a ruby is saying they are beautiful and special.

The Proverbs 31 woman is remarkable in the eyes of her husband. She is a woman beyond measure, someone he cannot imagine living without. She's precious in his sight and he can't say enough good things about her. It's a love relationship made in Heaven. She sets a standard that most women would be proud to uphold even in lesser measures.

The beauty of being a ruby, though, is that you have every reason to shine. You know that you are loved and trusted. You know that the work of your hands is a blessing to those around you. You know that you have set a high bar for your home and your work, which you achieve by staying connected to God. You know that because no matter how dear you are to others, you need God's help to be a treasure. You need Him to keep you strong and polished, to guide your steps and give you courage.

You are a ruby who can shine for Him every day simply by being your loving and beautiful self. With you around, others have a remarkable friend or an amazing example of what it means to be a person after God's own heart. You are such a gem!

*Lord, thank You for the gift of Your presence. Let my heart be filled with the **rubies** of Your love so I can shine Your light for others. Amen.*

# WATER

*Jesus answered, "Everyone who drinks this water will be thirsty again, but whoever drinks the water I give will never be thirsty. The water I give will become a spring of water gushing up inside that person, giving eternal life."*

John 4:13–14 NCV

**Water** is a necessity for life. Many people around the world suffer from a lack of clean drinking water. Many are thirsty. Some are doing all they can to alleviate these problems and provide for those in need. Here in John, Jesus is suggesting that the water we drink and use each day on a physical level can only have a short-term effect. It is good only for a certain point in time. He wants us to come to Him, then, so we can have Living Water, the kind that is effective all the way through eternity...

Jesus is the fountain, the Source of Living Water. He not only refreshes your spirit and nourishes your soul, but offers the kind of water that will cause you never to thirst again. How is that possible? It's possible because thirst means we lack something vital to being able to live well. Thirst means we're dehydrated and we can't function well physically and mentally. Thirst means that we can hardly think about anything but ourselves because our needs are so great. Thirst means we feel deprived of the necessities of life. We don't want to be thirsty; we need water.

If you haven't already done so, stop everything and simply go to the well. Go to Jesus and offer Him your heart. Put your life before Him and lower it into the well, and when you raise it again, you will discover that He has met you right there and is ready to shower you with blessing, to fill you with refreshing joy and all that you need to live now and evermore. Once you taste this Living Water, you will never be thirsty again. You will have all that you need gushing up inside you with every thought and prayer.

*Lord, thank You for giving me Your Living Water. It refreshes me and causes me to want to refresh others in any way that I can. Amen.*

# ENTER

*Now whatever city or town you **enter**, inquire who in it is worthy, and
stay there till you go out. And when you go into a household, greet it. If the
household is worthy, let your peace come upon it. But if it is not worthy, let
your peace return to you.*                              Matthew 10:10–13 NKJV

Have you ever known anyone who simply fills your house with a sense of
peace as soon as they **enter** through your door? There's something that is
hard to explain about the presence of the Lord that radiates from their
face even if they don't say a word about it. They enter your space, your
office, your home, and suddenly there is gentle light. For what appears to
be no reason at all, you feel more at ease, more at peace.

As the disciples walked around the towns and villages and visited with
people, Jesus gave them an example to heed. He suggested that when they
were welcomed and when they detected that His Spirit was being accepted
by people they stayed with or visited, they could give a gift to those people. They could give them a kind of peace that was rare, a kind that they
seldom experienced. Jesus said that the kind of peace He gives is unlike
any other; it is precious and beyond human understanding.

Test yourself a bit today. Wherever you walk, imagine that you are wear-
ing the full armor of God, the light of His Spirit, and the peace that only
Jesus can provide. As you go about your business, share your joy and your
kindness. See if you can recognize the people who draw closer to your light
versus the ones who prefer that you stay away. It could make your whole
day more interesting. Share the peace with those who allow you to enter
their space with love.

*Lord, thank You for being the one to **enter** my heart and for granting
me Your peace and love. Amen.*

# CAST

*Humble yourselves, therefore, under God's mighty hand, that he may lift you up in due time. **Cast** all your anxiety on him because he cares for you.*

1 Peter 5:6–7 NIV

**Cast**, in this Scripture, means to throw, or to send away, to get rid of. You want to send your cares and worries as far away from you as you can. You want to scrape them off, and not have to deal with them. How do you get to do that?

The first thing you can do is simply stop trying so hard to be the one who handles everything. You're not alone. You're not even the one who is expected to come up with all the solutions or relieve all the problems. You have to remember that as brilliant and helpful and loving as you are, that you can't take care of all these concerns. What that means, then, is that you have to step aside from being the superhero and realize that it's not your job. Lay down the burdens. Go to Jesus, Who is better able to handle them. Bow down with your heart and mind and body before God and seek His Divine presence, seek His help.

Once you've done that, once you've recognized that only God can carry the weight of your concerns, then you have a starting point. You can stop trembling. You put the burdens at the cross, cast them away from yourself, and then let Him come and lift you up. Let Him help you lighten the load. Do you have to keep a few worries just so you don't overburden Him? *No!* You don't have one misery, one complaint, one worry that He doesn't already know about. All you have to do is give them up. Put them in His hand because He cares so much for you that it breaks His heart to see you suffer so. Cast away your worries and you'll feel better instantly.

*Lord, thank You for allowing me to **cast** my concerns on You. Grant me wisdom and courage to deal with things according to Your mercy. Amen.*

# WRONG

*Make sure that nobody pays back **wrong** for wrong, but always strive to do what is good for each other and for everyone else.*

1 Thessalonians 5:15 NIV

You've been learning about right and **wrong** your whole life. When you were young, you were taught to share and play nice. You may have been scolded or rewarded for your actions. Sometimes, you knew something was wrong, but you did it anyway. Other times, you were innocent of the wrongdoing, but had to suffer the consequences, as when the teacher punished the whole class for something one person did wrong.

As an adult, you're still learning right and wrong. You have to choose what it means to you to do the right thing. Sometimes there really aren't any guidebooks to help you. You simply have to trust your heart and take your choice to God.

This Scripture asks you to deal with the consequences when someone else does something that feels wrong to you. What do you do when you're suffering over an incident, but it doesn't appear the other person feels any remorse for their actions? The answer is that you leave it to God. You let Him weigh the situation and the circumstances and decide on the necessary consequences. He will take care of the matter. You can go on with your life, helping others, being kind, and doing the things that feel good and right.

The beauty of moving on is that you don't have to waste time or energy or worry or anger or any other emotion on that problem. You're free to live again and enjoy the day. Let God take care of those that do wrong. He doesn't need your help.

*Lord, I know that I have done **wrong** things more often than I can count and I'm so sorry for each one. Help me to make it a priority to do what is right in Your eyes every day. Amen.*

# RIGHT

*Yet to all who did receive him, to those who believed in his name, he gave the* **right** *to become children of God—children born not of natural descent, nor of human decision or a husband's will, but born of God.*

John 1:12–13 NIV

A backstage pass gives you the **right** to meet with the entertainers you just saw in a show. Citizenship in the United States gives you the right to vote. Turning sixteen in some states gives you the right to apply for a driver's license. You've been dealing with "rights" for a long time.

The day you signed up to follow Jesus, God gave you some special rights as well. He gave you the right to call Him Daddy or Father. He gave you an opportunity to be in His will. He gave you the right to be called His child. Of all the rights you could ever attain, this one is the treasure, the ticket to everlasting happiness.

It's interesting that when you get arrested for doing something wrong, they often read you your "rights." You are told what your rights are because suddenly they seem limited; there are only a few things you can do in that situation. This is just the opposite of what God does. When He starts reading you your rights, even though you've done a multitude of wrong things, He starts widening your possibilities. He starts telling you that from now on you have free access to the One who created the universe. You have the right to call on His name anytime at all. You don't get just one call; you get a multitude of calls. You get unlimited opportunities to stand in His Presence, and He welcomes you with open arms.

Your natural parents call you their own for a lifetime. Your Heavenly parent calls you His own for eternity. That gives you the right to smile and be glad in your faith.

*Lord, thank You for giving me the* **right** *to be with You. Help me to honor all that You've done for me with the work I do and the people I meet. Amen.*

# HANDS

*Into your **hands** I commit my spirit; deliver me, Lord, my faithful God.*

Psalm 31:5 NIV

These words that Jesus spoke from the cross came from what we know as the Psalms. Like David before Him, Jesus knew that His life and His Spirit were safe in God's **hands**. Perhaps it would be helpful for us to utter something similar in the context of our own lives:

Into Your hands I commit my life.
Into Your hands I commit my spirit.
Into Your hands I commit my work.
Into Your hands I commit my family.
Into Your hands I commit my fears.
Into Your hands I commit my health.
Into Your hands I commit my finances.
Into Your hands I commit my children.

You can continue the list however it suits you, but if you do this and give over the concerns of the day to the Lord, who protects you and keeps you safe because He is faithful, you will have a brighter day.

Your life, your spirit, your work, and your family are matters of great concern to your loving Heavenly Father. He wants incredible things for you, and He can help you the most when you are willing to surrender everything that matters to you and place your concerns and priorities in His hands.

*Lord, I commit my life into Your **hands**, and I thank You for knowing me and loving me so well. Watch over each person I love today. I put each one in Your amazing hands. Amen.*

# WIDE

*I am the Lord your God who brought you up out of Egypt.*
*Open wide your mouth and I will fill it.* Psalm 81:10 NIV

It's hard to read this little love note from God without thinking of a mother bird, filling the mouths of her little babies as they open their beaks as wide as they can. She's already done the work of foraging for tasty treats and has the food ready to give them. All they have to do is open their mouths nice and wide.

How often does God do that very thing for us? How often does He have all the pieces together that will sustain our lives or nourish our spirits, only to have us not bother to look up? We focus on our worries and our concerns, keeping our heads down, and we miss the opportunity. If we focused instead on opening our mouths with praise, we might be filled to overflowing, and we might discover we have more than we even need because He is so generous.

Think of how generous you like to be with your own children. You provide for their welfare as they are growing up and you look for ways to help them even as they become adults. You want them to have everything they need. Since your love is a mere reflection of the kind of love God has for you, imagine what He wants to provide for you today. All you have to do is show up, sing His praise, open your heart and your mouth and your eyes and your ears, and you will find Him ready and waiting to fill you with delight.

Wherever you happen to be today, look for those moments when you can thank God for being so close to you that He's ready at any moment to feed and nourish your body, mind, and spirit. He wants more for you than you want for yourself, so just open your mouth wide.

*Lord, thank You for being willing to feed and nourish me. I will open my mouth wide to sing Your praise and to be filled up and over with You. Amen.*

257

# WITHOUT

*Without wood a fire goes out; without a gossip a quarrel dies down.*
*As charcoal to embers and as wood to fire, so is a quarrelsome person for*
  *kindling strife.*                                    Proverbs 26:20–21 NIV

There are a lot of things you'd be happy to do **without**. You could do without any opportunity to quarrel with people in your household or your neighborhood. You could do without somebody spreading unhealthy gossip about you or the people you love. You could do without those negative things that add fuel to the fires of discontent. God knows you do better without any of those things.

Proverbs 26 remarks on the things you are happy to do without because, despite your interest in staying away from them, they happen. You meet friends after church and they want to share a story about one of the people in the choir. As soon as you know it's all gossip, you are instantly faced with a choice. Do you become part of the fuel that fans the flame and keeps the rumor burning brightly, or do you step aside from the group and leave them to create their own embers?

Gossipy people show up in churches, in neighborhoods, and in workplaces. Sharing other people's tragedies or secrets makes the teller feel more interesting or powerful. The problem with listening to these stories, though, is you have to deal with information that may or may not be true. You become part of the process that passes on the strife. You don't want to be kindling; you want to be kindly. You want your heart to choose the best way to handle those heated conversations. Leave them alone and they will simply burn out. God has better things for you to do with your time and energy.

*Lord, I can do **without** the gossip and the arguments that some people love to bring to conversations. Let me always find it better to only tell stories when they are mine to share. Amen.*

# PORTION

*Whom have I in heaven but you? And earth has nothing I desire besides you. My flesh and my heart may fail, but God is the strength of my heart and my **portion** forever.*                              Psalm 73:25–27 NIV

**Portion** is a great word because it reminds you that no matter what your expectations might be in life, you truly are only meant to have a piece of the pie, an allotment, a portion. The thing to consider, then, is how you will determine when you have enough, when you've received your fair portion of all that is possible.

Some of the struggles in the world center around a misunderstanding of what it means to have a fair share. Some people assume they deserve more than others. Their lives are in total discontentment and chaos because they imagine they have been short-changed and they have to find a way to beat the system and get more. They want a bigger portion than what others receive. If they become obsessed with this idea, they may even steal the portions that rightfully belong somewhere else. Think of the story of Jacob stealing the birthright of Esau.

What is your portion? The psalmist has one answer. He says that God is your portion. Think of it! If God is your portion, then there can be nothing you lack. You always have enough. You experience abundance. God is your strength. If you were to be served anything else, it would only be superfluous because you truly don't need a helping of this world's material goods to keep you healthy and strong. You don't need this world's power or politics. All you need is your portion of the One who designed you, and you're top notch, good to go. When God is the strength of your heart, then He is indeed your portion forever.

*Lord, You are my **portion**. You are enough for me. Help me to keep You as the priority in my life. Amen.*

# GUILTY

*This is the way we know that we belong to the way of truth. When our hearts make us feel **guilty**, we can still have peace before God. God is greater than our hearts, and he knows everything.*     1 John 3:19–20 NCV

It isn't until you feel the remorse over something you've done that you realize the cleansing power of God. God allows you to feel the regret of your actions, so you can also understand what He has done to clean up your heart. Your sense of **guilt** reminds you even more of your daily need for your Savior.

When we watch villains on the big screen, we wonder at how inhumane they can be, when they have no sense of guilt or regret over the terrible things they do to others. Those same villains exist in our world, and our hearts are saddened by their actions, ones that apparently don't shame them in the least.

When you're a person seeking after the truth of God, the evil that exits in the world becomes harder and harder for you to bear. You have no way of fixing the messes of guilty parties and you are stunned. The actions of those people may well be outside your ability to cause any immediate change, but you do have a place to start.

Start with yourself and any action that causes you to feel guilty. Notice what you've done that doesn't please God, but gives you a chance to fix it by stepping closer to the truth. Go directly to God and seek His forgiveness and His truth. He will guide you away from temptation and help you stay on the path you desire most in your own heart, the one that connects you more securely to Him. Even when you feel guilty, you can find peace with God. Isn't that an amazing thing to consider?

*Lord, thank You for not causing me to continue to feel **guilty** for the wrong things I've done. Instead, You offer forgiveness and peace. I thank You and praise You for Your grace and mercy. Amen.*

# PANTS

*As the deer **pants** for the water brooks, So pants my soul for You, O God.*
*My soul thirsts for God, for the living God.*          Psalm 42:1–2 NKJV

The psalmist isn't thinking about your favorite pair of khakis as he writes this Scripture. He's thinking of the feeling you may have when you hike straight up a mountain trail, or after you've just finished an amazing workout. Your body can think of only one thing—getting a drink of water, and getting it quickly.

Imagine the deer running through the forest, **panting** for the babbling brook, hoping to quench his considerable thirst. It's been a long day, and nothing will satisfy him like a cool drink.

That desire for water, that drive to find a cool stream, is the same one that drives you when you're in need of the Lord. You are tired. You are worn out from the day. You've gone for miles and run through hoops to make decisions at work or at home. You've walked everywhere trying to make sure things are as they should be, but now you're parched. You've done everything you can and you can't wait any longer. You need to be filled up and nourished. You need to draw nearer to God, and you desperately want Him to draw closer to you.

When your soul thirsts for the living God, there's only one thing to do. Put down your business plan, your book, your cooking pot for making dinner, and go to Him. Don't delay. Don't wait even a moment because your life depends on you finding your way to be refreshed and revived. Only God can meet you in the place where your deepest needs can be realized. He bids you to come. He's ready with your unending cup of joy. He wants you to breathe normally and naturally and simply rest.

*Lord, when my soul **pants** for You, I know that I need to spend time with You in real ways. Help me to stop everything and come to Your side so that You can fill me again with Your love. Amen.*

# CLEAR

*Nothing in all the world can be hidden from God. Everything is **clear** and lies open before him, and to him we must explain the way we have lived.*

Hebrews 4:13 NCV

Blue skies, bright sunlight, crystal **clear** waters—these are the windows of God. No matter how dark the night sky or how dark the soul who wanders the streets, God sees everything. He knows our movements and our thoughts because we have no way of hiding from Him. Yet it is the first thing human beings try to do when they fail God. When we have done something that will not please Our Creator, the One who supports and sustains our very existence, we run and hide. From Adam and Eve on, we've been ducking down low every time we know we made a mess of things. The problem is God sees everything clearly; He already knows what we have done.

Perhaps when we make a mistake that grieves our spirits and disappoints us at the soul level, we need to stand before God and share our grief and seek forgiveness. We need to be clear and come clean.

God receives you heart first the moment you show up. He looks to see if you're going to explain yourself in truth, or if you're going to try to dance around what you did wrong. He needs to know that your heart is clear about your mistake and that you truly know you need His forgiveness. When you approach Him with a humble heart, He can offer you grace and mercy.

You may want to get your misdemeanors cleared up here on Earth so that God can cast those sins as far away as the east is from the west. You don't want to have to explain the way you lived at the end of your soul's life. Clear the air now. If you've got anything to lay at the cross, go ahead. You will feel better. God will forgive and forget. Sound good?

*Lord, thank You for making it **clear** that You will forgive me when I seek You with all my heart. Bless all those who come to You today and offer them grace. Amen.*

# RAN

*But when he was still a great way off, his father saw him and had
compassion, and **ran** and fell on his neck and kissed him.*

Luke 15:20 NKJV

The story of the prodigal son never gets old. It is one of the most beautiful
descriptions of forgiveness in the Bible, and it resonates with most of us
because we've been all three of the main characters. We've been the father
whose heart is broken because his son wastes his inheritance and goes his
own way. We've been the good son, who takes care of the family business
and tries to do what is right in the eyes of the father. We've also been the
wayward son, going off to do our own thing, squandering our resources,
living loose lives, and wishing we could figure out how to go back home
again.

One of the most dramatic parts of this story is that when the father
sees the son coming, he stops everything. He doesn't wait for the son to
get to him. He doesn't yell at the son and tell him to go away. He doesn't
ignore the son and not speak to him because he has been such a dreadful
child. He does one thing. He **runs**. He runs to his son, wraps his arms
around him, and hugs him. He cries tears of incredible joy as he kisses
his child and holds him tight. The father is so happy to see this boy that
nothing else in the world matters. He doesn't care what the boy has done
wrong, because he cares more about the boy himself.

Imagine your Heavenly Father. You are coming up the path. You are
sorry for your sins, and you are coming back to Him. You are seeking His
forgiveness because nothing else matters to you. You start back in His
direction and your heart nearly breaks as you see your Father run to meet
you, wrapping His arms around you and hugging new life into your weary
bones. He ran joyfully to you and He says, "Welcome home, I love you."
You weep now too. It feels so good to be home.

*Lord, let me always act like the father who **ran** to forgive his own son
because I know that is the way You forgive even me. Amen.*

263

# READY

*So while the five foolish bridesmaids went to buy oil, the bridegroom came. The bridesmaids who were **ready** went in with the bridegroom to the wedding feast. Then the door was closed and locked.*

Matthew 25:10 NCV

As you prepare for any event, you may need a checklist. Will you need special attire? Will you need to bring a gift? Will you need to get a babysitter? You may even need flight information or a map to get to the right location. Whatever it is you need, you want to get ready, organized, informed, and prepared.

A recurring theme of the Bible is the one that talks about being **ready** for a future event. Often the event being noted concerns Jesus' return. Are you ready? Are you prepared for His arrival?

The five foolish bridesmaids in the Scripture were nearly ready for the bridegroom to come, but because he was delayed, they ran out of oil. When no one else would give them more oil, they had to go out to buy more. When they returned, the bridegroom had already come, and they were locked out of the event. How sad that they had gotten that far and still missed being invited to the party.

It appears the best thing for any of us to do, then, is simply to be ready all the time, because we don't know the day or the hour when Our Lord will return. Only God knows when He will send His Son back to Earth. We need to be ready. We may be somewhat equipped, nearly there, but we probably are already aware that we are not all ready. Keep the oil of love and the faith in your heart strong and get ready.

*Lord, thank You for guiding me in the best ways to stay **ready** for Your return. Help me to stay alert and ready for Your call. Amen.*

# SIGHED

*Jesus **sighed** deeply and said, "Why do you people ask for a miracle as a sign? I tell you the truth, no sign will be given to you."*     Mark 8:11 NCV

Think about the things that cause you to heave a **sigh**. Sometimes you sigh when you feel slightly exasperated or frustrated. You've tried over and over to help your kids understand the importance of your house rules, but they simply don't seem to get it. You've tried to get your spouse to put the dishes in the dishwasher and not leave them in the sink, but there they are, in the sink again. It is a small thing really, but it bothers you just the same.

Jesus often explained the things of God to His followers in detail. He wanted them to understand things in ways that nobody else could do. He hoped He was getting through to them, but right about the time He thought they understood something, they would come back with one more question that showed they just didn't get it. Sound a bit familiar?

In this passage from Mark, we see that Jesus not only sighed, but sighed deeply. He took in their words and the realization that they were still lost, and it made Him sad. He heard their words in His heart and soul. It was a deep, pondering, sad sense that His followers had so much to learn.

You may feel that way as you look at the things people you work with do, as they make the same mistake over again, or the way your best friend can be so unreasonable. Whatever it is, the depth of your sigh will come from a heart that is sad and concerned. That was perhaps the heart of Jesus as He listened to the people around Him. When would they understand the truth of who He really was? Sigh! May you be filled with wisdom and understanding of who He is to you today.

*Lord, thank You for taking care of me and the people I love. I, too, have **sighed** over feeling misunderstood, and it is my prayer that I do not cause You to sigh over me. Amen.*

# PRAY

*Seth also had a son, and they named him Enosh. At that time people began to **pray** to the Lord.* 	Genesis 4:26 NCV

It's interesting to note this first reference to human beings putting their requests and thoughts before the Lord in prayer. This Scripture says that it wasn't until after Adam and Eve's third son, Seth, became a father himself that people began to **pray** to the Lord. Being able to pray is now a natural part of the life of a Christian, but after the fall of Adam and Eve, generations passed before the prayer connection with God was established.

The generations from Enosh to Enoch, and on to the family of Noah, found few people who desired a relationship with God. Few turned their thoughts into prayer as Noah did. Most people went their own way and didn't acknowledge God at all.

Imagine what it would be like if you could not talk with God. What would you do with your concerns or your heart of praise? What would you do when you need direction or a sense of peace over decisions you are making? What if there was no way to communicate with the Creator?

Prayer is a gift. It is one of the greatest privileges of being human. It is the most important heart-to-heart dialogue that exists. God hears your call and He answers. He answers because you are important to Him. He knew you would need a Savior, and He knows your immediate needs and worries. He knows what you will ask before you utter a word. He loves to talk with you, so He listens. The opportunity to pray is not something to take for granted, but something to do continually, to appreciate as a holy and blessed conversation between you and God.

*Lord, thank You for teaching me how to come to You and **pray**. Help me to remember how holy and special our time together is. Amen.*

# FAILS

*Love never **fails**. But where there are prophecies, they will cease; where there are tongues, they will be stilled; where there is knowledge, it will pass away*

1 Corinthians 13:8 NIV

This simple three-word sentence from Scripture is quoted at wedding ceremonies and often repeated at anniversaries, and yet it is difficult to truly understand. Oh, we like the idea that love, real love, true love, the love you waited for all your life, won't ever break down or fall apart. We love that thought, but we can't prove it with statistics or today's headlines. In fact, some have become jaded because of love's continual failings. "Love never **fails**" seems a bit overstated.

Your personal relationship experience in this world will likely determine how much you resonate with this Scripture. You assume that nothing lasts forever. At least you imagine that everything will pass away at some point, and yet here it is, a Scripture that says "love never fails," never truly goes away, never dies. So how can this be true, and what does it really mean?

Scripture tells us that God is love. You can reason then that if God is love, love never fails because God never fails. God succeeds at all He does. God keeps His promises. God knows every heart and He knows what to do for the good of each human being that ever existed. God knows that every philosophy and culture, every ideology and theology and scientific thought, will one day pass away. Since God is love and He will never pass away, love never fails. Love is never depleted, used up, or gone.

Human love fails because it isn't centered in the true Source of love. When human love seeks God's connection and that love is wrapped into one with Him, then success is assured. Your love and His love together can only mean one thing. Love never fails!

*Lord, I have experience with the kind of love that **fails**, but I know that Your love for me will never cease, that it will always be there for me. Thank You. Amen.*

# AROMA

*But thanks be to God, who always leads us as captives in Christ's triumphal procession and uses us to spread the **aroma** of the knowledge of him everywhere. For we are to God the pleasing aroma of Christ among those who are being saved and those who are perishing.*

2 Corinthians 2:14–15 NIV

You may remember that the patriarchs and priests of the Old Testament always made sacrifices to God that offered Him a pleasant **aroma**. To honor the gifts of their hearts' desires, their need for forgiveness, or their praise for special events, God demanded a sacrifice. That aroma pleased God and He heard their prayers. He forgave their sins and He gave them knowledge, insight, and direction.

We, too, are the pleasing aroma of Christ. God not only sees Christ within us when our hearts are right, but recognizes us from the very scent, fragrance, smell of Jesus that we emit. Perhaps without realizing it, we, too, spread the aroma of the awareness of Christ's presence within us. Others not only see His light as we do our work in the world, but unconsciously, they take in the fragrance of His Holy Spirit. This aroma of Christ within us connects us even more closely with our Heavenly Father.

Think of the wonderful scent of a baby, fresh from the bath, washed and powdered, sweet and clean. That baby makes you want to hug it and squeeze it and hold it close to your heart. It's a scent of pure innocence and joy. Perhaps in some way, that sweetness of spirit emanates from each person who works for the Lord with a clean heart and a gentle soul, innocent, because of Christ's sacrifice.

We are the fragrance of our Lord on Earth. What could be more wonderful than being a pleasant aroma, breathed in by the Spirit of our amazing God?

*Lord, thank You for the sacrifice that Jesus made for me. I ask that the sweet **aroma** of His Presence will fill my heart and soul today. Amen.*

# SLIP

*The mouths of the righteous utter wisdom, and their tongues speak what is
   just.*
*The law of their God is in their hearts; their feet do not **slip**.*

Psalm 37:30–31 NIV

This passage from Psalm 37 fills you with the love of God from head to
toe. Your mouth utters wisdom because of Him and your feet do not **slip**.
You're faithful and just and the things you do are done with grace and
mercy. God has placed His Spirit within your heart, and He upholds you
everyplace you go.

It's interesting to look at the word "slip" in the sense of the way we
speak and the way we act and the places we walk. As human beings, we
are often prone to a slip of the tongue where we say something foolish or
unfair. When we carry the light of Christ within our hearts, we find those
moments somewhat horrifying because our hope and our intentions are
always to be better than that. We want to be examples to others of what it
means to be a follower of Jesus and to speak well of each other.

The psalmist says that we will say the right thing and we will speak
kindly because we know that we are the temples of God and that we carry
His Presence with us all the time. We are protected, then, perhaps even
from our own foolishness so that we don't fall into behaviors that would
cause us to blush before God.

Remember today that you won't slip up anytime you remain conscious
of who you are in Christ. You are the heart of God for those who know
you, and what you say and do are shining examples to each person you
meet. Give God thanks and praise that He keeps you wise and He doesn't
let you fall.

*Lord, thank You for helping me to stand on solid ground so that I
don't **slip** by my actions or my words. I give You thanks and praise
for lifting me up each day. Amen.*

# MONEY

*The love of **money** causes all kinds of evil. Some people have left the faith, because they wanted to get more money, but they have caused themselves much sorrow.* 1 Timothy 6:10 NCV

**Money**, all by itself, is neither good nor bad. What is it about money that causes the good, the bad, and the ugly to appear out of nowhere? Money is a blessing when you have enough to keep the roof over your head and keep your family clothed and fed. Money is a blessing when you share it with others, giving to charity, tithing, or doing good deeds.

The struggle with money seems to come about when we are possessed by what it can do for us alone, and when we find it difficult even to imagine life without it. The difference between the rich young man in Luke 18:23, who did everything to follow Jesus but give up his money, and the poor widow who put all the money she had in the collection plate, is an issue of trust. The young man didn't know if he could trust God enough to let go of his money. The poor widow trusted God to provide for her daily.

In the United States, much of our money claims, "In God we trust." It's interesting that we print that phrase right on our money, and yet so few find it easy to live in that truth. Having a little cash is always a good feeling. Worrying that you might lose your fortune is not.

God wants you to have money, as much as He wants you to have every form of provision. All He asks is that you see money the same way you see everything else, as just one aspect of His provision. Where your treasure is, your heart is also. Let your faith be your treasure, for it alone will bring you joy.

*Lord, help me to truly love You and Your provision and be grateful for the ways You bring **money** into my life. Amen.*

# VICTORY

*In fact, this is love for God: to keep his commands. And his commands are not burdensome, for everyone born of God overcomes the world. This is the victory that has overcome the world, even our faith.*   1 John 5:3–4 NIV

You can't have **victory** without having a challenge. After all, you must overcome something in order to get to the goal, the winning moment, the Oscar opportunity. Most of us love victory, and we may even love a good challenge, at least in the areas where we have expertise. It's not as easy, however, to take on the challenges we don't feel equipped to handle.

God knows you and He equips you so that you are ready for anything you have to face. It's called faith!

Every morning you awaken to new challenges of faith because you have continual choices to make about how you will live your life. God didn't make His commands difficult or incomprehensible for you, but He placed them close to your heart so that, with each decision, you're aware of Him. You choose whether you'll try to please God, or simply to please yourself. One choice brings the victory; the other choice brings you short of the goal.

You are poised for victory anytime your work and your heart's intent are all about pleasing God. Whether you do big things or things that seem inconsequential to anyone else, the work of your hands is important to God. He blesses everything you do and gives you the winning moment when you are working for Him. It's your call. Every day is yours to determine the course, and the victory awaits you. Go for the gold today!

*Lord, I know that I only have **victory** in this life when I do the things You've called me to do. Help me to live out Your commands as fully and lovingly as I can. Amen.*

# VAST

*How precious to me are your thoughts, God! How **vast** is the sum of them!*
*Were I to count them, they would outnumber the grains of sand—*
*when I awake, I am still with you.*                    Psalm 139:17–18 NIV

**Vast** is one of those words that instantly brings a picture to your mind. It may be of a panoramic view from a mountaintop, or it may be of a nighttime sky with millions of twinkling stars. You can't count them because there are so many; it's a massive, enormous, uncountable number. It's a vast starry sky!

If you can't count the stars in the sky, of which there are billions, can you count the number of times God thinks about you on any given day or the amazing thoughts He has about you? The psalmist says that His thoughts are vast, uncountable, unknowable. They are beyond anything we can fathom and are more than the grains of sand.

Perhaps you imagine that God doesn't think about you personally, or that He is so busy with the rest of the world that He can't possibly have time to muse about how you're doing. The idea seems reasonable to a human mind, but to the mind of God, you are every bit as important as anything else He must do. Watching over you and making sure that you are protected and loved is a privilege to Him. He likes to check in on you many times a day.

The psalmist says that that awareness is very precious to him. He knows that God is there when he's fast asleep, dreaming through the night, and that God is still there, still thinking of him vast numbers of times, when he is wide awake. It's an amazing thing to him. It's an amazing thing to each of us.

Wherever you are today, be reminded once again that you are never far from your Father's thoughts or from His heart.

*Lord, I have no idea how **vast** Your thoughts are about me, but*
*I thank You for always being with me. I pray that I will think*
*continually of You as well. Amen.*

# CONFUSION

*God is not a God of confusion but a God of peace.*

1 Corinthians 14:33 NCV

Probably nothing robs you of a sense of peace as much as when you are in a state of **confusion**. You're driving your car and your GPS has marked the route for you, but suddenly, the designated road is under construction and the directions are not clear and people are passing you as you try to understand how to move forward. You are full of confusion and angst.

Your day can get muddled up quickly, almost anytime your plans don't go as you expected or you're suddenly thrown into a problem you aren't sure how to handle. It doesn't take much. Sometimes it's as simple as too many people talking at once, trying to get points across to one another, but no one can understand because of all the confusion and because no one is really listening.

You have choices even during this kind of chaos. You can stop and surrender. Seek God's help to turn down the noise. Pull over on the road and look at your options. Give God the details and then ask Him to guide you back to peace so that you can take care of things without the confusion.

You may have to start by doing a simple exercise. Breathe in. Breathe out. Repeat the process until you are calm and quiet and sitting closer to your Lord. Let Him help you anytime confusion is stirring up your mind and your spirit, making it difficult for you to move ahead. Remind yourself that your God is not a God of confusion, but He is a God of peace. He is there with you, and He knows the exact way that you should go.

*Lord, I thank You that I can turn over any **confusion** I might feel today and that You will do all You can to guide me back to peace. Amen.*

# TALK

*These commandments that I give you today are to be on your hearts.*
*Impress them on your children. Talk about them when you sit at home and*
*when you walk along the road, when you lie down and when you get up. Tie*
*them as symbols on your hands and bind them on your foreheads.*

Deuteronomy 6:6–8 NIV

What kinds of things do you **talk** about? Most of us talk about what interests us, or what troubles us. We like to discuss issues we're trying to understand or share things that inspire or motivate us. We want to talk about the stuff that matters.

Unfortunately, there's a lot of talk these days that does nothing to create greater understanding between two people or groups of people. There is very little talk that is intended to inspire our hearts or help us to have a more loving perspective toward others.

The writer of this Scripture reminds us of the important things God desires us to talk about. He wants us to talk about Him! He wants us to share His stories and tell everyone who will listen what He has done for us. He wants us to tell each other the meaning of a life of faith and why it can make a difference. He wants every generation to know that He is God and that He still exists today as much as ever. He wants to know that we never forget that He is near. Talk about Him, write about Him, wear your Jesus T-shirt or your jeweled cross. Do all you can to remind yourself and everyone else around you that the God of your heart, the Creator of the Universe, is alive and well and He lives in you. Talk about Him everyplace you go today.

When you love someone, it's easy to talk about them. When you feel loved, it's wonderful to talk about that too. Live, love, laugh, and talk about your Father in Heaven.

*Lord, thank You for Your steadfast and enduring love. It is my joy*
*to talk about You every opportunity that I get. Bless all those who*
*share the stories of Your incredible love today. Amen.*

# SHOES

*"If I were in your shoes, I'd go straight to God, I'd throw myself on the mercy of God."*                    Job 5:8 MSG

You may recall that Job was surrounded by people who were offering advice about how he might handle the situation he was struggling to endure. After all, he had been a faithful man of God, yet everything he had was taken from him, and life was unbearable. Job had all he could do to hang on, and yet someone suggested that, in his **shoes**, they would throw themselves on God's mercy.

Perhaps you've noticed that people are good at dispensing advice when they are not the ones suffering. All kinds of answers are available from those who don't have to bear the consequences. Interestingly, Job's friends felt they were in a place to dispense wisdom. They thought they understood him so well that they could feel what it would be like to stand in Job's shoes.

It's an interesting theory and one that each of us has dealt with somewhere in our lives. When we're trying to understand why our whole world is upside down and what we may have done to cause that to happen, we seek advice. Our friends have theories for us, just like Job's friends did. The difference is that Job hadn't done anything wrong to get himself into his troubles. He was faithful, and even when his friends suggested that he must have done something to offend God, Job knew in his heart that he had not. He knew that he was willing to die, placing his life in God's hands, even if he didn't understand what God was doing.

As you know, God rewarded Job for his faithfulness and restored everything to him. If you had to walk in Job's shoes, what would you do? Job walked the walk and he wouldn't even let his friends talk him out of his faith in God. Job trusted God no matter what.

*Lord, thank You for the example of Job. I have to admit I don't know what I would do if I had to walk in his **shoes**, but I pray that I would serve You well. Amen.*

# FISH

*When they landed, they saw a fire of burning coals there with fish on it, and some bread. Jesus said to them, "Bring some of the fish you have just caught." So Simon Peter climbed back into the boat and dragged the net ashore. It was full of large fish, 153, but even with so many the net was not torn. Jesus said to them, "Come and have breakfast."*　　　　John 21:9–12 NIV

This breakfast on the beach is amazing. Simon Peter and some of the other followers of Jesus have been out doing some early morning **fishing**. They come back to the shore and they see this guy standing there.

He tells them to come on over and bring their catch with them. Simon Peter jumps back into the boat and drags their net ashore. They have 153 fish. It's going to be quite the barbecue!

The fishermen are in a daze. They don't quite know what to make of this fish sandwich opportunity. They see the guy. He looks a lot like Jesus. They feel pretty sure it is Jesus, but how could it be? He was crucified several days earlier, and they are still in mourning.

It's interesting that one of the first acts of Jesus as He appeared to His followers and His friends after His resurrection was to have a little cookout. After all, He had taught them how important it was to catch fish. He had taught them to catch human beings. It had to be an incredible moment for all of them as they realized that it truly was Jesus who was cooking for them.

Jesus wanted His disciples to know that everything He had told them before the crucifixion was true. He appeared to them and ate with them and spent time with them so that they would know the truth that He was truly alive, once and for all. They would be His messengers, His hands and feet in the world, and so He chose to meet them in love and friendship. He meets us the same way.

*Lord, thank You for teaching me how to **fish** for Your followers. Thank You for sharing Your loving kindness with all of us. Amen.*

# EYE

*"The eye is a light for the body. If your eyes are good, your whole body will be full of light. But if your eyes are evil, your whole body will be full of darkness."*
                                                    Matthew 6:22 NCV

Your **eye** illuminates the world around you and allows you to see whatever your heart and mind are willing to take in. You know that's true because no two people describe something they see in the same way. Each one sees according to the influences of physical, emotional, and spiritual things that are going on in the body, mind, and heart.

Jesus often said something to the effect of, "If you have eyes to see and ears to hear..." It was a condition, not because people were largely blind or deaf, but because people were often both blind and deaf in emotional or spiritual ways.

The eye is a light, a lamp for the body. It shines a light on others, and it brings in the light from the outside world. Perhaps one of the lessons from this Scripture in Matthew is that it's important to recognize what you take into your mind with your eyes. Some things illuminate your heart and shine through your eyes: things like Scripture reading and beautiful scenic views, or the love you see in the face of a friend. Other things simply confuse your thinking and cause darkness to emerge where light wants to be. You must be aware all the time about the things you allow to come through your senses from television shows or even conversations around the office. The darkness hovers everywhere.

If you have an eye for the Lord, you will focus on the things that are good and you will make an amazing difference to everyone around you, lighting the way when they cannot see which direction to turn. May the eyes of your heart be full of goodness and love so that light shines through in all you do.

*Lord, thank You for giving me a heart for You so that I can keep an eye on all that is good and walk in Your light. Amen.*

# SHINE

*"Arise Jerusalem! Let your light **shine** for all to see. For the glory of the Lord rises to shine on you. Darkness as black as night covers all the nations of the earth, but the glory of the Lord rises and appears over you. All nations will come to your light."*
Isaiah 60:1–3 NLT

Most of us are happy when the light comes on when we enter a dark room or walk down a darkened street. We feel relieved and safer when we can see just what is going on around us. We're drawn to the way the light **shines**.

When the prophet Isaiah talked to the Israelites about rising to the light, rising to the glory of God that shone all around them, he did so to remind them who they were. They were not people of the same darkness that covered the rest of the Earth. They were people who were set apart and blessed by God's glory, His Presence. He wanted them to shine that light so that others would be drawn to them.

When God created all things and said, "Let there be light!" He caused the light to come out of the darkness. He set the sun and the moon into that darkness so that they could shine and bring day into what had been endless night.

Those who live in the Light of God's Presence and grace are blessed then to reflect His goodness and let His light shine so that others will find Him. Our job is to be dazzling, glowing, always willing to shed light into the darkness wherever we go.

Christians have the opportunity to carry the light of God's Presence. We reflect the One who loves us and mercifully guides our steps. When we stand up and let His light shine within us, we are a neon sign that flashes to others a message and an invitation to draw near to God. The world is dark. Shine God's light!

*May Your light **shine** through me today. Let me be a beacon that draws others closer to You no matter where I may be. Amen.*

# DIFFERENT

*The Spirit of the Lord will come powerfully upon you, and you will prophesy with them; and you will be changed into a **different** person. Once these signs are fulfilled, do whatever your hand finds to do, for God is with you.*
1 Samuel 10:6–7 NIV

When the Spirit of the Lord comes powerfully upon a person, you can rest assured that things will be **different** from then on. When Samuel told Saul in this Scripture that he would be a different person, a changed person, a person that he might not even recognize, it all came to pass. In the case of Saul, He discovered that he was filled with insight and wisdom, able to prophesy with the power of God. He was in God's favor.

When Jesus was preparing to leave His disciples and return to Heaven, he told them to wait for the Helper, the Holy Spirit. He said this Spirit would guide them into all truth and would fill them. As you may remember in Acts, when they were filled with the Holy Spirit, people everywhere began to prophesy, and they had incredible wisdom about the things of God. They were different. Just like Saul, years before them, the same Spirit filled them and made them understand everything in a different way.

The day you invited Jesus Christ into your life and into your heart, you were filled with His Holy Spirit and you became a different person. You were changed so that you could be a worthy vessel for the Spirit of God. You were changed so that you could do the work He requires of you for the good of the kingdom. Today, you're a different person because your heart is right with God and you can live in His grace and favor.

Dare to be different. Dare to become everything God designed you to be today.

*Lord, help me to love the idea that I am **different** because of You. Thank You for changing me a little bit more every day with Your love. Amen.*

# CLAY

*So I went down to the potter's house, and I saw him working at the wheel.*
*But the pot he was shaping from the clay was marred in his hands; so the*
*potter formed it into another pot, shaping it as seemed best to him.*

Jeremiah 18:3–4 NIV

If you're a creative person, you know that you aspire to perfect your craft.
If you paint, then you may go through several drawings or colors before
you decide your painting is done. If you write, then you work on your
manuscript until it meets the standards you've set for yourself. In any
case, you as the artist get to choose when your work is done. You decide its
value and its use.

Jeremiah describes his visit to the potter in this same way. In the
skilled hands of the artisan, the clay can become a multitude of things. It
can be used in a variety of ways, but only the potter knows exactly what he
wants the piece to be. If he sees a slight imperfection, he can use it to his
advantage to create something new or he can simply reshape and redesign
it until he gets it exactly right.

It's fitting that we use this same illustration to help us understand the
way our Father in Heaven created us. He molded us from the clay of the
Earth and He perfected us according to His intentions for the work He
would have us do. If He sees flaws in your design, He knows the ways to
reshape or redirect those flaws to make you even more useful or valuable.
He knows you are dust and He knows what He wants you to do.

As you consider the clay pots you may have around the house, or the
drawings you've done, imagine that you are, even now, a work of art in
the Creator's hand. He may yet be shaping and molding what you are to
become, but you know that in the end, you'll be incredibly beautiful.

*Lord, thank You for keeping me as the clay secure in Your hand.*
*Mold me and shape me to be all that You know I can be. Amen.*

# EMPTY

*And do not turn aside; for then you would go after **empty** things which cannot profit or deliver, for they are nothing.* 1 Samuel 12:21 NKJV

This verse is kind of like what Alice did as she searched for the white rabbit in Wonderland. Everywhere she searched, she came up **empty**-handed. She couldn't make sense of things, and she wasn't even certain how she would find her way back home. Most of the time, she felt foolish for having gone after the rabbit at all.

Sure, that is a fantasy story, but when you consider how easy it is to become distracted during the day, or how many times you feel like you get off track for almost no reason at all, you can understand that turning aside and going after the empty things is a lot easier than you might wish it to be.

God wants you to stay the course. He wants you to look to Him always to help you stay on the path He designed for you. He wants you to win at this game of life, and He's already declared the victory. His hope for you is that you will do everything in your power to complete the work He has for you, and that you will not turn to the right or to the left. He understands the foolishness of this world and its unlimited distractions.

Today, seek the things that will profit your faith, your heart and soul and the people around you, so that you can continue to deliver the light of God's love to each one of them. You don't want anyone around you to ever feel empty.

*Lord, thank You for filling me up with Your love so that I am never empty. Help me to stay on the path to Your purpose and let me never turn aside from You. Amen.*

# FIRST

*For your heavenly Father knows that you need all these things. But seek first the kingdom of God and His righteousness, and all these things shall be added to you.* Matthew 6:32–33 NKJV

You know what they say, "**First** things first!" Perhaps you've never stopped to think about what that little adage means to you, but we can discover one definition of putting things first in this Scripture from Matthew.

When you seek the kingdom of God first, and you strive to discover what He would have you do in ways that please Him, then you are on the right track. You are looking up, so that He can look out for you.

You may have days when things seem totally out of control. You have barely stepped out of your cozy night's sleep when you find that all your plans for the day are haywire, derailed, simply not going to move ahead the way you expected. When that happens, your first thought may well be to figure out how you can fix the plan. That's not a bad thought, but Matthew wants to offer you a better idea. He suggests the first thing you do is get on your knees. When you go to Him first, the sense of panic will be replaced with peace. After all, your problem is not too big for the One who totally designed everything.

God sees you right now. He feels your concern. He has a plan. Don't make a move without Him, because when you seek Him first, He can work on your behalf. He wants even impossible things to work together for your good. Trust Him! Trust that He will be your first responder!

*Lord, thank You for being first in my heart and in my life. Bless each person today who comes to You for help and guidance. Be our first thought! Amen.*

# KEY

*The key of the house of David I will lay on his shoulder;*
*So he shall open, and no one shall shut;*
*And he shall shut, and no one shall open.*          Isaiah 22:22 NKJV

When something is important to us, or needs to be secure, then we often put it under lock and **key**. We have keys to our cars and our houses, our offices and the mailbox. The key means that not just anyone can open the lock; not just anyone can come to share in our possessions. Isaiah talks about the key to the house of David, which shows how much God entrusted David with His love and His work.

As we just mentioned, Jesus did the same thing with Simon Peter, when He gave Him the keys to the kingdom, the keys to building His church on Earth.

What would be the key to your relationship with God? What kind of responsibility do you have to further God's work and to open doors for others to get to know Him? The answer is simple. You have Jesus in your heart and He is the key to your salvation, the door for every person to come back to the heart of God. Any chance you get, open the door for someone else to know Him. God knows your heart, and He knows He can trust you to help others find their way to Him. You hold the key to His love, and He has total confidence in you.

As you lock the door of your car or your house, reflect for a moment about what that key does to give you a small sense of security. Imagine now that, with the turn of that key, all the forces of Heaven come together to protect you and those you love. When you turn the key, they act on your behalf. Why? Because Jesus is the key and He secures the way for you!

*Lord, thank You for trusting me with the **key** to salvation through*
*Your Son, Jesus. Help me to open doors for others any chance I get.*
*Amen.*

# HOLY

*"Do not come any closer," God said. "Take off your sandals, for the place where you are standing is **holy** ground." Then he said, "I am the God of your father, the God of Abraham, the God of Isaac and the God of Jacob." At this, Moses hid his face, because he was afraid to look at God.*

Exodus 3:5 NIV

It's likely that you don't have a good sense of what it means for something to be **holy**. You may be in awe of God and realize that He is indeed holy, but you might struggle with what it means for you to be holy. "Holy" is a Divine word, a hallowed word. It feels like something beyond our reach as human beings, and yet we are asked to do our best to be holy.

Of course, nothing holy exists apart from God, so we must start there. The only chance we have at striving to be holy is because we are connected to God through Jesus. Jesus is our conduit to holiness. When God told Moses that he was standing on holy ground, he directed Moses to take off his shoes. Perhaps in his bare feet, Moses could feel God's Presence and Spirit more effectively. Perhaps it was simply that the living God was sharing a special moment with a human being, and wherever God is, the place is holy.

Coming back to you, then, it's helpful to remember that most of the time you are walking this Earth with your shoes on. You are doing what you can to please God, moving closer to Him with the work you do, and yet not coming as close to Him as He might wish. He wants you to be holy and that happens every time you remember to ask God to draw near to you. It happens every time you give priority to who God is because wherever He resides is holy. He is the living God of all generations.

Where would you like Him to reside today? Draw near to Him, take off your shoes, and bow your head. You will indeed share a moment that is holy.

*Lord, thank You for those moments that we share that are **holy** and loving. Help me to draw near to You each day. Amen.*

# EVIL

*Good people have good things in their hearts, and so they say good things. But evil people have evil in their hearts, so they say evil things.*

Matthew 12:35 NCV

A quick way to understand what makes people tick is by listening to the things they say. Their words are indicators of what is going on inside their heads and, more important, inside their hearts.

A good person listens as much as they talk. That person seeks to understand even before they feel the need to be understood. They speak first from the heart, and when that person is also a believer, you're in good company.

Some people have **evil** hiding in their hearts. They say unkind things and they leave a path of destruction for themselves or others almost any-place they go. They don't give; they take. They are absorbed in themselves, and they imagine they are entitled to more than others would receive. Their hearts have misguided them and turned to stone.

You choose how you will speak to others. You listen with your heart, so that each thing you say and do brings out the good in those around you. You see the best in people and commend them for being gracious and kind. Others embrace your goodness, because you cause them to want to be better people themselves. The Spirit of God lives within you. It is important that the good people, the ones with truly good hearts, bring a balance to the evil in the world. It is important for each of us to turn up the light of God's love.

*Lord, I ask that I can tip the scales away from **evil** and bring out the good in others, because of all the good that You have done for me. Amen.*

285

# PLEASE

*By myself I can do nothing; I judge only as I hear, and my judgment is just, for I seek not to **please** myself but him who sent me.* John 5:30 NIV

A lot of us are people **pleasers**. We do our best at home, at church, or in our jobs to make sure we do things that will create a positive atmosphere. It's all good, and it brings joy to our lives.

In this Scripture from John, we see almost the opposite of that kind of thinking. Jesus isn't out to be a people pleaser. He's out to be a God pleaser. He wants everything that He does to give God the glory. He doesn't need anything for Himself. He doesn't need to get His name in lights or in print. He simply has one mission. He wants to please God in every possible way.

How often do we begin the day, wondering what else we can do to please God? We know we have a purpose, we may even understand that we have a calling, but whatever is happening in our daily routines may still not reflect the desire to simply please God with our actions and our words.

Since we know that we can do nothing on our own, at least nothing that will advance the kingdom of God, then it's a good thought to simply remind ourselves of our one true job. We must strive to please God each day. If we're honest, we can then look at the day we spent and ask ourselves at bedtime whether we achieved that goal.

It's fun to be a people pleaser because we all appreciate being admired or at least affirmed by those around us. No doubt, it's even more fun to be a God pleaser because His admiration goes beyond anything we can imagine. His admiration helps us to shine a light all the way up to Heaven.

*Lord, thank You for Your willingness to work with me and help me discover more ways that I might serve You and **please** You. I ask that You guide me each day to follow Your example. Amen.*

# LOST

*If a man has a hundred sheep but one of the sheep gets lost, he will leave the other ninety-nine on the hill and go to look for the lost sheep. I tell you the truth, if he finds it he is happier about that one sheep than about the ninety-nine that were never lost.*                    Matthew 18:12–13 NCV

It's interesting that Jesus talked so often about the relationship of a shepherd over his flock and His wisdom in reminding us that He is our Shepherd. He is the one who makes sure we are not lost.

When a shepherd watches over his sheep, it is his responsibility to guard them from predators. He makes sure that they find nourishing pasture and clean water. He keeps them healthy and doesn't let them wander away where they can be hurt. The shepherd knows his sheep and he will not let anything happen to them under his watch.

So Jesus gives an engaging parallel here. Human beings are often like misguided sheep. We can be lost and led astray without even realizing that we've fallen into the path of a predator. Fortunately, those of us who have invited Jesus to be our Shepherd can listen for His voice so we know where to look for Him. We stay close to His side so that He can protect us from the evils of the world. When we don't, we are easily blindsided and can quickly become weak and unstable.

When even one sheep is lost, the shepherd makes haste to find it and bring it back to the fold. Your Savior does the same thing with you. When you are lost, even for a moment, He draws closer to you, encouraging you to turn around and look for Him again. He sees you and you can be sure that all the angels in Heaven celebrate with Him when you return to the fold. His hope is that no one would be lost eternally. The Shepherd continues to call for those who are part of His flock.

*Lord, thank You for saving me when I was lost. Even now, I ask that You keep me close to Your side so that I never wander far from You. Amen.*

# FOREVER

*We set our eyes not on what we see but on what we cannot see. What we see will last only a short time, but what we cannot see will last **forever**.*

2 Corinthians 4:18 NCV

**Forever** is a difficult concept. After all, in our life cycle, we are born, and we expire. Besides God Himself, nothing we know of exists forever. God is from forever ago to forever from now.

We like to imagine that love lasts forever. In the sense that God is love, we can maintain that perspective. His eternal love and existence are the reason we have hope in our temporary state.

We love the idea of forever because when things are good, we do not want them to end, ever! We want forever love, and forever success, and forever happiness.

The truth is, God wants those things for us, too, and that's why He provided a door that leads us into forever. It's the only door of its kind. It is the One that He invites us to open nearly every day of our lives. He continues to guide us toward that door until we draw our last breath because He wants us to exist with Him eternally. He wants us to live forever inside His love and care.

He asked Jesus to be the forever door, to keep it open for you. Once you walk in, your eyes will be opened as well. You will begin to see the things that others cannot see. You will understand that being temporary is only an issue if you remain outside the door.

Thank God for holding the door wide open. He invites you into His love forever.

*Lord, thank You for being the One we can count on both here and in eternity. I will love You **forever**. Amen.*

# PERFECT

*Do not be shaped by this world; instead be changed within by a new way of thinking. Then you will be able to decide what God wants for you; you will know what is good and pleasing to him and what is perfect.*

Romans 12:2 NCV

No matter how much exercise you do, or how much weight you lose, or what kind of clothes you wear, you probably won't get to your **perfect** physical self because there's only one thing that truly transforms your appearance. You can shape and reshape your outward look, but only God can shape your inward understanding and your heart, which guides you in all things. Only God can make you truly beautiful so that you will be perfect in His sight!

The writer of Romans wants you to remember that, with Christ, you are not just changed for eternity, but you are changed in your everyday life because you no longer think the way you once did. Your new thoughts give you a perspective of faith that really makes you beautiful. You never have to worry about a bad hair day or whether your outfit is just right because the only thing that matters emanates from within. You can leave all the old baggage behind and travel light because anytime you need to understand more of what God wants from you, you can look within yourself and connect with Him heart to heart.

God will transform you and inform you and help you to become all that He intended anytime you spend time with Him. The closer you are to Him, the more you will become like Him, the more you will please Him in ways that are perfect. You know what they say about people who spend a lot of time together? They say that they reflect each other, and they even start to look like each other. They can finish each other's sentences because they know each other so well. That's your goal. Become so intimately acquainted with your Savior that you begin to resemble Him and to act more like Him. You may not get to perfect, but you will be closer every day and you will most certainly please Him.

*Lord, thank You for shaping my heart and mind and helping me to desire to be more perfect in You. Amen.*

# FEET

*If I, your Lord and Teacher, have washed your feet, you also should wash each other's feet. I did this as an example so that you should do as I have done for you.*                                John 13:14–15 NCV

Let's face it. Your **feet** are not especially attractive. They work hard, they make your life a whole lot easier, and you appreciate them. Since they spend a lot of their time sweating in shoes, it's not easy to let someone else wash them for you. It's very humbling.

Imagine how the disciples must have felt when their teacher, the one they adored, chose to wash their feet. Who knows how far they had walked that day and how much dust remained between their toes. Personal hygiene aside, this was not an act of a king to his people. This was an act that servants did for a king.

They were rightly confused because even today leaders often forget that the best leaders know how to serve their people well. Jesus was asking them and us to lead others to Him by loving them and serving them. We can wash their feet and He will wash away their sins.

As you walk the walk with Him, you will discover more about what it means to serve His people. So get up on your feet and serve others, following Jesus' lead.

*Lord, I pray that You will bless the work of my hands and the paths that I walk with my feet. Help me to serve others in ways that please You. Amen.*

# HUNGRY

*If you feed those who are **hungry** and take care of the needs of those who are troubled, then your light will shine in the darkness, and you will be bright like sunshine at noon.*                    Isaiah 58:10 NCV

Everybody you know is **hungry** and needs to be fed. They hunger for their physical needs to be met, their emotional needs to be understood, or their spiritual needs to be nourished. They need to be given tender, loving care, and God in His infinite wisdom assigned you to the task. He knows that you will do what you can to shine His light on those who are troubled in any way.

And He knows that you hunger also. You hunger and thirst after the things that will turn the world right side up. He knows that you need His encouragement and His help to continue doing the amazing things you do for Him each day. Even when you are not aware of Him, He is aware of you. He knows what you need and goes before you to provide everything. He understands the sadness you feel as you look around at so many people in such dire need, many of whom do not even realize how starved they really are.

As a child of God who is fed by His mighty hand, give God the thanks and praise today for encouraging your work and for guiding you into the kingdom. He's proud of the work of your hands and He knows how much you love to spread the Word and shine His light. It's a great day because God will make sure that you and each person you touch will never go hungry again because your spirit will be fed by His grace and mercy.

*Lord, I do my best to feed the **hungry** in body, soul, and mind in every way I understand. Help me to be willing always to unleash Your power into the darkness. Amen.*

# JOY

*Nehemiah said, "Go and enjoy good food and sweet drinks. Send some to people who have none, because today is a holy day to the Lord. Don't be sad, because the joy of the Lord will make you strong."*

Nehemiah 8:10 NCV

If **joy** was a weightlifter, it could probably do the work of Atlas and carry the world on its shoulders. After all, the joy of the Lord is what makes you strong, and when that joy bubbles over into everything you do, there's almost nothing that is beyond your ability.

For many people, though, joy is elusive. And when it wanders away, the feeling of strength, the willingness to share and give, and the possibilities of any given day seem to go away too. They are deprived of strength, and hope, and dreams.

God did not just make joy an attribute for a few people, however. He said through Jesus that He came to Earth to give abundant life so that everyone's joy could be full. Can you imagine what it would be like if you were full, filled up, overflowing with this thing called joy, happiness, giddiness, gratitude, every single day?

Imagine it! Try it! Since you are a child of God, this gift is always available to you. Of course, you'll have troubles and conflicts and even heartbreak, for this is part of the life of every human being. But you will have more than that—you will have comfort and blessing and joy in every circumstance because of the One who seeks your good and showers blessing after blessing upon you. Go ahead and be merry and celebrate with those you love, because the joy of the Lord is your strength. Let every day be wholly given over to the joy of the Lord.

*Lord, You cause me to see the joy in so many areas of my life and through that joy You give me strength. Bless everyone who seeks Your joy today. Amen.*

# GLORY

*Then the Lord said, "There is a place near me where you may stand on a rock. When my **glory** passes by, I will put you in a cleft in the rock and cover you with my hand until I have passed by. Then I will remove my hand and you will see my back; but my face must not be seen."*

Exodus 33:21–23 NIV

Close your eyes and picture this scene. It is a Divine moment like few others in history. God is passing by the Patriarch, Moses, and He is protecting Moses from His **glory**. He knows that it is not something that a human being can take in, and in our vision, even in imagination, it is difficult to realize the utter, amazing glory of the Presence of God. We, too, would be overwhelmed. God covered Moses with His own hand to protect Moses from too much exposure to Him. Scripture speaks of the glory of God in many different passages. You recall that the angels were surrounded by His glory and that they sang praise and honor and glory to God at the birth of Christ.

Have you ever experienced even in small ways the glory of the Lord? You know the feeling, the moment, the sense of God's Presence that is unmistakable? You feel His light cover you, or you sense His holiness surrounding you. You feel transported, unable to even remember where you were when you started your prayers and drew near to Him. Nothing on Earth can quite compare with those moments, those little reflections God allows you to experience of His glory.

God will shield you, like Moses, from receiving more than you can handle, but He will enlighten you, illuminating your soul as He passes by, causing you to know without any doubt that He is with you.

*Lord, thank You for passing so closely to me at times that I can truly sense Your **glory**, Your unmistakable Presence. I praise You and give You glory. Amen.*

# PAST

*For everything that was written in the **past** was written to teach us, so that through the endurance taught in the Scriptures and the encouragement they provide we might have hope.*                    Romans 15:4 NIV

It's been said that if we forget the **past**, we are destined to repeat it. The past is often a great teacher. It shows us where we've been, and with the perspective gained from our history and our present awareness, we're able to be wiser. When things feel difficult, we can draw on what happened before and make better choices. Our own history offers us guidance, and memory serves to shine a light on what we need to know.

God's Word comes to us in part as a historical document. It reminds us of the choices others made and shows us how that worked out. If we choose to learn from what they did, knowing the consequences of their actions, then we benefit from their experiences. The past is our teacher. God's Word is also a living document, which means that it is still relevant; still able to help you with the situations you face in the present.

You have a family history, and a work history, and personal experiences that have taught you how to respond to difficult circumstances. You have a relationship history and a friendship story. Everything about you is guided by the experiences and the knowledge you gained from years past. You've grown into your present self because you learned helpful lessons. God honors your past and He helps you move closer to Him with every choice you make. He is there for you, steadfast and sure, unchanging; the same yesterday, today, and forever!

*Lord, thank You for always being near me and loving the **past**, present, and future me. I am grateful for all I've learned from You. Amen.*

# LONELY

*God sets the **lonely** in families; he leads out the prisoners with singing;*
*but the rebellious live in a sun-scorched land.*          Psalm 68:6 NIV

One of the worst conditions for people comes from the days and nights when we feel **lonely**, abandoned, or left to navigate the world all on our own. Being lonely feels like you are a tiny vessel on a vast ocean. It's hard to know which way to turn.

It's interesting that in the world of computers and cell phones and Facebook and all the intentional ways that people can stay connected, that we are still lonely. In some ways, we use technology to build walls around ourselves, which isolates us.

God does not want His children to be lonely. He set us in families, either biological or in community with others, with people who can share our joys and concerns. He knew when He created Adam that it wasn't good for the man to live alone, and so He created Eve. God's heart was intent on His creations feeling love and comfort and knowing that they did not exist alone. He knew we needed each other.

We don't have to disappear into technology. We don't have to build walls and create deserts. With God's help, we can create bonds between us that will sustain our hearts and minds and not allow loneliness to prevail. Set down your phone or your tablet and spend time with those who are near you. Make it a point to step away from those things that draw you off into a cyber world, so that you connect more fully with those who need your comfort and your love. Take someone's hand today and connect to them with joy.

*Lord, I have often been **lonely** in my life, even in my own household. Help me to be willing to connect face to face with my friends and family today. Amen.*

# OAKS

*They will be called **oaks** of righteousness, a planting of the Lord
for the display of his splendor.*                                    Isaiah 61:2–4 NIV

**Oak** is often used to build lovely furniture, or to create beautiful doors and window frames. It is the kind of wood that you can count on to perform well no matter how it is put to use. If you burn oak in your fireplace, it will provide warmth and a gentle fragrance that lasts for hours.

How wonderful that Isaiah compared the people of God who returned to Him with joy, and who would be blessed with His favor, as oaks of righteousness, ready to be on display, able to show what God does. That is the work of God's people and always will be, to stand tall and reach up, sharing the work of God with others so they can see His possibilities.

What a compliment it is to any of us to be thought worthy of God's favor, ready and willing to add richness and warmth to those around us, sharing His blessings and standing strong. Believers are called oaks of righteousness, sharing in the splendor only God provides and giving light and shade to those around them.

God designed your limbs, and He helped to create the foundation of your faith, by planting you among others who could strengthen and nourish your spirit. Through His love, you have become eternally His, an oak of splendor and joy.

*Lord, thank You for planting me among the **oaks** of righteousness so
that I could grow stronger and stand firm for You. Amen.*

# REFUGE

*These six cities shall be for **refuge** for the children of Israel, for the stranger, and for the sojourner among them, that anyone who kills a person accidentally may flee there.*       Numbers 35:15 NKJV

When you're afraid, you need somewhere to turn, perhaps even some-place to run. You need to know that you can find safety and be protected. We all desire sanctuary when trouble looms.

In the days of the patriarchs, God set up cities of **refuge**, places where people could go if they committed manslaughter, accidentally killing someone. The thinking was something like this: What if the axe blade breaks off the handle and hits an innocent person nearby? The person who was using the axe had no idea that it would fly off and hit someone. But the person who was killed would have family members who would seek revenge.

In our culture, we have sanctuary cities or policies that try to protect immigrants from being deported and those are places of refuge, and so the idea is to have a safe place to be. The reminder here is that God is our refuge, our safe place when a crisis hits us or when we know we have sinned against Him or people around us. We ask His forgiveness and hope for His mercy. He alone sustains us right where we are.

Don't wait for a crisis, an accident, or something out of your control before you seek God as your refuge. You can ask Him to keep you protected in the shadow of His wings. Let Him be your Source of peace, your personal place of refuge.

*Lord, thank You for being my place of **refuge** when concerns of the day overwhelm me. Grant me the gift of Your peace and presence always. Amen.*

# SERVE

*And she had a sister called Mary, who also sat at Jesus' feet and heard His word. But Martha was distracted with much serving, and she approached Him and said, "Lord, do You not care that my sister has left me to serve alone? Therefore tell her to help me."*  Luke 10:39–40 NKJV

Imagine that you're getting ready for a big family dinner and you're excited because you have some of your favorite people gathered together to share a festive meal. At first, everyone seems to be helping here and there to pull things together, but then as the guests begin to settle in, you're the only one left in the kitchen. Everyone else is having fun chatting, playing board games, and watching videos. Suddenly, you feel overwhelmed with the work to be done. It irks you just a little bit.

As sisters, Mary and Martha often shared the domestic duties of their household. We don't hear other stories of Martha complaining that no one helps her around the house, so we assume something else is going on in this Scripture. Mary is so excited that Jesus is there that she just leaves Martha to the task of doing all the preparations for their meal and goes to sit at Jesus' feet, so she can hear His stories. It was expected that women would **serve** guests who came to their home, so it was even more unusual here for Mary to abandon Martha and simply sit down to hear the stories of her friend Jesus. When Jesus tells Martha that Mary has chosen the best thing to do, He's reminding everyone present that listening for His voice is always the right choice.

How is it that we can best prepare to serve others? Is it by always being in the kitchen and dishing up the potatoes, or could we learn more about serving others if we sat a little longer and listened closely to the Master? Practical issues aside, perhaps to serve, we have to first prepare our hearts. When we do that, we are no longer serving people, but the Lord Himself. No doubt, there's a mix of Mary and Martha in each of us.

*Lord, thank You for allowing me the chance to serve You and the people I know You've placed in my care. Let me be willing to truly serve You in the best ways. Amen.*

# ENDUED

*And you are witnesses of these things. Behold, I send the Promise of My Father upon you; but tarry in the city of Jerusalem until you are **endued** with power from on high.*                    Luke 24:48–49 NKJV

**Endued** is probably not a word that slips easily off your tongue since it isn't used that much in today's English. It is used in the Scripture from Luke as a way to be filled with the power of God, something worth waiting for. After the resurrection of Jesus, the followers were concerned about how they would be guided to spread the word about Him. They were His witnesses, but they knew they needed help and they feared being separated from Jesus.

They didn't have to worry, though, because Jesus made them a promise. He said that they would be endued with power by His Father. They would receive a gift that would give them power, spiritual power, to continue their training in matters of the kingdom. They would be endued with the Holy Spirit.

We, too, look to be endued with, filled with, or given the gift of the Holy Spirit, because just like our ancestors in faith, we are facing a world that will strive to take it from us. Ideologies, and philosophies, and political slants, and even theologies abound, but our job is to know Christ, the resurrected Savior of the world. Our hearts have been endued with grace and the Spirit of Christ.

*Lord, I pray that I will be **endued** with Your Spirit every day and that, through Your power, I will be able to continue in Your presence. Amen.*

# TELL

*"My God, I want to do what you want. Your teachings are in my heart."*
I will **tell** *about your goodness in the great meeting of your people.*
*Lord, you know my lips are not silent.*                    Psalm 40:8–9 NCV

When you can **tell** a story to the people around you, what kinds of things do you talk about? Typically, we tell stories about the things that concern us, make us laugh, or mean a lot to us. We tell stories about love, and life, families and friends.

David reminds God that he loves to tell others about the things God has done, about His goodness, and about His teachings. David wants to spread the word about God because he loves God and he has a special relationship with Him.

What do you suppose it took for David to speak of God's love and His mercy in the great meeting rooms of his people? Did he care whether they believed him or whether they were on the same page spiritually as he was? We can imagine that he did not care about what others thought. Why? Because his love for God was so important to every aspect of his life. David couldn't imagine handling one detail without bringing God into it. David wanted to tell others about God because he had an amazing story to share. He knew what God had done for him. He was a boy shepherd who became a king, and he knew only God could orchestrate that. He was also a man who had made many poor decisions, rebelling against God when it suited him. He knew that He needed God's forgiveness and steadfast grace. No doubt, David was greatly relieved to know that God had forgiven him and restored him to become, as it says in Acts, a "man after God's own heart."

You have stories to tell today. When you think of the things that you love, the ones that are key to who you are and the life you live, share your heart. Share your stories and tell others about your faith in God.

*Lord, thank You for giving me so many awesome stories to **tell** about You. Amen.*

# UNDERSTAND

*David said, "All these plans were written with the Lord guiding me. He*
*helped me **understand** everything in the plans."*

1 Chronicles 28:19 NCV

People have incredible abilities and talents. They have natural gifts that help them understand the nuances of the things they do well. They can take a math formula or a scientific theory apart and put it back together because they have learned about and **understand** those things.

Your faith walk is like that. You know and understand things that God has shown you. You are inspired to walk with Him in ways that others simply don't get. You have a gift for sharing your stories of His love and grace.

When David needed guidance, he asked God to show him what he needed to know. He believed that God would directly influence his thinking and help him to understand whatever it was that concerned him.

You can know what a math formula is, but not truly understand how it works. You can know what someone said, but not understand how they came to their conclusions. It's one thing to know something. It's another thing to understand what it truly means.

We try to learn and grow every day. We look for ways to know more about our business, parenting skills, or Bibles. We can know a lot of things, but only God can truly give us the kind of understanding that will make a difference. Seek His guidance so that you can understand all that He has for you to share.

*Lord, I know that I have not begun to **understand** You in the ways*
*You hope I will. Help me to know You, guide me to understand You*
*more today. Amen.*

# WAY

*Jesus answered, "I am the way, and the truth, and the life. The only way to the Father is through me."* John 14:6 NCV

This Scripture from John anticipates the questions "How do I get there? What is the **way**?"

Jesus' answer is direct and forthright as He talks with His disciples. Of course, they are still trying to understand all the events of the past few days. They were there when Jesus was put in the tomb, and now He's back with them, talking to them, still trying to show them the way. They want to follow Him still, but they are not sure they know the way.

Jesus is very clear. He doesn't say that He is one of many paths. He doesn't say why He is the way. He simply makes a statement and tells the disciples that He is the way. He is the only way to the Father. There's no other option, no other possible entry point.

You may not always be certain about the various paths you take in this life. You might lose your way in the process of trying to get there. You might go the wrong direction, take a circuitous route, and chase a few wild geese. You may stumble and fall over and over again as you seek the best relationship, or you work your way up the corporate ladder, but none of that really matters. We'll always know how to get to God because we'll follow Jesus, who is the way, the path to truth and life.

Some people want you to do things their way. They may even say something like, "My way, or the highway." Jesus doesn't have to intimidate you. He only speaks the truth. "I am the way." May you be blessed as you follow in His footsteps.

*Lord, thank You for showing me the way to be with You and the way to meet my Father in Heaven. Bless all those who follow You with their whole heart. Amen.*

# INCLINE

*O Lord, you will hear the desire of the meek; you will strengthen their heart, you will **incline** your ear to do justice for the orphan and the oppressed,*
*so that those from earth may strike terror no more.*

Psalm 10:17–18 NRSV

God doesn't just hear what you have to say. He doesn't sit passively by and let your words fall randomly around Him. He is far more intentional than that. He is predisposed to your prayers and willingly listens for your voice. For your sake, He will **incline** His ear toward you, leaning in to hear the things you say because you mean so much to Him.

You don't have to say perfectly crafted prayers, weighing every syllable to make sure you've got it right. He hears your voice and immediately strengthens your heart. He feels your need and is prepared to help you the moment you call. He is ready at every hour of the day to rescue you from any kind of oppression.

You have no reason to question or doubt His intention or His ability to take care of your needs. You simply lean into Him, lift up your heart, and seek His guidance. He will incline His ear to you and offer comfort and mercy as you speak. He will look your way as soon as He hears your voice, no matter what the circumstance or situation is that you must face. His every inclination is toward you, to show you His great love and kindness.

Today, walk confidently with your gracious Creator, knowing that He is actively caring about you and listening to your heart.

*Lord, thank You for leaning in and **inclining** Your ear to me. I pray that You will hear the prayers of the hearts of all Your children around the world. Amen.*

# EXTOL

*I will exalt you, my God the King; I will praise your name for ever and ever.*
*Every day I will praise you and extol your name for ever and ever.*
*Great is the Lord and most worthy of praise; his greatness no one can*
*fathom.* Psalm 145:1–3 NIV

Can you remember the last time you were so excited about something or someone that all you could do was talk about it, share your unbridled enthusiasm, and do a happy dance? That's the idea of what David is saying as he prays to God and praises God's name. He says, "I will exalt you," meaning "I will lift up your name, put it on the marquee at the movie theater, make sure everyone knows about it. I want the whole world to know that you are my God and my King because nothing means more to me than that."

In his exuberance, David also says that he will **extol** or "highly praise" God. He will go on and on about God's great deeds and the amazing and miraculous things God has done. He won't stop talking about God all day long and he will tell anyone who will listen how great God is.

You may have never thought about a way that you could extol someone on Earth, but perhaps from now on, you will look up to your Father in Heaven and praise Him with the same kind of enthusiasm that David had. You can extol Him forever and ever.

*Lord, thank You for doing the most amazing things in my life to support me and show Your love for me. I will extol You all the days of my life. Amen.*

# FIELD

*He answered, "The one who sowed the good seed is the Son of Man. The field is the world, and the good seed stands for the people of the kingdom."*
Matthew 13:37 NIV

Imagine as you look at the globe, this planet designed for human beings, that it is in reality one large **field**. This field has been intentionally created, and the gardener knows every bit of the turf. He knows which parts of that field will be productive at harvest time and which areas will not.

He knows where to plant the good seed and just what it will take for it to grow. He made the field big enough to take in a variety of seeds, a variety of good seeds, and He nourishes every part of it with His love and mercy. He waters it and watches as the roots form and the blossoming begins. He loves this field, every inch of it, and He won't begin to harvest it until every little seedling has had a chance to get grounded in Him. He's adamant that none should perish, that none would miss the opportunity to bear fruit.

You have a home on God's field. You are one of the seeds that He planted, one of the seeds that causes Him delight. He does all He can to give you the proper balance of sunshine and rain, and He watches over you as you grow. You are never out of His sight. He looks to you to dig your roots deeply into His soil so that nothing can take you out of His hand.

Just as He did to Adam and Eve, God planted human beings in His field, His garden, this thing we call the world, and waits patiently, watching us grow, hoping we will produce great abundance at the harvest time.

*Lord, thank You for putting me in Your field and watching over me all the days of my life. Help me to dig deeper into my study of Your word and Your ways so that I can produce the fruit that pleases You. Amen.*

# IMITATE

*We do not want you to become lazy, but to **imitate** those who through faith and patience inherit what has been promised.*  Hebrews 6:12 NIV

You've been learning to **imitate** what you see in others since you were born. You heard your mother talking to you and you eventually began to imitate the sounds you heard. You watched your classmates at school, and imitated their behavior, both good and bad. When you tried a new work-out class, you tried to imitate the movements of those around you. So it isn't new for you to consider what it means to imitate Christ or to imitate those who walk the walk of faith.

It's interesting to think about the difference between imitating classmates or workout buddies and imitating Christ. Those situations meant everyone should do exactly the same thing at the same time.

When you imitate Christ, though, you seek the teacher, not the crowds, for each situation. Jesus often acted in ways that were contrary to the other religious leaders. He ate with sinners and He talked with tax collectors and women. He ministered to those who were considered off limits to the priests and Pharisees. Part of the reason for this is that He was following the voice of His Heavenly Father, a voice that few of them could hear.

As you imitate Jesus in the world, you might be doing things differently than the people around you. You might stand out from the crowd. But you will also be sure to shine the light of his love to those same people.

*Lord, thank You for teaching me to **imitate** You as much as possible. Help me to learn from You with every beat of my heart. Amen.*

# APPLE

*For the Lord's portion is his people, Jacob his allotted inheritance.*
*In a desert land he found him, in a barren and howling waste.*
*He shielded him and cared for him; he guarded him as the **apple** of his eye,*

Deuteronomy 32:9–10 NIV

An **apple** is an amazing fruit because it comes in such a variety of colors and tastes and sizes. If you were to ask any three people which type of apple is their favorite, they would probably each list a different one. After all, some people prefer hard, crunchy, tart apples and others like them mellow, soft, and sweet. Whatever your taste, it's fun to consider this metaphor about what it means to be the apple of God's eye.

God designed humans so that He could have a relationship with them. He wanted to keep us close to Himself because we are His joy, His children, and He sees us as "the apple of His eye." God wanted people to love and provide for and protect. He wanted to talk with us about things that matter and things that bring Him delight. He wanted His heart to be reflected through His children; His own family.

God hoped His love would cause us to respond to Him with joy. He wanted to be loved and respected and honored for who He is. He wanted to know that we were grateful to have His love and guidance because He wanted to be able to enjoy His own people as the apple of His eye.

What that means is that you can be yourself. You can be whatever variety of apple you might choose, if you strive to serve God and please Him with the work of your hands and heart. You can be a bit tart and He'll applaud your spunk. You can be sweet and kind and He'll love your spirit. You can be a beautiful, fragrant, unique you, because you have a cherished relationship with Him and you, too, are at the center of His heart and the apple of His eye.

*Lord, I am glad to be the **apple** of Your eye and I pray that I will always do the things that please You as You shield me and care for me. Amen.*

# DISCERN

*He gives one person the power to perform miracles, and another the ability to prophesy. He gives someone else the ability to **discern** whether a message is from the Spirit of God or from another spirit.*

1 Corinthians 12:10 NLT

Much as we like to imagine it, human beings can't really read each other's minds. We can be familiar with our friends in ways that mean we can sometimes finish each other's sentences, but we can't truly know their deep thoughts. Being able to **discern** someone's actions takes a gift that God gives through His Spirit. He allows us to separate out what someone does from what someone says so that we can be guided in our treatment of them. When we recognize the truth of what they say, we are able to give sound advice or direction.

Being able to discern or discriminate between an action and the cause of an action may be two different things. Usually, we need to know someone very well in order to read them correctly and differentiate the possible meanings of their words or actions.

God knows you so well that He can indeed discern or "observe" your movements and your thoughts. He knows everything about you, and that's a good thing for you because no matter where you are or what you're doing, He understands your heart. He knows what motivates you because He looks beyond the surface and separates the sin from the sinner. He adores you and wants to see your willing and loving heart so that He can help you in all the best ways.

When you discern the actions of others, you provide helpful advice and you can love them right where they are.

*Lord, I am so grateful that You **discern** my thoughts and actions, sifting out the best parts of what motivates me to guide me with Your grace. Amen.*

# CAN

*God **can** see what is in people's hearts. And he knows what is in the mind of the Spirit, because the Spirit speaks to God for his people in the way God wants.*                                                              Romans 8:27 NCV

God **can** do amazing things and one of the best things is that He can look at you and remove the mask you wear, get rid of the superficial disguises you use to face the world, and get right to the heart of who you really are. He knows that when you are troubled in your spirit, He can help because His Spirit speaks about what you need. The Holy Spirit helps God hear your prayers in ways that are meaningful to Him.

When you imagine God's ability to look into your heart, the first thing you want Him to see is your love for Jesus. When He knows that Jesus is there, He can open the door to greater possibilities for you and He can lean on the Holy Spirit to shine a light on what you need. You don't have to be concerned that you will be misinterpreted because you have a team of loving experts at your side, helping you make wise choices and gifting you with greater faith.

When God looks inside your heart, He sees you as the innocent lamb you were on the day you were born. He sees the ways you've grown to become more of what He created you to be. He sees your kindness and your willingness to try harder to do better when you fail. He sees a soft heart that calls out to Him when you're afraid or when you need strength and courage.

God sees your heart because He loves you and that's the best place for the two of you to connect, heart to heart, friend to friend. God can do and can be all that you need right now.

*Lord, thank You for being a **can**-do kind of God. I know that You can do all things, and I am grateful that You see me heart first. Amen.*

# FALSE

*False Christs and false prophets will come and perform great wonders and miracles. They will try to fool even the people God has chosen, if that is possible.*                                        Matthew 24:24 NCV

It's become increasingly more difficult to know the good guys from the bad guys these days. Fake news runs across the headlines and truth is buried in the midst of chaos. It's no wonder that the time will come for even **false** Christs and false prophets to make bold moves across social media. The trappings are everywhere, and it will take a lot of discernment for Christians to be able to recognize the answers on the true-false tests.

Perhaps the best thing to do is to keep alert and prepare yourself ahead of time so that you stand on solid ground, no matter what is going on in the world. The Bible shares the truth of God and it's there for you anytime you are willing to spend time with it, reading, praying, digesting it, and taking it into your heart. It will give you invisible armor to wear and keep you safely in the range of God's truth and love. It may not be easy. You may find that people challenge your faith and insult your intelligence because you've chosen to bear witness to the God of the universe. You can handle that.

Stay close to your Heavenly Father and to the people who can remind you who you are in Christ. You will never have to worry then about false teachers and false prophets, because you will have the truth as your guide and that truth will carry you anyplace you go.

*Lord, thank You for choosing to love me and share Your truth with me. Bless the lives of all the people I love so that they will know Your truth and simply dismiss the fake news and the **false** teachers who try to persuade them away from You. Amen.*

# HARMONY

*Live in **harmony** with one another. Do not be proud, but be willing to associate with people of low position. Do not be conceited.*

Romans 12:16 NIV

What would your day be like if it was lived in perfect **harmony**? You would wake up and thank God for all that you have, get a little wisdom on how to deal with the day, and then move on to greet your family. The kids would all get along and everyone would have a sense of purpose and hug each other good-bye. You'd go to work and your agendas would work out well. You'd accomplish your goals and you'd find that every person you connected with was somehow a little kinder and a little more compassionate than you'd ever noticed before.

It doesn't really have to be a fantasy to live in harmony. It all starts with you. You can wake up and acknowledge your Creator, spend some time in prayer, and quietly enjoy a few peaceful moments. You can offer a cheerful face to your family as everyone separates to go on their way, and then you can be considerate of each person you meet. The traffic jam you're in doesn't have to cause your mood to change. It can be a chance to look out at the others, slowly moving along the path of life with you. You can pray for them. You can think warm thoughts about the people you love. You can bring peace and harmony to your own soul simply by making that one decision.

Sure, that sounds like it could be difficult to really do, but is it truly easier to spin negative remarks, even in your head, about perfect strangers? Is it any more difficult to be kind to a person who works for you than it is to be kind to the person you work for? Kindness and harmony have nothing to do with the social, economic, or physical attributes of any person you know. They are matters of the heart, and this kind of harmony is a choice you can make today.

*Lord, help me to desire to live and to act in every way that brings **harmony** to others. Amen.*

# HARVEST

*Even now the one who reaps draws a wage and **harvests** a crop for eternal life, so that the sower and the reaper may be glad together. Thus the saying "One sows and another reaps" is true.*　　　　　John 4:36–37 NIV

There's always some kind of **harvest** taking place: Your long-term project is done, finals are over, your child graduates from kindergarten. Whatever has taken place, a lot of effort and time went into it, and more than one person participated in the success of the venture. Others helped you meet the goal and reap the reward so you could get to the harvest moment.

We have little harvests along the way of life, because seeds were planted, and some were nourished and well watered and came to fruition. Some died on the vine for a variety of reasons. The grand finale of all harvests, though, will be the one God has planned for His entire creation. He knows those who sow and those who reap firsthand because of all the time they have already shared with Him. He knows the good seed, and He knows those that have withered on the vine.

One of the reasons we celebrate occasions like Thanksgiving is that they remind us to be grateful for the harvest, the bounty that we have because of God's grace and provision. We know that one may plant, and one may water, but only God can make things flourish and grow. He loves you and He planted you in your family, in your community, and in the very place you happen to be, where you're becoming more each day of all He intended. He is proud of who you are, and He knows you will work with Him from now to that grand harvest. Give Him thanks and praise today for all that is, and all that will yet be in your life.

*Lord, thank You for planting seeds of love within me so long ago. I pray that I will be worthy of the **harvest** and bring joy to You all the days of my life. Amen.*

# GIFTS

*There are different kinds of gifts, but the same Spirit distributes them.*
*There are different kinds of service, but the same Lord.*

1 Corinthians 12:4–5 NIV

What is it about **gifts** that makes them so special to us? In part, we love receiving gifts because, most of the time, they are given with genuine love and affection. We know that someone took the time to think through what gift would mean the most to us. We know that they value our relationship and the gift is a token of the joy that we share together.

We love gifts also because of the great variety that we can both give and receive. No matter how many gift ideas you come up with for the people you love, nothing you give even begins to compare with the One who already gave you the gifts of a beating heart and life-giving water, and people to love you. Those are gifts that are beyond measure.

God gives each person who draws a breath His exquisite gifts. He makes one person a healer, and one an encourager. He makes one a gourmet chef and one a minister of His Word. He goes about giving each one a different gift, unique and special. Some are gifts of service, and some are gifts of intellect. Some are gifts of kindness, and others are gifts of sharing.

If you wonder what your gifts are, you don't have to look very far. Your smile, your kind word, your giving and gentle spirit, your willingness to accept all people with love—these are incredible gifts. Give God thanks and praise today for the gifts He gave you and the ones you appreciate so much in the people around you.

*Lord, thank You for the **gifts** that You have lavished upon me. You have done more for me than words can ever express in gratitude. Amen.*

313

# INHERIT

*Blessed are the meek, for they will **inherit** the earth.*     Matthew 5:5 NIV

As Jesus was offering blessings for the various types of people on the planet, He didn't give any homage to the arrogant, the loud-mouthed, or the bullies. He didn't offer an inheritance to the rich or the famous or the skilled or the talented or the athletic. Instead, He offered blessings to the humble, and the gentle in spirit, and the ones who kindly watched out for the good of others.

Now, He didn't tell those people they would **inherit** some farmland over by the lake, or that they would receive the best high-rise that would ever be built near Central Park in New York City. He gave them instead the whole, entire, incredible riches of the world He had created with His Father in Heaven. He gave them the Earth.

He said you are God's sons and daughters, and you will inherit this world and the next. All you must do is be kind, be humble, and be willing to live a quiet and gentle life.

Some people think that the person who dies with the most toys wins. But Jesus says that the person who dies with the most heart wins. We already know what we will inherit, so celebrate and live generously.

*Lord, thank You for the blessing of knowing that if I can live a gentle and loving life, I will **inherit** the Earth. Thank You for teaching me how to live. Amen.*

# GUIDE

*The Lord says, "I will make you wise and show you where to go.*
*I will **guide** you and watch over you."*                    Psalm 32:8 NCV

When you are preparing to travel to a new city or country, it's always a good idea to look for a **guide**book or person to tell you the best places, restaurants, and other points of interest. You don't have time to simply wander around hoping you will stumble across the best things to see. So you ask someone to help you.

Some people haven't figured out yet that God has given them a guide for their trip here on Planet Earth. Most of us didn't come with a built-in understanding of the best sights to see or the most important things to know. In our brief span of years, we don't have time to just hope we'll run into the things God would have us know. So He provided multiple resources.

The Holy Bible is like a guidebook. It shows you where the people before you came from, the mistakes they made, and the things that you can learn from them. Learning from their mistakes means you don't have to do them yourself. It also shows the pitfalls in the ways people think or perceive the world. God wants you to know that there's a better way to do things.

Along with the Guidebook, God provided a Master for you to follow. He knew it would be easier for you to stay on the path if you simply followed the Guide. After all, He wouldn't let you fall into any traps or obstacles. Jesus would know exactly where you should step because He would go before you and watch over you. God wants you to be wise and to have confidence wherever you are. Just remember to go to the Guide and leaf through the Guidebook when you're not quite certain where to go next.

*Lord, thank You for being my **Guide**. Please direct my steps*
*according to Your will and purpose in all that I do today. Amen.*

# PENNY

*Two sparrows cost only a **penny**, but not even one of them can die without your Father's knowing it.*                    Matthew 10:29 NCV

The value of a **penny** may be a matter of perspective, but the point of this Scripture is that God values His creation. He knows when the smallest bird dies, or when your heart breaks, and He knows when you need His help. You never have to wonder if God is with you or if He cares about the way your life is going. He cares.

It's fitting for us to stop and consider the things that we value and hold dear. Some of those things are priceless, at least to us, and some of those things have no significant value at all. The value in either case does not depend on the market price that could be realized, but on the worth of it to the owner.

Every living thing is valuable to the Creator. When you struggle to take care of an issue with a family member, or you wonder how you'll pay all the current bills, or you feel anxious over the report you must do for your job, it all matters. It matters to God because He values you above all else.

As the saying goes, "If you had been the only person that needed saving, God would still have sent Jesus to come to Earth and die for you." That means you are always in God's heart and He antes up for you every day. He put up more than a penny, or a million dollars. He put up His Son to live and love, die and live again, just for you.

*Lord, thank You for loving me and for giving me the kind of worth that cannot be measured like a **penny**. I bless Your name today. Amen.*

# NOISE

*When the day of Pentecost came, they were all together in one place.*
*Suddenly a **noise** like a strong, blowing wind came from heaven and filled*
*the whole house where they were sitting.*                    Acts 2:1–3 NCV

If you have ever sat in a shelter and listened to the wind of a hurricane as it wreaked its havoc on the landscape and everything else in its path, you might have some idea of the **noise** the first believers experienced as they sat all together awaiting the Holy Spirit.

Jesus had told them to wait for the Presence from on High, the Holy Spirit of God, who would fill them with the gifts of His Spirit and cause them to be changed. They waited and then they began to hear the sound. It may have been a bit of a whistling wind at first, gathering in strength, blowing and pounding like a hometown drum and bugle corps. It shouted and echoed and whipped and swirled its way around the room as it moved among the people. It was a blowing, beating, pounding wind from Heaven, and it rested on each person in the room, causing them to speak in different languages. It was a Holy fire of the Presence of God, and though it was a mighty noise, it was music to their ears.

When we read a phrase like "suddenly a noise" happened, we're alerted to something important that is coming next. The noise signals the entrance of something that will change the story line, and will make a difference in the way the story is told from that moment on. This noise, this moment, when the Holy Spirit arrived from Heaven and fell upon the people gathered in that room, changed the story of our belief system. It signaled the beginning of life in the Spirit. It was indeed a joyful noise and a sound that can come to us as well.

*Lord, You often announce Your Presence and I'm grateful that You*
*help me hear Your voice above the **noise** of the world. Thank You for*
*Your Holy Spirit. Amen.*

# PROVERBS

*He spoke three thousand **proverbs**, and his songs were one thousand and five. Also he spoke of trees, from the cedar tree of Lebanon even to the hyssop that springs out of the wall; he spoke also of animals, of birds, of creeping things, and of fish.* 1 Kings 4:32–33 NKJV.

You remember those little things your mom always said, bits of advice that she probably got from her own mom? They were sayings like, "Don't run with scissors," or "If you can't say something nice, don't say anything." They were just common sense usually, but you remembered them, at least sometimes.

**Proverbs** are something like that, bits of wisdom to help you make good choices and decisions. They remind you about the differences in working hard or being lazy, or doing a good thing for someone, or doing something unkind. Solomon was given a depth of wisdom that no one before him or since has had. He asked God to favor him with an ability to know how to rule God's people.

One Proverb says, "A friend is always loyal, and a brother is born to help in time of need." If you carry this thought around, or embroider it on a pillow, or hang it like a plaque on your wall, you'll think twice about being a good friend or a good brother.

Another Proverb says, "A truly wise person uses few words; a person with understanding is even-tempered." Perhaps using few words is good advice, since explanations are often dangerous.

Wherever you are today, consider one of the Proverbs of Solomon and take it with you through the day. Repeat it and work with it until it becomes part of your thinking. It will serve you well.

*Lord, I love the wisdom of **Proverbs** and appreciate each helpful nugget of advice. I pray that You would give me wisdom today in all I do. Amen.*

# SAND

*"But everyone who hears these sayings of Mine, and does not do them, will be like a foolish man who built his house on the **sand**: and the rain descended, the floods came, and the winds blew and beat on that house; and it fell."*                                    Matthew 7:26–27 NKJV

Some of us must admit that we've been known to build some houses on the **sand**. Oh, we may not be foolish enough to literally build a house on sand, but we've built our thoughts and expectations on things that simply had no foundation. Can you remember any of those sandy thoughts, the ones that you look back on now and cringe to realize you were silly enough to pursue?

Maybe you thought you could run a marathon, simply because you walk around the block a couple times a week. You didn't realize you would have to really prepare for a marathon. You didn't and so the whole event was not very satisfying. You may have thought you could write a book. You wrote some of the book, but you didn't know how to keep your plot going. You didn't know that writers practice, join writers' groups, and do a lot of background work to write books. They build a foundation.

Nearly any important thing you want to do with your life requires preparation. You can't build ideas or friendships, or anything else, unless you build on a firm foundation. All the sand thinking in the world won't help you when any sign of difficulty emerges. You need to be able to withstand the storms of life. Fortunately, God has provided you with a house built on a rock, the rock of His Son, Jesus. You'll always be standing on a firm foundation with Him. Watch out for those foolish thoughts that leave you knee-deep in the sand.

*Lord, I stand on Your rock and not on the **sand**. Keep me strong and help me continue to build a firm foundation in You. Amen.*

# TABLETS

*Then Moses went down the mountain, and in his hands he had the two*
*stone tablets with the Agreement on them. The commands were written on*
*both sides of each stone, front and back. God himself had made the tablets,*
*and God himself had written the commands on the tablets.*

Exodus 32:15–16 NCV

If we talk about **tablets** today, most of us think about the easy-to-carry, electronic devices that we can take anywhere and use for a hundred different reasons. Tablets help us get the word out, quickly and easily.

Now slip back in time and consider the tablets that Moses carried in his hands. They weren't lightweight, easy-to-carry tablets. They were made of stone, and they had been written on both sides, front and back, by the finger of God. These tablets contained some of the most sacred Scriptures of all time called the Ten Commandments. These were the agreements God wanted to make with His children. They were so incredibly important, God wrote them Himself.

God continues to try to get human beings to listen to Him. He keeps intervening in our lives in ways that will help us know how to please Him. He uses any resources at His disposal to get the word out, even tablets. The good news is that He has even written a portion of Himself into your heart, which means you don't need any clever device at all to draw near to Him and understand what He wants.

*Lord, You have provided guidance with the tablets of old, and with*
*the help of devices in our current culture. Help me to seek Your*
*wisdom every day. Amen.*

# USEFUL

*But I said, "I have worked hard for nothing; I have used all my power, but I did nothing useful. But the Lord will decide what my work is worth; God will decide my reward."* Isaiah 49:4 NCV

Most of us want to feel like we're valuable, **useful**, contributing to a project or to our communities. We want to be guided and have a purpose and work hard to fulfill that purpose. We want that, but sometimes we're not exactly sure what we do that is really useful. We wonder if we still have a purpose or if anyone really needs what we do or cares about what we can do.

These are all good questions and here's the answer. When you seek the Lord's help, ask for His guidance about the work you do. Whether your Earthly accomplishment is impressive or not, your Heavenly accomplishment may be far more than you know. God can use all that you do for the good of the kingdom, and He can make it useful to get His work done.

Sometimes His work is found in simple things, and sometimes it is blessed by amazing things. You may not be asked to slay a Goliath, but you may be asked to be kind to the woman who sits in church week after week and feels invisible. You may have to step up and be willing to speak God's name proudly to those who might laugh. You don't ever have to worry that your efforts will not be rewarded. Your Father in Heaven sees each one of them, and He smiles each time you accomplish the smallest deed.

You are useful, valuable, appreciated, and loved by God for the work of your hands. Stay the course today and He will continue to bring you favor.

*Lord, thank You so much for accepting my small efforts to share the good news of Your salvation. I pray that I will be **useful** to You today. Amen.*

# WEEDS

*"The seed cast in the weeds is the person who hears the kingdom news, but weeds of worry and illusions about getting more and wanting everything under the sun strangle what was heard, and nothing comes of it."*

Matthew 13:22 MSG

You may not realize you've been walking in the **weeds** until you come to a crisis in your life. Sometimes the lure of reaching the top rung on the ladder can blind you to what is really going on. You may have a good reason for the efforts you make to be the best CEO in the world, but the fact is, if you missed the work of the kingdom in the process, then you're just laboring under illusions. You're stuck in the weeds.

Weeds can be deceptive. They can look like beautiful plants as they blossom among the good seeds into flowers, as though they won't be any trouble at all. After all, what can be wrong with having a few dandelions on the lawn?

You might be able to stand the dandelions in your yard, but the dandelions that crop up in your faith are enormous trouble. They come in all kinds of forms: worry, or visions of grandeur, or elusive success. They tempt you and taunt you and keep you thinking that weed walking is okay, because, eventually, good will come out of it. Really? Can good come from the weeds?

Today, look around you, and if you notice weeds of doubt, or worry, or illusions of greatness loitering in your heart and mind, seek God's help. Pull those dandies out by the roots as quickly as you can. You don't need them. They are lions waiting to devour you. Don't walk in the weeds. They will surely strangle your faith.

*Lord, thank You for plucking me out of the weeds today and keeping me on Your steady and beautiful path. Amen.*

# ZEAL

*Be devoted to one another in love. Honor one another above yourselves.*
*Never be lacking in zeal, but keep your spiritual fervor, serving the Lord.*

Romans 12:10–11 NIV

Perhaps one way to define **zeal**, or passion, or a certain fervor for something is to describe it as a thing we give singular focus. We go to sleep thinking about this object of our affection and we rise the next morning, ready to pursue it again. We believe in it! We know that it is important. It feels inspired and we know that God is with us to get the job done. That's passion! That's zeal! It occupies the spaces in our hearts and minds like few things can.

It's funny how we admire passion in those who pursue a dream, going after it, rising and falling and trying again until they succeed. We applaud their efforts and think highly of them for being so focused on this thing that draws them to keep going each day. We love their zeal! However, when we think of people who are passionate for their faith, who have zeal for the Lord, we often laugh at that and attack them. We call them zealots, or "Holy Rollers," or some other less than complimentary name because they make us uncomfortable.

You can imagine that John the Baptist made some people uncomfortable. Some of the prophets of old—Jeremiah comes to mind—made the people uncomfortable. They had one focus. They were a one-note song. They only said and did what God called them to say and do.

What about you? Could you stand a bit more passion, more energy, more zeal for the God of your heart? Keep your spiritual fervor and serve the Lord.

*Lord, I know that my spiritual fervor and zeal come and go. Help*
*me to stand more firmly for You in all that I do today. Amen.*

# CATCH

*Later they sent some of the Pharisees and Herodians to Jesus to **catch** him in his words.*                    Mark 12:13 NIV

When certain disciples put down their nets in the waters around Galilee, they hoped to **catch** a lot of fish. They worked to trap them in their nets. They were fisherman and they knew how to do this well enough to make a living.

The Pharisees of Jesus' day had something like this in mind nearly every time they spoke with Him. They were threatened by His faith and His preaching. They never knew anyone who had such a command of the Scriptures or who taught in parables with such authority as He did. They schemed in every conversation with Him to catch Jesus in some kind of lie, something that they could label as heresy or that would cast Him as a rebel against the local authorities. Jesus knew their tricks, and so He was skillful in not allowing Himself to be taken in by their questions. Perhaps this is a skill we need to develop ourselves.

Believers are often confronted by those outside the kingdom who hope to be able to label them in some way, to catch them in the act of being human, or to set up a trap for them so they are open to ridicule. As human beings, we can easily fall into those traps. God will protect us, though, and help us to maintain our focus on Him. We simply must remember to be calm, to pray for His Spirit to direct our words and our actions, and to let others catch us only doing good.

When you feel concerned about those who would try to catch you and belittle your faith, stand firm, because you and God together are always going to win the day.

*Lord, I thank You for **catching** me anytime I start to weaken and fall. You know the best ways to catch those who might try to deceive us. Help me walk closely with You today. Amen.*

# FIRE

*There the angel of the Lord appeared to him in flames of fire coming out of a bush. Moses saw that the bush was on fire, but it was not burning up. So he said, "I will go closer to this strange thing. How can a bush continue burning without burning up?"*                              Exodus 3:2–3 NCV

Moses was in the presence of Holy **fire**. He had never seen such a phenomenal thing before. He couldn't help but ask the practical question, the one that showed the human mind at work: "How can this bush be on fire, but not burn up?" He did not yet understand what he was seeing. He decided to move closer to the spot.

The beauty of this Scripture is that it shows us the totally human side of Moses. He was the man God had protected since his birth, and he had to learn to listen for God's voice and act as God requested him to act. He grew to know that God could do powerful and miraculous things. He learned how to walk with God.

This is important for you to consider as well. After all, you're doing your best to walk with God each day. You're listening to His voice and seeking His guidance. You may have to move closer to Him, though, just as Moses did, before you can recognize Holy fire.

The flame that God put inside your heart draws you to Him, hoping to melt any hardness that might remain, hoping to cause you to see Him more clearly as you do His work each day. You, too, may be walking on Holy ground. Seek God's help and stay close to Him so that you always know when to take off your shoes, so you can feel His Presence and listen for His voice.

*Lord, I believe You have put a Holy fire within my heart. Help me to move so close to You that I will always know Your direction for my life. Amen.*

# FOUND

*So Enoch lived a total of 365 years. Enoch walked with God; one day Enoch could not be **found**, because God took him.*          Genesis 5:23–24 NCV

We tend to think that the opposite of **found** is lost. That may often be true, but it is not the case with Enoch, who could not be found. Enoch was not lost. He was far from it. He walked with God for 365 years and he did it in such a way that God found favor in him, and finally God simply picked him up in His chariot and said, "Come on home!" No doubt Enoch smiled as the chariot arrived, perhaps feeling like a prince who was being picked up in a royal carriage. The King knew him by name and was pleased to bring him home again.

Enoch found his faith in God, and he never departed from it. He stayed with it every day and year of his life, learning more about how to be the man God wanted him to be. Enoch taught his children and his grandchildren about God. He was the great-grandfather of Noah, and most likely influenced Noah to walk with God as well.

Human beings spend a good part of their lives as lost souls. They are lost because they simply do not understand, nor do they seek the ways of God. They imagine that their intellect or their money or their good deeds will be sufficient to take them through this life. They would be right, of course. Those things will take them through this life, but they may not be found in the next life, the one that lasts eternally.

Take a little time today to ponder what it means to you to be found by God. Spend your day as one who is not lost, not wandering, not wondering what to expect in the life to come. You have been found and God is pleased.

*Lord, I know that You **found** me a long time ago and I am eternally grateful. I know there is nothing I can do on my own to merit Your love. I'm so glad You found me. Amen.*

# END

*Because of the increase of wickedness, the love of most will grow cold, but the one who stands firm to the end will be saved. And this gospel of the kingdom will be preached in the whole world as a testimony to all nations, and then the end will come.*                Matthew 24:12–14 NCV

That chill in the air may well signify the declining rays of the sun as you head into the winter months. Summer is gone, the fall has come to an **end**, and winter is upon you. It's a natural part of the way the system of weather works around the globe.

If we read the words of Jesus as He presented them here, we might also notice that there is something akin to Spiritual weather. We can see that the climate is changing, and oftentimes it doesn't seem to be changing for the better. It feels as though the bad guys continue to make themselves known, and their evil deeds crush our spirits. They have hardened their hearts and their love has grown cold.

To be sure, none of us want to come to the end of love. We don't want the day to ever arrive when no one remembers what it means to love a neighbor or help a friend. We don't want the Good News to go unheard or the voices of the people with a heart for God to be silent. We want good to prevail and we want that to happen from here to the end of time.

How can we safeguard that possibility? What can we each do to make a difference? The solution seems to be that we must watch the Spiritual climate of our churches and communities and even our households. We must keep love alive and continue to share the gospel of Christ. When we do, God can continue to work in the world, changing the hearts of many, until the day He chooses to return. Let's hold on to Him and His love all the way to the end.

*Lord, thank You for loving me from the beginning of my life, and staying with me to the **end**. Let me share Your love wherever I am today. Amen.*

# HAVE

*Therefore consider carefully how you listen. Whoever has will be given more; whoever does not have, even what they think they **have** will be taken from them.*

Luke 8:18 NIV

You know that moment when the light of understanding dawns? You've been trying to learn something new, and for whatever reason, you simply couldn't get it. Then all of sudden, you're in, you've got it, you **have** it down, and it feels so good. Once you've got it, you're ready for the next steps; you're ready to learn more and build on the foundation you now have.

Sometimes, though, you don't get it and you never seem to understand what to do with what little you know. Eventually, since having that information didn't serve you well, you simply forget about it. It's akin to learning French in high school, but years later, because you didn't continue your study of French, you're reduced to a few common words, but you never have enough words to actually converse in that language.

In some measure, these analogies are similar to your understanding, your enlightenment, your willingness to seek more about your faith. When you have it, meaning that your faith is strong and you build on your foundation, then you continue to learn and grow. If by chance, though, you began to embrace faith some years ago, but you never really got it, that is, you never made the transition from head knowledge to heart knowledge, then you're in jeopardy of losing what you have. You don't have enough understanding to seek more and grow your faith.

You don't want what you have now to be lost or taken away from you. You want to continue to nurture and build on your foundation of understanding. Thank God for continuing to teach you His ways.

*Lord, thank You for all that I **have** in You. Help me to keep growing and building my understanding of all that You would have me know today. Amen.*

# KEPT

*You have recorded my troubles. You have **kept** a list of my tears.*
*Aren't they in your records?*                                    Psalm 56:8 NCV

Imagine now that God has made a list of the troubles you've experienced since birth. He noted what happened, how you responded, and even **kept** your tears in His records. He knows each thing that broke your heart as you journeyed through life. Perhaps He saved each one so that you would realize how important you are to Him, and that nothing about your life has gone unnoticed. He wanted to be able to show you that He knew what you were going through even when you didn't know He was there.

He's kept your baby book up to date since your first breath and He won't close the book until you're safely back in His arms. He knows you. He knows everything about you and He always wants to be there to dry your tears.

Wouldn't it be something if you kept a record of all the times God made a difference in your life? Maybe you could note when He came through and healed someone for whom you had prayed. You could note those times when the job happened that you didn't expect, or the financing for something important for you was delivered. After all, when you are in continual relationship with God, you recognize those times when His Presence made all the difference in the world. What a fun conversation that will be when you one day exchange stories of how you were there for Him and He was there for you.

It's wonderful to have keepsakes and memories. You know where to turn anytime you want to look through your treasures. That's what God is doing, treasuring each moment that the two of you have shared, collecting your tears in a bottle, and bringing the smiles back to your face.

*Lord, thank You for keeping little treasures about me. I have*
***kept** joyful memories of You as well. Bless all those who live in*
*relationship with You. Amen.*

# DISCIPLINED

*We do not enjoy being **disciplined**. It is painful at the time, but later, after we have learned from it, we have peace, because we start living in the right way.*

Hebrews 12:11 NCV

We may not enjoy being **disciplined**, but sometime in our lives, we come to respect it, knowing that along with gentleness and kindness and love, it helped shape us into the people we are today. We may remember moments in our childhood that didn't go so well for us when we stepped over the line. Yet what would we be like if no one cared enough to guide our behaviors and our mistakes?

If you're a parent now yourself, you know the value of disciplining your children. You don't do it to anger them or to be cruel to them; you do it to remind them that they can make better choices, and you hope that the next time visions of right and wrong fly through their minds, they'll know what to choose.

Your Heavenly Father also wants to lovingly mold and shape your heart and mind. He wants you to feel great joy when you do well, and He wants to help you make a better choice when you don't. Saying you are disciplined out of love may not feel true as you go through the experience, but as the writer of Hebrews says, "Later, after you have learned from it, you have peace and you start living in the right way."

Perhaps you're not always certain whether you are being disciplined by God or by someone simply being unkind. If you learned something that opens your heart to God in a new way, then peace will fill your spirit and guide your steps from that moment on.

*Lord, thank You for knowing when I need to be **disciplined**. I pray that I will learn my lessons quickly and honor You each day. Amen.*

# NEED

*He and all his family were devout and God-fearing; he gave generously to*
*those in **need** and prayed to God regularly.*                    Acts 10:2 NIV

As we approach the end of the fall season, Thanksgiving is celebrated by families all around the country. Our celebration honors God, the provider of all that we have. It honors those who labor to prepare the foods that feed our hearts and bodies and spirits, those that are nutritious and those that simply bring delight. We come to this celebration with hearts of gratitude, often reaching out to those less fortunate to be sure their **needs** are met as well.

We're grateful to have enough, and it is in that spirit that we share what we have with those who do not have enough. The beauty of Thanksgiving is that any of us can give generously despite our own circumstances. If we have plenty, then we can give food or funds or other donations to our favorite shelters or charities. If we don't have material possessions, then we can give of ourselves, volunteering to serve those who cannot serve themselves. If we cannot volunteer, then we can bow our heads in prayer for those in need everywhere on the planet and God will hear our heartfelt requests.

One of the best parts of being a person who honors and serves others is that you feel God's peace and His pleasure as you serve. You recognize that apart from God's grace, you, too, could be the one in great need.

Be grateful today and make every day Thanksgiving in your heart. You have so much to give and there is so much need in the world.

*Lord, thank You for taking care of the things I **need**. Help me to bless*
*others by sharing from the bounty You have given me. Amen.*

# REPENT

*Peter replied, "**Repent** and be baptized, every one of you, in the name of Jesus Christ for the forgiveness of your sins. And you will receive the gift of the Holy Spirit."*
Acts 2:38 NIV

**Repent** is one of those "old-fashioned" words. We tend to think of it as a call of Scripture or the sandwich-board sign and the voice of some "preacher" on a street corner. It feels like a word that simply points fingers at others, trying to tell them what to do.

Yet the fact is that being willing to repent, apologize, surrender, give up, admit wrong, is exactly what any of us must do if we want to move closer to God and find ourselves enjoying His Presence for all eternity. It's part of the process of how we get to the goal called eternal life.

To repent is not simply an action of doing; it's an action of being; being straight with God about the things you've done that you knew at the time were wrong for you to do. It's a heart thing. It's a moment when your own heart breaks because you realize how much you have disappointed the One who loves you and who created you. When you repent, you are saying to God, "I am ready to turn things around. More than that, I am ready to turn my life over to you."

Because of the sacrifice of Jesus, God sees your heart and He forgives your sins. God wipes the slate clean and fills you with His Spirit so that you can be made perfect in His sight. Praise Him for His act of love and the blessing of His Son to redeem you from your sins. It's a gift that will leave you feeling lighter than air.

*Lord, I **repent** of those things that I have not yet turned over to You, and I ask that You forgive each thing I've done that offends You. Help me to live a better life. Amen.*

# LADDER

*Jacob dreamed that there was a **ladder** resting on the earth and reaching up into heaven, and he saw angels of God going up and coming down the ladder. Then Jacob saw the Lord standing above the ladder, and he said, "I am the Lord, the God of Abraham your grandfather, and the God of Isaac."*

Genesis 28:12–13 NCV

The beauty of dreams is that they manage to mix up the common and the uncommon in interesting ways. In Jacob's dream, he sees a **ladder**. What does a ladder normally do? One thing it does is allow you to reach something that is up higher than you are. It causes you to have to take a step and climb intentionally toward the thing you desire. It's a tool that gives you the chance to move up or down as you see fit. It may even serve as an extension of your right arm.

Jacob's ladder was not a tool for him to use, but it provided a way for the angels to go up and down. Jacob could see that these beings were real and that they served God. No doubt he was in awe of this vision. When he saw God standing at the top of the ladder that reached into Heaven, he knew that something significant was happening and he listened with his whole heart.

In worldly terms, we like to talk about climbing the ladder of success. In Heavenly terms, there couldn't be a better metaphor than this one that allows us to understand that God has provided a bridge, a ladder, between Earth and Heaven. He stands and waits and calls to each of us to discover He is there. Look up, because God sees you as well.

*Lord, thank You for giving me a chance to reach up and stand on the **ladder** that brings me closer to You. Bless all who look for You today. Amen.*

# PRESENT

*That is the way we should live, because God's grace that can save everyone has come. It teaches us not to live against God nor to do the evil things the world wants to do. Instead, that grace teaches us to live in the **present** age in a wise and right way and in a way that shows we serve God.*

Titus 2:11–12 NCV

It may well be true that there's "no time like the **present**," as you consider whether to start something new. However, it could be better to accept the fact that there's "no time *but* the present." What you did yesterday is gone and what you hope to do tomorrow is all well and good, but that's tomorrow.

This present is all there is, and the writer of Titus agrees. He wants you to know God's grace is alive and well, right here and now, ready to help you, embrace you, guide you, and give you strength. There's no need to wander back into the past to try to find it. You don't have to wonder about whether you will stumble across it in the future. You have it. Today! You live in the grace, mercy, and peace of God, and all you must do is accept it, and embrace it for your good.

So how does living in the present moment affect your life today? Perhaps it means you'll take an action that you've been postponing for some time. Maybe you will sign up for that course you've wanted to take to get a degree. You might decide to offer forgiveness to an old friend. You may visit a shut-in. Your choices are about now, about this moment, because the truth is, this is the only moment you truly have. You can wait until another day, and by the grace of God that day will come, but if you want to get your life on track quickly, then do it today. If you're running on empty, the best way to get filled up is by the Holy Spirit of God, who is ready to help you make great choices wherever you are. Be present with His Presence every day of your life.

*Lord, thank You for helping me to live in the **present**. I pray that I will serve You well today. Amen.*

# QUIT

*People who **quit** following the Lord will be like a name written in the dust, because they have left the Lord, the spring of living water.*

Jeremiah 17:13 NCV

If there's one theme throughout the Old and the New Testaments, it's the one that asks us to listen and to follow the Lord's commands. The mystery of God is that He has always been, and He always will be. Long after we're dust, He will still be there. He does not change. He offered Himself to humankind so that we could learn what it means to love, to give, to forgive. He wants us to know Him and to love Him, each other, and ourselves. The best thing we can do, then, is to immerse ourselves in His love, swim in His Spirit, and take in more of Him every chance we get. The worst thing we can do is **quit**, leave, call it a day!

What do we lose if we quit following the only Source of Living Water that has ever existed anywhere? In truth, we lose all that it means to live. We are dust in the wind, and all things are meaningless. Without Him, we are nothing and we can be nothing. We have no breath, no life in the Spirit.

What do we gain if we follow His path? We live with more positive attitudes built on God's blessings. Our hearts are warm and generous. We remember that God provides for our needs, and so we share what He has given us because He will give us more. We learn that serving Him is not some kind of chore that we dislike having to do, but it is a privilege that we can enjoy and take part in as we do His loving work. To quit means we've abandoned Him, left our post, walked away from His incredible love and His desire to build a relationship with us. We never want to quit following the Light of the World, the One whose name means Love. He is the Source of all that brings us hope and possibility.

*Lord, thank You for keeping me close to You and never letting me **quit**, even when I'm discouraged. Thank You for loving me more than I can truly understand. Amen.*

# MERCY

*The Lord answered, "I will cause all my goodness to pass in front of you, and I will announce my name, the Lord, so you can hear it. I will show kindness to anyone to whom I want to show kindness, and I will show mercy to anyone to whom I want to show mercy."* Exodus 33:19 NCV

God knew Moses very well. They had walked together for many years, and God was pleased with Him. However, the children of Israel were a stubborn group of people, and God continually worked to teach them how to live. He showed great restraint and **mercy** toward them because they made one mistake after another. They had stubborn, wayward hearts.

This Scripture from Exodus reminds us that God does not owe human beings any explanations for His behavior. He is the Creator. He is the only being with such authority. There is no one greater than God now and there never will be. God can show mercy to whomever He chooses to show mercy, compassion, kindness, leniency, and forgiveness.

When we walk closely with God, we have more opportunities to get to know each other. God can soften our hearts and work with us so we become what He intended, what He knew we could be, before we drew our first breath. When we surrender our lives and step away from our stubborn natures, He can come closer, announce Himself to us and help us recognize His voice. We want to live in such a way that His goodness can pass in front of us and become part of us. We want to share His kindness with those who still do not know He exists. Let us remember to show kindness and mercy to everyone we meet today.

*Lord, thank You for Your tenderness to me and for Your continual mercy. Help me to show that same patient love to others today. Amen.*

# RULES

*But the Lord **rules** forever. He sits on his throne to judge, and he will judge the world in fairness; he will decide what is fair for the nations.*

Psalm 9:8 NCV

Chances are the word **rules** puts a little fear and trembling in your heart. After all, we don't like "rulers" because we tend to think of rulers as intolerant and overbearing. We don't like "rules" because that sounds like we must color within the lines for everything we do and that hinders our growth and creative expression.

However, knowing that the Lord rules forever is something to take to heart in a positive way. Knowing that He rules and will always rule and that nothing in this world can change that means we can depend on Him. He can offer us unconditional and steadfast love and we can trust that it will be there until our dying day.

He rules, and along with His ruling comes His judgment. Again, judgment is a scary word because we imagine only the worst. We see the spotlight on those aspects of ourselves we don't like, and we fear He will judge us. He will judge us, but the psalmist reminds us that He will judge with fairness. That means He will weigh all the evidence, the good and the bad, and He will then determine what is fair. He will judge us with love and discernment. He will judge us as a loving parent, who looks at a wayward child and hates the sin, but loves the sinner.

Seek the One who rules forever and come before Him with repentance and a contrite heart. He will lift you up from the mud you have gotten yourself into and free you. He rules you with compassion, love, and mercy.

*Lord, thank You for **ruling** over all of us, judging us with tender mercy and kindness. Help me to live up to all that You want me to be. Amen.*

# SPIRIT

*After they had crossed over, Elijah said to Elisha, "What can I do for you before I am taken from you?" Elisha said, "Leave me a double share of your spirit." Elijah said, "You have asked a hard thing. But if you see me when I am taken from you, it will be yours. If you don't, it won't happen."*

2 Kings 2:9–10 NCV

The word **spirit** gets bandied about with a meaning that shares your love for God with your love for your favorite sports team. We cheer together with team spirit when our team is running behind, hoping they will feel our enthusiasm and that it will help them win the day.

As a human being, as a child of God, you have a body, a mind, and a spirit. Sometimes you know that the spirit within you is guiding your choices and helping to direct your steps. Sometimes you feel the Presence of Jesus deep in your soul and it's a glorious thing.

Look what Elisha asked for, from his mentor, Elijah. He said, "Leave me a double share of your spirit." Why? Why would Elisha want the same spirit, and then some, that he witnessed in Elijah? Elijah was a man who walked with God, and his spirit was connected to God in obvious ways. When he prayed, things happened. When he spoke, it was with clarity and authority. When he worshipped, it was with his whole heart. He knew God and God knew him.

Since Elijah didn't know whether God would honor Elisha's request, he put a condition on it that totally left the outcome to God. As the story continues, you know that Elisha received a double share of Elijah's spirit. We, too, can seek more of God's Spirit. All we must do is ask.

May God's Spirit grow within you and shine on you each day.

*Lord, thank You for giving me Your **Spirit**. Help me to learn more from You and to desire more of You. Amen.*

# UPHOLD

*The Lord makes firm the steps of the one who delights in him;*
*though he may stumble, he will not fall, for the Lord* **upholds** *him with his*
*hand.*

Psalm 37:23–24 NIV

In your own strength, you might not recognize it. You might not notice the One who sustains you, **upholds** you, and maintains the things that bring life to your soul. In your own strength, you might even imagine that you are doing these things for yourself out of your own brilliance or cleverness or ability. Can a tree uphold itself? Can the Earth maintain itself as it circles the Heavens?

Of course, you already know that a tree needs to dig its roots deeply into the ground so that it can withstand the tempests and the trials of winds and rains and the storms of the world. It needs to be able to stand tall no matter what happens. The Earth needs the gravitational pull of its orbit and the proper tilt of its axis to continue on its daily path around the sun. It can't do anything on its own.

In the same way, you need the One who upholds you every day, for only when you are deeply rooted in His love and care can you withstand the trials and tribulations life presents. Only when you are properly aligned with Him can you feel drawn to Him in ways that will keep you on the path He has designed for you. The Lord upholds you in every way, and though you may have talents and abilities and strengths, they all depend on His grace and love and mercy. You may stumble from time to time, but you will not fall, for God Himself upholds you with His right hand. Thank Him for keeping you steady and strong.

*Lord, thank You for the great love and mercy that* **upholds** *me,*
*giving me the strength I need to do the work You've called me to do. I*
*give You thanks and praise today. Amen.*

339

# CHOSEN

*For you are a people holy to the Lord your God. The Lord your God has
**chosen** you out of all the peoples on the face of the earth to be his people, his
treasured possession.*                                    Deuteronomy 7:6 NIV

Perhaps you recall a time when you were growing up, when you were chosen to take part in something special, like a competition, an election, or a
team sport. It felt good to be **chosen**. Sometimes you were chosen without
even knowing that you were under consideration.

Think about what it means to you to be a chosen child of God. That
means you were selected by His grace and His desire to be with you all
through your life. You were handpicked because God wanted to shine His
light upon you and give you the opportunity to grow in your relationship
with Him. God put His Spirit within you when you accepted Jesus so that
you could build on that foundation of holiness and learn from Him. He
chose you purely out of love. You didn't deserve to be chosen. You didn't
earn any special favor or have any particular talents. You simply were
selected by His love and mercy.

You may be chosen to be a leader, or a member of a group where you
serve as an example to others. You are blessed to be a blessing. Being chosen simply means that God opened the door of His heart and He called
you to come in. He always chooses you and He always will. All He wants
in return is for you to choose Him right back...not just once, but every
day of your life. He wants you to serve Him with your heart, mind, and
soul. You'll never make a better choice.

*Lord, thank You for allowing me to be **chosen** by Your love. Help me
to serve You with joy and thanksgiving. Amen.*

# IMPOSSIBLE

*Jesus looked at them and said, "With man this is **impossible**, but not with God; all things are possible with God."*     Mark 10:27 NIV

When life goes smoothly for us, we imagine that we can do anything. In the grace of God, we have some of those good days and we're grateful. The problem, or the question of what is possible, then, comes up only when we face an obstacle. It happens only when we are suddenly thrown off course, or illness strikes, or something goes dreadfully wrong and possibilities fly out the window.

The life of a human being always has limits. We face each day with what we can do and what we can't do. According to Scripture, though, when the Holy Spirit came to Earth, He brought with Him the possibility that would allow us to do the things that Jesus could do. In fact, Jesus offered that we might do even greater things than He did. So what happened?

Few of us can heal the sick or bring someone back from the dead. We don't seem to have abilities to allow five fish to feed five thousand people or to get our tax payment out of a fish's mouth. We have limitations. We cannot bring about miracles that require altering physical or biological facts.

Perhaps what we could consider, though, is this: Yes, we are limited. We cannot do the **impossible**, at least not by ourselves. But we may not know what we can do with God's help. We may not exercise our abilities in the light of the One who makes all things possible. When it serves Him, God will use even His human children to do amazing things. All we must do is remain totally devoted, connected, aligned with our God of the impossible. He gives you the strength to do all things.

*Lord, help me to realize that when something seems **impossible** to me, it simply means I have not surrendered it to You. Amen.*

341

# NEIGHBOR

*"Which of these three do you think was a neighbor to the man who fell into the hands of robbers?" The expert in the law replied, "The one who had mercy on him." Jesus told him, "Go and do likewise."*

Luke 10:36–37 NIV

Perhaps no one in our current culture has done more to promote being good neighbors than the late and beloved Mr. Rogers. He sang out each day how much he hoped to have a "**neighbor** just like you." But the idea of taking care of our neighbors, especially the ones near us, is still a challenge. Most of the time, we're lucky if we know a couple of people who live on our street. We usually have no real understanding of what is happening in the lives of our neighbors.

As Jesus shares the story of the man who fell into the hands of robbers, He asks the Pharisees, which one of those who saw the beaten man acted like a neighbor? Jesus is still asking us what it means to be a good neighbor. Sometimes, we need to have mercy, grace, kindness, and gratitude for the people across the street. Other times, we need to understand that human beings across the globe are truly our neighbors as well.

If we lived in Mr. Rogers's neighborhood, we could be sure he would have a pretty good idea when we needed help. He would know because he would make us, his neighbors, a priority. After all, each of us appreciates those nearby who offer to lend a hand when things happen outside of our control. We need good friends and we need good neighbors. Perhaps the best way to have a good neighbor is to be one yourself.

*Lord, thank You for each **neighbor** that I have now, and help me to be willing to reach out and lend a hand anytime they need me. Amen.*

# REQUIRE

*And now, Israel, what does the Lord your God **require** of you, but to fear the Lord your God, to walk in all His ways and to love Him, to serve the Lord your God with all your heart and with all your soul, and with all your mind.*
Deuteronomy 10:12–13 NKJV

If you were going to make a little laundry list of exactly what God wants from you, one that you could frequently refer to so that you wouldn't forget the details, this Scripture might be it. What does the Lord **require**, want, expect, hope for, and desire from you?

It appears that the first thing God wants is for you to fear Him. This fear is the trembling kind because you have so much respect for Him you cannot imagine doing anything that would displease Him. You are in awe of Him in ways that far surpass your devoted fandom for your favorite celebrity. He is amazing and awesome!

He also desires that you would walk in all His ways. You do that by showing Him your gratitude and your love. You do that by humbly serving others in His name. You walk in the ways that God leads you and instructs you. You follow in His footsteps without hesitation or reservation. You are intentional about everything you do for God.

Finally, you serve Him with your whole heart, every bit of it, not withholding one thing from Him. You sing His praises, and your soul rejoices every time He crosses your mind. You honor God above all else. This is your life purpose and it goes way beyond your daily routine, your parenting skills, or current occupation. You serve with a heart that is dedicated to God. Check the list each day so that you can see where you might fall short of the things the Lord will require of you. He'll help you be a good and faithful servant.

*Lord, thank You for showing me what You **require** of me and help me to daily devote my heart and soul to You. Amen.*

# TRUTH

*The time is coming when the true worshipers will worship the Father in spirit and truth, and that time is here already. You see, the Father too is actively seeking such people to worship him. God is spirit, and those who worship him must worship in spirit and* **truth**. John 4:23–24 NCV

When you worship God in spirit and **truth**, it focuses the way your heart and mind seek after God. It is sometimes different from the way your head and body choose to operate your life. God is Spirit. God is truth. God is love. God can only speak in truth and love, and He does everything in His power to relate that truth to His children.

God wants you to share His heart. He will encourage you to speak from your heart and mind when someone needs advice or direction. He will ask you to help guide the perceptions of those who are getting it wrong and falling. He will simply choose to sit with you and enjoy the friendship you share spirit to Spirit.

Sadly, the world has let go of its desire for truth. Half-truths and fake facts have replaced what once was considered sacred, oaths sworn on Bibles, ceremonies with vows, love at its finest. Truth is seldom part of the equation because we've bought into the lies that keep us slipping farther and farther away from what the Creator hoped for us.

As a believer, you are a truth-seeker. You know that your heart discerns the realities of what may appear to be true, and what is certainly a God-given understanding. Sit close to your Maker and seek His integrity and upright Spirit. He guides you to know everything, so you will not slip and fall. He comes to you anytime you ask, and He will teach your heart to know Him. He's near you now in wisdom, truth, and love.

*Lord, help me to know Your* **truth** *so that I might worship You with my whole heart and mind. Amen.*

# LEAST

*Then Jesus said, "Whoever accepts this little child in my name accepts me. And whoever accepts me accepts the One who sent me, because whoever is **least** among you all is really the greatest."*                    Luke 9:48 NCV

Wait a minute! Is that right? Did He say that whoever was the **least** among you all is really the greatest? How can the least be the greatest? Humanly speaking, these two words seem like direct opposites. Godly speaking, though, they are in direct correlation. Here is where the least and the most mean the same thing and what it means is that God is pleased.

Jesus is reminding us that when we accepted His invitation and asked Him to come in and live inside our hearts and stay with us eternally, we received a double portion. We received Him, and we received the One who sent Him to Earth. He offered the Holy Spirit as well, so our lives could be complete.

What is it about childlike faith that brings us even closer to the heart of God? Perhaps it is that there is an innocence in childhood that does not exist anywhere else in our lives. There is a willingness to trust and to believe and to seek the gifts of life, the miracles of every day. A child surrenders heart first to the love of a parent, knowing that the parent will ensure that protection and kindness and forgiveness reign.

Sometimes we become a little too much adult. We forget what it is like to simply trust and believe and surrender our lives to our Creator. No matter where we are on a social, political, educational, or spiritual scale, from the least to the greatest, we are one in Christ. He causes us to be more than we could ever be without Him. Praise God!

*Lord, thank You for causing me to accept You a long time ago and raising me up from being the **least** to the most I can be in You. Amen.*

# EAGER

*So be **eager** to do right, and change your hearts and lives.*

Revelation 3:19 NCV

When we were kids, we were **eager** to please the people in our lives. We did what our parents wanted and imitated their good behaviors. Sometimes we were eager to please our friends because we wanted to be liked and to fit into their circle. Somewhere along the way, though, we stopped being eager to make a good impression. We stopped trying to please anyone but ourselves.

As believers, once we get in line behind Jesus, we still need to be willing, ready, and eager to serve Him. We must be eager to do right so that we please Him and live in ways that reflect His kindness and mercy. If we enthusiastically serve others with humble hearts and help when we can, then we are doing those things that please God. We are eager to show Him that we have changed our hearts and our lives, and we want only to walk closely with Him. With eager intent, we feed and nurture and provide kindness and sustenance for others. We demonstrate our persistent desire to shine the light of God's love.

Humble yourself before Him and surrender your heart to God so He can see how willing you are to be His child. Give your spirit full permission today to be excited and eager in everything that you must do. Imitate goodness, faithfulness, and service to God and you will inherit all that He has promised to those who believe. The good news is that God's promises are never broken because He is eager to keep them.

*Lord, thank You for giving me a heart that is **eager** to share Your love for others. Help me to do my best to stay true to the calling You have placed on my life. Amen.*

# WANT

*The Scripture says, "I want kindness more than I want animal sacrifices." You don't really know what those words mean. If you understood them, you would not judge those who have done nothing wrong.* Matthew 12:7 NCV

When we **want** something, it usually means we don't have it. We are in want of it; it's lacking in our lives. Jesus was quoting His Father when He offered this thought, this desire. Jesus says that God wants kindness, more than animal sacrifices. As you know, animal sacrifices were required in the Old Testament as a way of offering God the first fruits of people's labors and as a way of honoring God and worshipping God. People brought animal sacrifices out of obedience to God and their pleasant aroma pleased God.

It's interesting, though, that Jesus suggests that even more than sacrifice, God wants something else. He wants kindness. Kindness means that we allow other people to make mistakes, or to be different than we are. Kindness means that we seek to see each other as God sees us. Kindness means that we don't set ourselves up as the ones who need to criticize or ostracize or otherwise do verbal harm to those around us. Kindness is a heart thing. Kindness is what God wants from us because it is what He gives to us. God sees that we are in want of kindness; it's lacking, yet we live every day in God's grace and mercy, undeserved and unmerited kindness.

The Scripture is sharing what God wants so that we know what to do to make our communities and our workplaces more humane and compassionate. God wants what He knows will help us to be better people. He wants us to change our judgmental hearts, stony and hardened as they may be, and serve Him and each other with soft, kind hearts. Kind hearts know how to love. Reflect His kindness wherever you are today. Let no one be in want of kindness when you are near.

*Lord, thank You for letting me know what You **want** so that I can try harder to be a kind and thoughtful person. Amen.*

# CREATION

*For since the **creation** of the world God's invisible qualities—his eternal power and divine nature—have been clearly seen, being understood from what has been made, so that people are without excuse.*

Romans 1:19–20 NIV

It's difficult to observe the wonders of the world, the beauty of **creation**, and not also recognize the handiwork of the Creator. Even suggesting that everything we see, the ground beneath our feet, and the starry skies at night are simply a matter of chance and happenstance seems ludicrous. God cannot be separated from His creation any more than He can separate His love from you because He can only be what He is: love.

If God is invisible to human beings, perhaps it calls into question our own willingness to see the evidence He has placed all around us. He put Himself into all the work of His hands, which includes the starry sky at night and the sunlit vistas of the day. He put a measure of Himself inside each heart, and we either see what He wants us to see, or we close our eyes, the eyes of our hearts, and simply choose to stay blind. God is not trying to hide out from us. Quite the contrary. He wants to be known and He wants us to know all He has done.

The more we seek His face, His Presence, His gift of life, the more He will become real, the more we will see Him in every aspect of creation. Today, may you see God in the skies above you and in the scenic beauty that surrounds you. May you see Him in the faces of people you love and those who simply reflect His grace and mercy. Let Heaven and nature sing in your heart today!

*Lord, thank You for putting so much of Yourself into all of **creation**. I see Your hand at work everywhere I turn. Amen.*

# FLEECE

*Gideon said to God, "If you will save Israel by my hand as you have promised—look, I will place a wool fleece on the threshing floor. If there is dew only on the fleece and all the ground is dry, then I will know that you will save Israel by my hand, as you said." And that is what happened.*

Judges 6:36–39 NIV

Gideon was a man of God. God chose him to do a special work. The beauty of this story is that it reminds us how far God is willing to go to help us understand His direction and His will for our lives. If we are people who talk to God regularly and are striving to do what God wants us to do, God will be clear about His message to us. God allowed Gideon to put out a **fleece**. Gideon knew how big the job was that he had to do. He knew he could not do it on his own. He knew he needed God to be with him, and so he asked for God to confirm the plan.

Not only did God do what Gideon asked in the Scripture above, but if you read further in the text, you'll note He allowed Gideon to continue the test of the fleece until Gideon felt confirmed that God called him to do this job. You may not feel called to save people, or you may not wonder whether you're doing what God wants, but the message is that you can ask God for very specific guidance. You can put your own "fleece" out before Him so you know exactly what He would have you do. When you have a relationship with God, you can ask Him anything, and you can trust His answers. Gideon got the guidance he was seeking and then he did not hesitate to do what God asked him to do. One more note: Before you set a fleece out, be sure you're ready to do what God is asking.

*Lord, thank You for allowing us to put a fleece of confirmation in front of You. I pray that You would bless the people who seek Your guidance today. Amen.*

# LAMP

*Your word is a **lamp** to my feet*
*And a light to my path.*

Psalm 119:105 NKJV

What does a **lamp** do? It brings light into the darkness. It helps you see more clearly so that you will not stumble and fall. A lamp illuminates your path so that it is easier to follow.

The psalmist compares God's Word, the Scriptures, the Holy Bible, to a lamp. He reminds us that Scripture is intended to shed light on those things that God wants us to know as we follow Him. His Word opens our eyes, so we see Him in a new or magnified light. When we are intentional about knowing more about God, He is quick to draw near to us, quick to give us light to see Him. He opens our hearts.

As a believer, you follow in Jesus' footsteps to do His work and to offer light to others. His light doesn't run on a double A battery. It runs on the power of God. You plug into His power, and He lights the way every time you engage with His Word. He lights up a passage for you to consider. He illuminates a Scripture you've read a hundred times before and makes it brand new. He always knows the Word for the day that will strengthen and renew you.

Your lamp may be a floodlight, or it may be a candle, but either way, it helps you navigate your world. It continues to shine when you stay closely connected to the Source of its power. Without His light, you may stumble along. But God is your Lighthouse, your beacon making the path bright and shiny for every step you take.

*Lord, thank You for being the **lamp** of my heart, the light that helps me to see where I'm going. I praise You for Your kindness and Your Holy Word. Amen.*

# TROUBLED

*Peace I leave with you, My peace I give to you; not as the world gives do I give to you. Let not your heart be **troubled**, neither let it be afraid.*

John 14:27 NKJV

Most days feel somewhat scrambled as you hurry to get things done and work to complete the tasks you set, but never quite accomplish. One day dissolves into the next and you're running to catch up. What happens in the busyness of life is that you fall into a never-ending cycle of turmoil, constantly churning and turning and bending and balancing and hoping to achieve. It's how you define a normal day!

What happens when you add illness or concern for a child or a friend, or when your marriage is struggling, or your bank balance is falling? What happens is that your life feels more like peril than peace. Your heart is **troubled** and overwhelmed and you hardly know where to start to set things back in order. Your worries turn to fear, and your fears turn to a troubled spirit, and nothing seems to move in your favor.

Is there an answer? Yes, but it isn't easy because it means you must surrender all those worries. It means you must be willing to put down that two-ton weight of troubles and let them rest at the feet of Jesus. You must seek His grace to give you something only He can give. You have to be ready to give up the wacky world of worries, and be willing to receive a big dose of peace. He knows the world only gives you troubling stuff. He gives you Heavenly stuff, peace that goes beyond the boundaries of Earth; peace that emanates from your Heavenly Father. Go ahead! Take heart and don't be troubled! Put down your burdens and wrap yourself in peace today.

*Lord, thank You for stepping into my **troubled** spirit and renewing me with Your amazing love and peace right now. Amen.*

# PREPARE

*There are many rooms in my Father's house; I would not tell you this if it were not true. I am going there to **prepare** a place for you.*

John 14:2 NCV

Isn't it a wonderful thought to know that God has already made room for you to spend eternity with Him? He has loved being able to **prepare** a special place for you because He knows you will thrive and love being there. He's already excited about sharing it with you when your mission on Earth is done. What do you suppose you can do to prepare for Him?

Imagine a mother preparing for the birth of her baby. She starts by thinking of the things her baby might like, setting up a nursery or a little bed that would keep the infant safe and comfortable. She does everything she can to nourish herself and care for the baby in utero until the baby is ready to see the light of day. Ideally, the baby comes into the world to a welcoming committee of people who are ready to love and help the baby grow to become all that baby is meant to become. They all prepare a place for the baby.

Just like there was excitement in the planning for the day that baby came to Earth, there is excitement around the day when you will go to your new home in Heaven. Those who have gone before you are already telling stories about some of the best things they know of you. They will celebrate your life with great joy when you come to the gate. It's nice to know that God has prepared a place for you. It's His way of saying thank you for all you've done to prepare a place for Him in your heart. Keep growing in His love today and help others prepare to know Him now and forever.

*Lord, thank You for all You've done to **prepare** for me on Earth and in Heaven. Amen.*

# AMEN

*For no matter how many promises God has made, they are "Yes" in Christ. And so through him the "Amen" is spoken by us to the glory of God.*

2 Corinthians 1:20 NIV

We often say **amen** as our concluding response to prayer. It echoes our surrender and our agreement with God. It declares "so be it" as we raise our hopes and our worries to God. It means that we have put our concerns in God's hand and that we trust Him to deal with those concerns. It even turns out that "amen" is our signature, the point where we sign off on the issues we've placed in God's hand.

Jesus is our ultimate "amen." He is God's answer to our questions. He is God's positive response and His willingness to watch out for us and to continue with us forever. He is God's "yes" and His total agreement for the lives of all creation.

Sometimes we say amen with a sense of agreement with others who have spoken prayers in our midst. Sometimes we say amen as we declare our needs and wants to God and then praise Him for taking care of us. We say amen in gratitude for what He will do on our behalf and we let Him know that we have given it over to His care.

Listen to your heart as you say the word "amen." Seek to understand what it means to you to know that God is with you no matter what you are going through and that He alone has the answers to bring peace to your life. Remember that you are loved, and that God sent His only Son to redeem you because nothing else was more important to Him than knowing you were saved. It's always a good day to lift up your heart in thanks and praise. Amen?

*Lord, thank You for holding me up and hearing my prayers with grace and love. You are my perfect "**amen**." Amen.*

# CHARACTER

*We also have joy with our troubles, because we know that these troubles*
*produce patience. And patience produces **character**, and character*
*produces hope. And this hope will never disappoint us, because God has*
*poured out his love to fill our hearts.*                    Romans 5:3–5 NCV

Most of us aspire to be people of "good **character**." We spend our life-time figuring out who we are in body, mind, and spirit, and in the process of that search we define our character. Let's consider this passage from Romans, starting at the end of it and going back to the beginning.

God poured His love into our hearts, knowing that love would drive us to desire more of Him: more guidance, more understanding, more con-nection to His Divine character. His love caused us to strive to know Him better even when we were not always conscious of the search. He created us with this desire to know Him and teaches us His ways, by the blessings and the trials we experience. He knows that learning to overcome adver-sity causes us to become stronger on the one hand, and more dependent on Him on the other. We look to Him to guide us through the mess, and as we patiently work through those trials, our character emerges. We get to know ourselves in new ways. We see that God is still with us as we experi-ence failure and adversity, and that awareness gives us hope.

Hope gives us every reason to keep trying. Each effort where we prevail reminds us that God is guarding our spirits, strengthening our hearts and minds and redefining us as people of good character. That building block of hope never disappoints us, and patience reveals His Presence and His power as He connects His Divine character to our human one.

*Lord, thank You for helping to build my **character** day by day*
*and year by year, through the power of Your Spirit and Your love.*
*Amen.*

# POWER

*At once Jesus realized that **power** had gone out from him. He turned around in the crowd and asked, "Who touched my clothes?"*

Mark 5:30 NIV

You've probably had plenty of opportunities to walk through a crowd in your life. Sometimes it was exciting and filled with amazing things to see, like at a big parade or a half-time show at a sporting event. You've been jostled about with the best of them and may not have noticed when someone walked a bit too closely to you. That was the scene as Jesus walked with the people that day. He was being jostled on every side, but at the precise moment, when a woman who had prayed to touch the hem of His garment was near enough to reach out, she did, and bam! Jesus knew something had happened. He felt Divine **power** go out of His body. It was amazing!

Even though His followers couldn't understand how Jesus knew something had happened, there were two people in that whole crowd who did know. Jesus knew and the woman who touched Him knew as well. She knew because His power had changed her. His power had healed her and made her whole for the first time in many years. She knew that she could finally consider herself clean and healthy. She was healed. She was normal. She was free.

The disciples may not have understood what happened because they were not full-time recipients of the Holy Spirit at that point. They were simply followers, perhaps like many of us, hoping to understand the power of Christ, the gift of God. When Jesus returned to Heaven, He left us His peace and His power so that we, too, could help others, offering Divine intervention as God leads us. May you understand that power and use it well.

*Lord, Your **power** is beyond my understanding, but I thank You for Your Holy Spirit, who is teaching me more all the time about what it means. Amen.*

# SEEK

*But if from there you **seek** the Lord your God, you will find him if you seek him with all your heart and with all your soul.* Deuteronomy 4:29 NIV

We don't often use the word **seek** in everyday conversation. It is one of those words that has more to do with searching for something than simply looking to see something. When you search, it means you have to be focused on it. It means you must know exactly what you're looking for or at least what you're hoping for. In this Scripture, the writer says that God wants you to seek Him, search for Him, pursue Him, and if you do so with all of your heart and all of your soul, you will find Him.

Why do you suppose that it's important for you to seek, to search for, to look with the eyes of your heart for God? Perhaps the reason is that when you go after God in this way, it lets God know that you are ready to find Him. If you must search for Him with everything you've got, then He knows that you want more than anything in the whole world to know that He is there for you.

So He agrees. If you pursue Him in the same way that you felt determined to get a college education, or that you were adamant about finding the right life partner, with real focus and intention, then you will find Him. He will not hide from you. God asks only this one thing, that you will desire His company and that you will want to spend time with Him for the rest of your life, heart and soul, day by day. Like those three kings of old who searched for baby Jesus, He wants you to be wise forever and always seek Him.

*Lord, thank You for inspiring me to look for You, to **seek** You with my heart and mind and soul. Thank You for allowing me to find You now. Amen.*

# SALT

*You are the **salt** of the earth. But if the salt loses its salty taste, it cannot
be made salty again. It is good for nothing, except to be thrown out and
walked on.* Matthew 5:13 NCV

**Salt** is one of the seasonings that make a difference in the taste of our
foods, enhancing the flavor, and bringing out the best in it. It preserves
some foods, and in the right balance is important to our bodies. But if
salt becomes neutralized, loses its saltiness, then it also loses its value. It
simply must be thrown out.

Most of us like the idea of being considered by those who know us as
"the salt of the earth." Generally, that means they think we bring value to
their lives, flavor our friendships, and add joy to life. Jesus said that you
are the "salt of the earth," and you can take that to be a good thing.

What makes you salty then? Perhaps the reason you're worth your salt
is because you are so kind to those around you. Maybe you have a generous and loving heart, and it's clear to everyone who knows you that your
intentions are honest and good. Maybe you bring out the best in others
simply because you see them as more special than they see themselves.
You're the salt. You're the one who makes a difference by the things you
say and do, and that's a wonderful thing.

Jesus also wanted to suggest to us that it's important to stay close to
Him so we will never lose our salty selves. Replenish and nourish yourself
by spending time each day with the One who knows you well, who sees
you always as the salt of the earth, designed to add more zest to living.

*Lord, thank You for giving me a chance to be **salt** to those around
me. Keep me close to You always so I continue to learn how I can
add flavor to the lives of others. Amen.*

# STAR

*After the wise men heard the king, they left. The **star** that they had seen in the east went before them until it stopped above the place where the child was. When the wise men saw the star, they were filled with joy.*

Matthew 2:9–10 NCV

**Stars** are a bit of a mystery as they light up the heavens on a clear winter night. As we approach the moment of Jesus' birth, we note that God even involved a star to play a significant part in this monumental event. The wise men, the scientists of the day, had been watching the heavens for a sign that the Messiah would indeed be born. An incredible star led them right to the place where the child was. Can you imagine their excitement as they realized the star they had studied and followed had stopped in the precise place they needed to go? Amazing!

We hear this story of the wise men and the star of Bethlehem every year at the Christmas season. We remain in awe of that special event and the Light that was coming into the world. Maybe we would get more from the story if we saw ourselves as those great wise men of old.

You're wise. You've been following Jesus, studying His Word and seeking to understand more of Him. You too, have followed His Star. Perhaps this holiday season, you can be a star for Him. You can shine a light so that others who are desperately looking for Him may follow and come to know Him.

As you consider that amazing star that led the wise and the lowly to the manger in Bethlehem, seek God's help to show you how to shine a light for those who are near you, those who are also seeking to find Him.

*Lord, thank You for being the **star** that I hope to always follow; You are the Light of my life. Amen.*

# PONDERED

*Great are the works of the Lord; they are **pondered** by all who delight in them.*                                                         Luke 2:19 NIV

Do you remember the last time you sat and **pondered** something important? Perhaps you were thinking about whether to accept a new job and it wasn't an easy choice because it meant moving to a new city and starting again. Perhaps you were wondering whether to accept a marriage proposal or whether it was the right time to have a baby. We ponder life's big decisions and think about them thoroughly.

It's interesting in the story of the Virgin Mary to read that Mary pondered in her heart what the angel Gabriel had told her. She accepted the angel's message because she had a great desire to serve the Lord, but the Scripture says that she then pondered these things in her heart. No doubt, it was a lot to take in. Few of us could have dealt with it as well, given her age and culture and status. It must have been mind-boggling, and yet she accepted God's call and continued to ponder it, think about it, wonder about it, and imagine it, probably for the rest of her life, and for the life of her Son.

Luke reminds us that we, too, have opportunities to ponder God's word. He comes to each of us with a call and He asks us if we will do what He desires. Sometimes, as in Mary's case, it isn't an easy task, but it's an important one. Think back on ways you have seen God's hand at work in your life, moments when you, too, may have had to ponder the decision, the choice you made. When God works wonders, He wants you to consider His actions. He promises to be with you, and He knows you will answer His call and delight in your opportunity to serve Him. Praise the name of the Lord!

*Lord, I thank You for times You've reached out to me as I **pondered** my choices, knowing I wanted to serve You. I bless Your name today. Amen.*

# BORN

*Today in the town of David a Savior has been **born** to you; he is the Messiah, the Lord.* Luke 2:11 NIV

Your calendar notes a variety of special holidays, including the birthdays of a few presidents, festivities to celebrate gratitude and love, and even to get you started toward a bright new year. However, no other holiday celebrates everything combined into one like Christmas.

The very fact that Jesus was **born** to be the Messiah, the Light, the Counselor, and Almighty God, makes this the most phenomenal day of the year. Our celebrations of the life of Christ, the day He was born, and the day He departed into Heaven are days that changed the calendars of the world. We mark time as BC, Before Christ, and AD, Anno Domini (the Year of our Lord). These two events of the birth and the death of Jesus make every other notable day pale by comparison.

Beyond the incredible sacredness and beauty of Christmas is the wonder that permeates the air as houses adorn themselves with lights and evergreens. Visions of sleigh bells and even a jolly old elf keep traditions of giving and generosity at a peak. Families draw near to one another, some to share in the story of the baby born to Mary and Joseph, and some oblivious to what God has done.

How you choose to celebrate this day is inconsequential in comparison to the true story, the story of how God redeemed His children everywhere. Those children rejoice like no one else can. The Spirit of God decorates their lives season after season. God bless you and your family at this Holy season.

*Lord, thank You for this amazing moment in history, the day You were **born**. Bless all people everywhere who celebrate Your love and majesty. Amen.*

# EVERLASTING

*But from **everlasting** to everlasting the Lord's love is with those who fear him,*
*and his righteousness with their children's children—with those who keep his covenant and remember to obey his precepts.*

Psalm 103:17–18 NIV

There's very little in our lives today that is **everlasting**. Our throwaway world considers few things worthy to be heirlooms and keepsakes. We make promises in marriage ceremonies to celebrate a life of everlasting love, but not all keep the promise. We offer to pray without ceasing, but prayer is not always uppermost on our minds. We hope that our relationships will always be satisfying and that our vows will be kept sacred, but our hearts suffer from brokenness and we lose our way.

God's promise, though, is endless, eternal, truly lasting forever and ever. He was and is and will be forever God, and so He can make promises that are indeed everlasting. God promises to be with you and to love you because you are His and you are trying your best to live according to His guidance and His Word. He has compassion for you when you pray and when you reach up to Him for help. He sees your heart and He knows what you are trying to accomplish with your life.

Before you put away the wrappings from your Christmas gift exchanges, or begin to return the things that you really don't want, take some time for you and God. Thank Him right now for the gift of His Son and for the everlasting love that He has for you and your family. Remember Him in all you do in the days ahead, and He will bless you beyond measure, giving you everlasting memories that will become keepsakes and treasures for a lifetime.

*Lord, thank You for Your steadfast and **everlasting** love and mercy.*
*Watch over all the people who reach up for You day after day.*
*Amen.*

# DOVE

*As soon as Jesus was baptized, he came up out of the water. Then heaven opened, and he saw God's Spirit coming down on him like a dove.*

Matthew 3:16 NCV

The **dove** has played a significant role in our faith history. You probably remember it was the bird that Noah sent out from the ark to determine whether the land was dry enough for habitation. He had initially sent a raven, but it was the dove that came back with an olive branch in her beak. The dove signified that God was ready to make peace with humans; He was ready for His creation to come back to life.

The dove is symbolic for all of us who seek peace in our lives. Beyond the idea of contentment and well-being is the image described in Matthew of the dove that came down from Heaven at the baptism of Jesus. That dove was the embodiment of the Holy Spirit of God, the Spirit that filled the heart of Jesus from the day He was lifted up from the waters of the Jordan.

Imagine Noah's ark as going through a kind of baptism, coming out of the flood waters that destroyed much of humanity, only to be brought back to God's grace and mercy on the wings of a dove. Imagine, too, that the baptism of Jesus brought a new opportunity for the Spirit of God to be revealed to all humankind. The dove once again symbolized God's Presence and His willingness to redeem His children from lives that could only bring them a flood of disaster.

May the Spirit of peace, as symbolized by the Spirit of God Himself, fill your heart and mind through the remainder of this season and all through the year.

*Lord, thank You for sending a dove to open the way to peace and to Your Holy Spirit. Bless the world with more of Your grace and mercy today. Amen.*

# ADORE

*Shout Hallelujah, you God-worshipers; give glory, you sons of Jacob; **adore** him, you daughters of Israel. He has never let you down, never looked the other way when you were being kicked around. He has never wandered off to do his own thing; he has been right there, listening.*

Psalm 22:22–24 MSG

As we go through the Christmas season, we often sing, "Come, let us **adore** Him!" We sing those words with humble hearts, and with deep gratitude. We feel within our souls that it is right, honorable, loving, and a privilege to have the chance to simply adore our Creator. Nothing quite compares to the feeling of singing God's praise.

Yes, we may adore our spouse or our children. We might adore visiting a certain city or a country, but those things come and go with our moods. The only truly sustainable Source or focus of adoration, worship, praise, and glory is to your only Redeemer, your Father, the true Prince of Peace.

You may have had moments over the past year when you left God behind, went on your merry way, and assumed you could get along just fine. You know how that worked out. One thing that's for sure is that God never once left you. He never once was too tired, or simply bored with you, or too busy solving the crisis of the moment so that He didn't have time for you. You have many reasons to adore Him... but His steadfast, never-ending, unconditional love surely ranks up there with the best of them. Come, let us adore Him!

*Lord, I do **adore** You, and I thank You with my whole heart for staying close to me always. I pray that You will draw near to each person who adores You today. Amen.*

# CONTENT

*I know what it is to be in need, and I know what it is to have plenty. I have learned the secret of being **content** in any and every situation, whether well fed or hungry, whether living in plenty or in want.*

Philippians 4:12 NIV

Ah, to be **content**! Now that is a concept that is somewhat of a mystery to modern culture. As we look around the world or even our own neighborhood, we are hard-pressed to find anyone who is truly content. Every place we look we see the result of those who feel deprived, depraved, depressed, and deeply troubled in every other sense of the word. We discover that human beings are restless souls that rarely know how to find the peace that eludes them.

The writer of Philippians, though, reminds us that it is still possible. It is possible to have a lot or to have a little and be untroubled by either state. It is possible to be somewhat hungry or slightly overfed and realize that life goes on. It is possible, he tells us, to be content in every situation.

Perhaps it is a good reminder, as the year comes to a close, to look back over our most recent events and memories and see if we can discover those moments when we were truly able to be content. If we cannot find very many days or hours spent in true peace, worry-free days filled only with the joy of the present moment, then maybe we need to begin again, make more of an effort.

If this is you, open your heart to your Father in Heaven and sing for joy for all that He has done to keep you safe and well and able to continue in His service. Ask Him to guide you into all peace and help you to be content with whatever may come in the days ahead.

*Lord, please be with everyone I love and help us to find our sweetest days in being **content** to serve You. Amen.*

# FAITH

*Now faith is confidence in what we hope for and assurance about what we
do not see.*                                    Hebrews 11:1 NIV

A key ingredient of **faith** is that in order to have faith, we have to know
what it is that we have faith in; we have to have confidence in something
or someone. If we buy a ticket for a cruise, we have faith that the ship
will float. If we go to work every day, we have faith that our paycheck will
arrive on time. If we have faith in God, it means that we buy into the idea
that God is there, always and forever.

Faith means we have confidence. It means we trust and believe in the
object of our faith. It means we know in our spirits that we are right about
our beliefs. We therefore, have assurance that what we cannot see doesn't
matter, because we trust in God.

Jesus continually tried to help His followers understand the meaning
of faith. He often said they had very little faith because they acted with
so little power. As we already discussed on an earlier day, He told them
that with a tiny bit of faith, perhaps the size of a mustard seed, they could
become like a mighty tree. Their faith would be an unshakable tree where
birds could build their nests.

How often do we imagine, think about, or read about faith, and yet find
our faith feels no bigger than a newly planted mustard seed? This year,
right now, look to God and ask Him to help you grow in faith. You are
already rooted in His grace and He alone can provide the confidence you
need to branch out. May you have ongoing faith, hope, and assurance for
the days ahead.

*Lord, thank You for giving me a growing faith. Help me to trust in
You in ways that cause me to become even more deeply rooted in
You. Amen.*

# RETURN

*"Men of Galilee," they said, "why are you standing here staring into heaven? Jesus has been taken from you into heaven, but someday he will **return** from heaven in the same way you saw him go!"* Acts 1:11 NLT

Some say that we're living in the last days, the days preceding the **return** of Jesus. Of course, there have been some who have said that very thing since our Savior was taken up into Heaven in the sight of many. Those "men of Galilee" stood and stared as Jesus went up into the skies and disappeared into the clouds. They watched until they could see Him no longer, but they were given the assurance that one day He would return. He will return for all those who wait for Him with heart, mind, and soul.

In the meantime, we can still feel His Presence. We know that He shows up when we need Him. We know that He draws near to us when we pray. Perhaps we can sense His return each time we do a good deed for a neighbor or a friend. When we make it a point to consider just what Jesus would say or do or act like in a certain situation, He comes back again. Jesus is alive and well on planet Earth, and He is living inside you. He makes His home with you now, and someday He'll come to take you to live in His home in Heaven. It's a lovely arrangement, because neither of you wants to be apart.

The next time you're pondering when Jesus will return, remind yourself that He lives all the time, anytime, for all of time in the hearts and minds and souls of His children. When you cause someone else to see Him or feel His Presence for even a moment, then He returns. Until the day or the hour that only God knows, Jesus will return each time we offer His love to those around us. May He return to you many times throughout the coming year.

*Lord, thank You for the blessing of knowing You will **return** and that You do come back for us time and time again even now. Amen.*

# What a Great Word!
## Alphabetical List

Able, January 4
Abundance, March 6
Accept, February 11
Act, April 2
Adore, December 28
Adversity, January 24
Afraid, January 27
Against, July 10
Aim, January 31
Alert, January 29
All, June 20
Also, September 2
Always, March 15
Amen, December 18
Angels, August 24
Anxious, February 28
Apple, November 2
Arise, March 26
Armor, June 1
Aroma, September 24
Asks, April 22
Assurance, March 9
Aware, February 21
Be, March 16
Beauty, May 9
Beginning, April 3
Believe, January 30
Belong, March 4

Bend, March 28
Better, August 27
Beyond, August 26
Big, August 13
Blind, July 26
Blot, July 7
Boldness, April 4
Born, December 25
Brave, June 27
Bread, June 21
Breath, July 4
Burdens, April 26
Calling, June 2
Calm, May 8
Camps, July 9
Can, November 4
Cast, September 9
Catch, November 19
Chance, July 25
Change, January 21
Character, December 19
Child, August 1
Choice, April 5
Chosen, December 5
Clay, October 6
Clear, September 18
Close, August 30
Cloud, May 4

Come, June 25
Commit, April 24
Compassion, March 17
Confusion, September 29
Content, December 29
Continually, January 9
Courage, February 8
Create, June 4
Creation, December 13
Crossroads, April 25
Cup, May 13
Daily, April 6
Darkness, July 17
Delight, February 12
Deserves, August 7
Different, October 5
Discern, November 3
Disciplined, November 25
Do, February 1
Done, April 27
Door, August 6
Doubt, February 9
Dove, December 27
Dust, June 13
Eager, December 11
Easy, July 12
Effort, July 31
Empty, October 7

Lambs, July 3
Lamp, December 15
Laugh, May 1
Learning, February 6
Least, December 10
Lesson, July 8
Letter, July 18
Life, June 7
Light, July 23
Listen, January 23
Live, March 11
Load, July 15
Lonely, October 21
Lost, October 13
Love, February 14
Mercy, December 1
Mind, June 10
Miracles, July 14
Money, September 26
Name, February 15
Natural, June 28
Need, November 26
Neighbor, December 7
Net, February 24
New, January 11
News, September 1
Noise, November 12
Nothing, May 10
Number, August 22
Oaks, October 22
Obey, July 13
Obstacle, April 1

Old, August 5
One, June 19
Only, January 15
Open, January 12
Overcome, May 14
Own, March 2
Pants, September 17
Part, August 4
Past, October 20
Patience, February 10
Peace, January 18
Penny, November 11
Perfect, October 15
Picture, May 15
Pities, June 11
Place, July 16
Plans, August 23
Planted, April 29
Please, October 12
Pondered, December 24
Portion, September 15
Power, December 20
Pray, September 22
Prepare, December 17
Present, November 29
Programs, August 3
Protect, February 16
Proud, January 13
Proverbs, November 13
Publish, May 16
Purpose, January 25
Questions, April 11

Quickly, January 14
Quiet, August 18
Quit, November 30
Race, August 15
Ran, September 19
Ready, September 20
Reality, August 31
Reason, August 20
Recount, March 19
Redeem, April 12
Refuge, October 23
Relax, May 17
Remember, June 9
Repent, November 27
Require, December 8
Respect, March 24
Rest, August 12
Restore, March 14
Return, December 31
Right, September 11
Rock, April 13
Room, July 1
Roots, May 7
Rubies, September 6
Rules, December 2
Rush, May 18
Sad, August 11
Safe, July 29
Salt, December 22
Sand, November 14
Satisfy, February 17
Seal, June 14

## *What a Great Word!* Alphabetical List

Seek, December 21
Self-Control, March 29
Serve, October 24
Shine, October 4
Shoes, October 1
Sighed, September 21
Sign, February 18
Simple, April 15
Sing, July 22
Slip, September 25
Slow, August 29
Small, July 20
Smile, May 19
So, August 25
Sorrow, August 19
Source, January 16
Spacious, March 27
Speech, April 14
Spirit, December 3
Stand, February 20
Star, December 23
Stones, July 28
Stop, August 9
Story, May 20
Strength, March 3
Struggle, March 25
Stubborn, August 17
Study, January 28
Success, January 20
Surely, May 2

Sustain, May 6
Tablets, November 15
Talk, September 30
Taste, March 22
Teach, June 16
Tell, October 26
Test, May 24
Think, March 13
Time, February 27
Tired, July 24
Today, June 17
Toward, May 3
Treasure, September 3
Troubled, December 16
Trust, April 16
Truth, December 9
Trying, May 23
Turn, June 15
Unbelief, January 5
Understand, October 27
Unity, August 10
Uphold, December 4
Useful, November 16
Vast, September 28
Victory, September 27
View, April 17
Vigilant, February 3
Vision, March 12
Voice, May 21
Waits, May 22

Walk, February 4
Want, December 12
Was, May 11
Washing, August 2
Watch, January 1
Water, September 7
Way, October 28
Weakness, April 18
Weeds, November 17
Whatever, June 18
Whole, May 25
Wide, September 13
Will, January 26
Wisdom, January 19
Wish, May 5
With, July 30
Without, September 14
Witnesses, March 23
Wonderfully, April 19
Wonders, June 29
Word, June 30
Works, June 22
Worrying, April 8
Worthy, January 17
Write, May 26
Wrong, September 10
Yeast, June 8
Yes, August 14
Yourself, April 20
Zeal, November 18

# Acknowledgments

When it comes to Scripture, I suspect I'll always be a student, a curious pursuer, trying to gain insight and perspective of the words I read in my Bible. Creating this book, *What a Great Word!*, has caused me to be even more aware of the richness and importance and understanding to be gained by each individual word. Some time ago, God inspired my husband, Bruce, to send me a simple word to consider each morning as he spent time doing his own devotions. Each morning, then, I gain a new perspective on words I've read many times before. I thank God for inspiring Bruce with these daily messages, and I thank Hachette for catching the vision to create a book that will inspire readers who are deliberate in their own pursuit to walk with God.

I thank Rolf Zettersten and Keren Baltzer, Nicci Jordan Hubert, and Grace Johnson and the amazing editorial team at Hachette who believed in this book and helped strengthen and develop its content. I thank Jody Waldrup, who designed the incredible cover to draw readers into the discovery of each word.

I thank my friends and associates who kindly endorsed the pages of this book. Each one of you encouraged my efforts and brought joy to the work. I especially want to thank Duane Ward, whose friendship and encouragement blesses my heart always; and Bob Bubnis, whose heart for God inspires everyone around him. My dear friends Pete Kersten, Kathy Davis, Terry Squires, and Brenda Golden amaze the world with the work of their hands each day. I am blessed by Ron Doyle, George Shinn, Daniel Rice, Joel Comm, Marty Roe, Joe Bataglia, David Hancock, and several others who offered endorsements to shine a light on this work. Finally,

## Acknowledgments

I thank Jean Ziglar, wife of Zig Ziglar and mother of our dear friend Tom Ziglar. Each of you contributed your gifts to this work, and I can't thank you enough.

I thank God, Who allows me to do this work in the world and continues to inspire my heart and mind every day. May He do the same for each one who reads through these pages.

# About the Author

KAREN MOORE is the best-selling author of more than 100 books for kids, teens, and adults with her inspirational daily devotionals. Karen teaches at writing conferences and is a keynote speaker for conference events and women's groups. Karen has also worked in the greeting card industry, creating thousands of greeting cards, as a product development specialist, and as a book publisher. Currently, Karen is working on screenplays for television and movies, with two licensed properties for children. She is married and makes her home in Richmond Hill, Georgia.